JUDAISM STATES ITS THEOLOGY

SOUTH FLORIDA STUDIES IN THE HISTORY OF JUDAISM

Edited by
Jacob Neusner
William Scott Green, James Strange
Darrell J. Fasching, Sara Mandell

Number 88
JUDAISM STATES ITS THEOLOGY
The Talmudic Re-Presentation

by
Jacob Neusner

JUDAISM STATES ITS THEOLOGY
The Talmudic Re-Presentation

by

Jacob Neusner

Scholars Press
Atlanta, Georgia

JUDAISM STATES ITS THEOLOGY

Publication of this book was made possible by a grant from the Tisch Family Foundation, New York City. The University of South Florida acknowledges with thanks this important support for its scholarly projects.

Library of Congress Cataloging in Publication Data
Neusner, Jacob, 1932–
   Judaism states its theology: the talmudic re-presentation/ by Jacob Neusner.
     p. cm. — (South Florida studies in the history of Judaism; no. 88)
   Includes bibliographical references and index.
   ISBN 1-55540-890-7
   1. Talmud—Theology. 2. Talmud—Criticism, interpretation, etc. 3. Judaism—Doctrines.   I. Title.   II. Series.
BM504.3.N45   1993
296.3—dc20   93-24475
                            CIP

Printed in the United States of America
on acid-free paper

Table of Contents

Preface

The Judaism, or Judaic system, of the Dual Torah, which through time became normative, took shape in the progression from its beginning as philosophy through its transformation into religion and onward to its re-presentation as theology. That Judaic system presented an account of the way of life and worldview of a social entity called (an) "Israel" formulated in response to the Pentateuch. Seen whole, its statement was set forth by the Written Torah and also by the first document to write down (part of) the oral component of the Torah, which was the Mishnah (ca. 200 C.E.).

That document made its systemic statement in philosophical categories. The framing of the statement of the Torah was then transformed into other, religious categories. This was by the categorical reformulation (the formation of counterpart categories) accomplished in the Talmud of the Land of Israel (ca. 400 C.E.) and its associated Midrash compilations, the earlier ones represented by Sifra and one of the Sifrés, the later by Leviticus Rabbah.[1]

---

[1]In this book I do not systematically deal with the several Midrash compilations, though each one of them finds its place in the scheme I set forth. Only Sifra is essential to this account of the Talmudic hermeneutics of the Mishnah, and that is because Sifra illustrates in a very clear way what I mean when I allege that hermeneutics forms the medium for theological expression. I do think a companion study would be of interest in showing how the modes of discourse of the Midrash compilations developed from concrete exegesis of words and phrases, in documents that depend for context and meaning on the Written Torah's text itself, to syllogistic arguments set forth through propositions not formed as commentaries to texts, and onward to abstract propositions everywhere restated in the form of commentary once more. That pattern – from commentary to syllogistic discourse abstracted from commentary and onward to syllogistic discourse effected through commentary – is fairly easy to discern in the documentary succession from Sifra and the two Sifrés through Genesis Rabbah and Leviticus Rabbah and upward to Song of Songs Rabbah, Lamentations Rabbati, Ruth Rabbah, and their several companions, respectively. It would form a separate path, running alongside the one I outline in this book.

The same Judaic system was finally restated as theology by the final document to write down the oral component of the Torah, which was the Talmud of Babylonia (ca. 600 C.E.) and its companion Midrash collections, exemplified by Song of Songs Rabbah, Ruth Rabbah, and Lamentations Rabbati. That accounts for my simple formulation: from philosophy through religion to theology.[2] This book explains the third and concluding stage in the formation of Judaism, defining the work and showing how it was done, both in theory and, for a single case at the end, in practice.

It remains to note that I have taken all texts in this book from my translations of nearly the entirety of the canon of Judaism in its formative age, Mishnah, Tosefta, Sifra, the two Sifrés, the Rabbah-Midrash compilations, the Talmud of the Land of Israel, and the Talmud of Babylonia. Each abstract given here is represented by me as typical and representative of a type of composition or composite common in the document from which it comes. Since most of the book concerns the character of the Talmud of Babylonia, it may have been valuable for me to provide an account of the proportion of the compositions or composites of that Talmud made up of a given type of composition or composite cited here. But I state very simply that the principal types of discourse portrayed throughout are routine and characteristic of the Bavli throughout. For an example of statistical summaries I have made in demonstrating some of the basic propositions given here, I refer readers to my *The Bavli's One Voice: Types and Forms of Analytical*

But to show the ways in which the Midrashic reading of the Written Torah runs alongside the Talmudic reading of the Oral Torah (Scripture, Mishnah, respectively) would carry us far afield and place much more weight upon the structure of this book than it should be asked to bear. So one thing at a time; but it is important even now to record that a corresponding story is to be told. It is to hint at that story that I make reference here to the Midrash compilations, even though only one of them figures in this account.

[2]We need not take seriously the mantra of the *Wissenschaft des Judenthums* and its modern (and even contemporary) avatars, "Judaism has no theology." Morning and night faithful Jews contradict that opinion when they say, "Hear O Israel," and numerous other liturgical statements of the dogmas of a well-composed theology likewise refute that ignorant position. The dogma of dogmaless Judaism confused the sociology of nineteenth-century Reform Judaism, which acknowledged the absence of consensus in its own midst by affirming as normative over a long past the character of pluralism in theology. Whatever the merits of theological pluralism, Judaism in its normative statement did not exhibit them, insisting on not only a variety of theological dogmas (the unity of God, the divine revelation of the Torah, the resurrection of the dead, for example) but also on their harmony and cogency, that is, on their character as a compelling system. In the introduction I deal with the confusion of sociology of religion and descriptive, historical theology, such as is the program of this book.

Discourse and Their Fixed Order of Appearance (Atlanta, 1991: Scholars Press for South Florida Studies in the History of Judaism). Since much of the argument rests not only on my characterization of the two Talmuds together but also on the differentiation of the second from the first, for the basis for my characterization of how the Bavli is unique in documentary context, I refer readers to the seven parts of my *The Bavli's Unique Voice* (Atlanta, 1993: Scholars Press for South Florida Studies in the History of Judaism).

Since this work brings to a conclusion a long-term inquiry of mine and further defines the three formidable projects I have now to address, I take the occasion of the end of my work on one considerable problem to state briefly what I plan as a sequel. The problems that now await attention are three: one of a historical, the second of a religious-historical and the third of a theological character. I have long maintained that, read in documentary sequence, the canon of Judaism yields an account of text, context, and matrix. Here I bring to a climax my account of the history of the formation of Judaism as worked out along documentary lines. The textual work accomplished, I turn to the matters of context and matrix and theological outcome: the historical, religious, and theological definition of Judaism in its formative age.

By context, I mean the historical context in which the Judaism of the Dual Torah took shape. What I want to know, in particular, is about the context in actual, lived history to which the texts at hand attest. Can we read these writings to find out about the people who wrote them and the world in which they lived? Of course we can, when we know how.

By matrix, I mean the larger world of religious faith and practice in which that same Judaism of the Dual Torah came to expression. Everyone understands that in the writings at hand, we have not only systemic statements of closed systems – their writers' – but also evidence of a sheltering and nourishing world of religious sensibility and conviction. I propose to find out about the matrix in which the very specific formulations that we have came to expression: What do they take for granted, what do they everywhere know to be true but never trouble to validate? What do our sages of blessed memory take for granted in the various documents that groups of sages set forth?

The theological work has already been clarified: Knowing that hermeneutics governs theological discourse, and identifying the hermeneutics of the Bavli as I do in these pages, how do I formulate some of the theological results that the right reading of the Bavli yields?

These represent, then, the logically consequent questions – historical, religious-historical, and theological – that I have now to take up. My present plan calls for the following studies:

Context in History

From Text to Historical Context. A Historical Reading of the Canon of Judaism.
  1. *The Mishnah and the Tosefta.*

From Text to Historical Context. A Historical Reading of the Canon of Judaism.
  2. *The Earliest Midrash Compilations.*

From Text to Historical Context. A Historical Reading of the Canon of Judaism.
  3. *The Yerushalmi.*

From Text to Historical Context. A Historical Reading of the Canon of Judaism.
  4. *The Later Midrash Compilations.*

From Text to Historical Context. A Historical Reading of the Canon of Judaism.
  5. *The Bavli.*

From Text to Historical Context. A Historical Reading of the Canon of Judaism.
  6. *The Latest Midrash Compilations.*

Rabbinic Writings as a Source of Historical Facts: What the Canon of Judaism Tells Us about the History of the Jews in Late Antiquity.

What Does Rabbinic Literature Contribute to the Understanding of the New Testament Gospels?

Matrix in Religion

From Texts to Theological Matrix: The Torah, One, Entire, and Whole. 1. Oral.

From Texts to Theological Matrix: The Torah, One, Entire, and Whole. 2. Written and Oral.

The Judaism That Is Taken for Granted.

The Theological Upshot of Hermeneutics:
The Message of the Torah's One, Whole Re-Presentation

The Yield of Hermeneutics: A Preliminary Theological Reading of the Talmud.
  1. *The Division of Appointed Times.*

The Yield of Hermeneutics: A Preliminary Theological Reading of the Talmud.
  2. *The Division of Women.*

The Yield of Hermeneutics: A Preliminary Theological Reading of the Talmud.
  3. *The Division of Damages.*

The Yield of Hermeneutics: A Preliminary Theological Reading of the Talmud.
  4. *The Division of Holy Things.*

As is clear, at this time these planned monographs represent matters for present reflection and future composition. In my experience, ideas have their own logic and direct me where they will.

I express my continuing thanks to the University of South Florida for providing ideal conditions – including a generous research expense fund

– in which to pursue my research, and to my colleagues in the Department of Religious Studies and in other departments for their ongoing friendship and stimulating conversation. They show me the true meaning of the word collegiality: honesty, generosity, sincerity. In the long, prior chapter in my career, now closed, I never knew such people of character and conscience.

I planned this book chapter by chapter and wrote the first draft of three-quarters of it while a Visiting Fellow at Clare Hall, Cambridge. The humble facilities of that research center conceal the wealth of spirit and intellect that flourish there; to the president and staff of Clare Hall and to the many friends and colleagues who accorded a warm welcome to my wife and myself, I express thanks.

I owe special thanks to my study mate and friend, Professor David Gunby, University of Canterbury, Christchurch, New Zealand – who also will be my colleague when I am Canterbury Visiting Fellow at the University of Canterbury in 1994. He surely learned more about Judaism than he ever thought he would, but in his work on John Webster, he also taught me more about hermeneutics, theoretical and applied, and thinking about the problems of analysis and formulation, than he may even have himself realized. Seeing the *Duchess of Malfi* through his eyes showed me how the hermeneutics exposes the meaning and serves as the medium for the message of a document, precisely what I mean to show here. I owe him thanks for guiding me into the intricacies of hermeneutics as worked out in matters of literary theory. That was only one, though the most important, among the many exceedingly pleasant relationships that my wife and I enjoyed at Clare Hall.

It strikes me as providential that, at just the point in my life that I found, at University of South Florida, a community of learned colleagues capable of genuine intellectual exchange and cordiality, too, I found in Cambridge a similar community, to which I have now been elected a Life Member. Not many people know even one such place, and I have the good fortune to participate in two of them. As I move toward harvest time in my career, having passed sixty and so survived the ages of *karet*, I find myself in truly fortunate, fertile fields. So I owe a *yama tava lerabbenan*, and here in my way I begin to make it.

JACOB NEUSNER

Life Member, CLARE HALL
CAMBRIDGE UNIVERSITY
Visiting Research Professor
ÅBO AKADEMI, FINLAND

Distinguished Research Professor
of Religious Studies
UNIVERSITY OF SOUTH FLORIDA
Tampa, FL 33620-5550 USA

Introduction

The re-presentation, as theology, of the Judaic religious system of the Dual Torah claims to afford knowledge of God through God's own self-manifestation. "Judaism" or "the Torah" (the external and internal name of the same system) claims to mediate God's self-manifestation, and the Torah promises to inform in the two senses: illuminate, but also, reshape. The mind is informed, given truth it otherwise cannot gain; it is informed, given the power of analysis and argument to gain truth it otherwise cannot gain. Defining and shaping intellect in particular, "Judaism" or "the Torah" inform by forming intellect in the model of God's. Here I shall set forth the context in the history of the religion of the Judaism of the Dual Torah where this took place and then define how this was done – and finally demonstrate through an exemplary case that that indeed is the intent and program of "Judaism" or the Torah. If this book succeeds, I shall have defined a productive program of theological description for the history of Judaism, one that will take some time to run its course.

Let me commence with a brief account of the program of the book. It is simple, resting on the single, self-evidently valid premise that the characteristics of documents (oral, written, or human, as in Dilthey's[1] "permanently fixed life-expressions") convey the traits of the systemic formations (the "Judaisms") that provoke the writing of those documents and come to expression in them. I build upon the claim that the character of the principal documents of the three stages in the formation of Judaism corresponds to – and reveals – the paramount character of those phases. I have argued in works cited presently, that the Mishnah presents a philosophical system derived from a philosophical mode of thought, the Yerushalmi a religious one, formed of a different, other-

---

[1]Cited by K.M. Newton, *Interpreting the Text. A Critical Introduction to the Theory and Practice of Literary Interpretation* (New York, 1990: Harvester/Wheatsheaf).

1

than-philosophical, mode of thought. And I now maintain that the Bavli shows us a theological way of restating a religious system.

The work begins, however, not with documents but with definitions. In Chapter Three I define the generative categories of my account of the formative history of Judaism and analysis of each of the stages of that history, philosophy, religion, and theology, with stress on the first and the third of the categories, the relationship of theology to philosophy. In Chapter Four I set forth the definitions that govern here: what I conceive to be the theology of the Judaism of the Dual Torah, its purpose and its sources. I offer a bilingual explanation of the matter, using the secular and philosophical category "Judaism" and the native and theological category "the Torah" and playing these off against one another.

The entire shank of the book, Chapters Five through Ten, is devoted to spelling out the point that hermeneutics forms the medium for the method and the message of theology as defined in Chapters Three and Four: when we are instructed in how to read the Torah, we also are afforded access to the knowledge of God that through the Torah God has made manifest to us. From this elaborate account of what I think was going on, I move in conclusion to a specific statement of a concrete result: the theology that I maintain hermeneutics yields, and how that theology is to be identified.

The entire question therefore draws us to the writings that define the Torah and mediate its messages: how these are read not only yields theology but itself conveys theology – that is my point. Hence I have to describe the more important documents' hermeneutics. I work on the two Talmuds in particular. The first Talmud and a fair proportion of the second are devoted to Mishnah exegesis. I have therefore to explain the character of that exegesis and show how that exegesis accomplishes a part of the hermeneutical, therefore also theological, work: the task of rigorous definition and clarification of the character (not just the words and phrases) of the oral part of the Torah. I maintain that there is no material difference between the category formation or consequent message of the two Talmuds; both say the same thing, which I show with reference to the treatment in each of two generative categories, Torah and Messiah. On these (and like) subjects I simply cannot differentiate sayings found in the second Talmud from those found in the first. But the second Talmud, as I show, differs in fundamental hermeneutical dimensions from the first in its reading of the Mishnah, and the difference defines the theological method and program of the second. To show how hermeneutics bears a theological method and message, I turn then to one of the earliest Midrash compilations. There I show how that Midrash compilation conveys a theological principle, concerning the Mishnah, never through articulation but solely through the hermeneutics that guides the exegesis of the book of the Written Torah upon which that compilation is focused. That sets the stage for what is to follow.

In Part Three we proceed to the second, and principal, labor of theologizing: the work accomplished by the Talmud of Babylonia and its companions of Midrash compilation, devoted to the Mishnah and Scripture, respectively. Here I find the work of stating a few vast but simple truths through countless cases. In Chapters Eight, Nine, and Ten I set forth what I conceive to be the unique hermeneutics of the Bavli and how it conveys a theological message. In a separate, companion work, *Judaism's Theological Voice: The Melody of the Talmud,* I shall elaborate on that point.

The argument therefore unfolds in the comparison of the two Talmuds to one another to show likeness, then contrast, thus to demonstrate and also account for difference. Specifically, I show that the two Talmuds define principal categories in the same way, saying the same thing about fundamental topics. In that they are alike. That is the point of Chapters Five and Six. Then I demonstrate that the two Talmuds differ in their definitions of how discourse is to be conducted. In that they differ profoundly, and the difference of the second of the two Talmuds from the first is the difference between theology and religion. That is the point of Chapters Eight through Ten. Accordingly, I address two complementary tasks, involving the close study of two documents, the Yerushalmi and the Bavli and their companions: show the documents say the same things, and, further, demonstrate that the second of the two makes its statement in ways vastly different from the first. The two Talmuds therefore are compared and contrasted, shown to be alike in religious propositions, but significantly (but not wholly) different in intellectual characteristics.[2]

---

[2]I recast and greatly revise the results of my *The Bavli's Unique Voice. A Systematic Comparison of the Talmud of Babylonia and the Talmud of the Land of Israel* (Atlanta, 1993: Scholars Press for South Florida Studies in the History of Judaism), I-VII. I. *Bavli and Yerushalmi Qiddushin Chapter One Compared and Contrasted;* II. *Yerushalmi's, Bavli's, and Other Canonical Documents' Treatment of the Program of Mishnah-Tractate Sukkah Chapters One, Two, and Four Compared and Contrasted. A Reprise and Revision of* The Bavli and Its Sources; III. *Bavli and Yerushalmi to Selected Mishnah Chapters in the Division of Moed. Erubin Chapter One and Moed Qatan Chapter Three;* IV. *Bavli and Yerushalmi to Selected Mishnah Chapters in the Division of Nashim. Gittin Chapter Five and Nedarim Chapter One. And Niddah Chapter One;* V. *Bavli and Yerushalmi to Selected Mishnah Chapters in the Division of Neziqin. Baba Mesia Chapter One and Makkot Chapters One and Two;* VI. *Bavli and Yerushalmi to a Miscellany of Mishnah Chapters. Gittin Chapter One, Qiddushin Chapter Two, and Hagigah Chapter Three;* and VII. *What Is Unique about the Bavli in Context? An Answer Based on Inductive Description, Analysis, and Comparison.*

To stake my claim about the second Talmud's unique formulation of matters – theology in the form of hermeneutics – I have to distinguish the traits of the Bavli from those of the Yerushalmi and thereby characterize the Bavli. Only when I can show what is unique to the Bavli have I defined the data that will sustain my claim that that Talmud theologized the religious system of the Yerushalmi. This I do by specifying what is in fact particular about that writing. When we examine with care the distinctive modes of inquiry that the Bavli, but not the Yerushalmi or any other document, undertakes, we are able to specify the elements of the documentary structure that require attention. In line with my definition of theology and its method in Judaism given in Chapters Three and Four, I concomitantly translate these literary traits into their theological principles. That characterization then validates my view that a theological statement of a religious system is conveyed through the documentary character and structure of the Bavli. It further defines the theological system of Judaism as its processes and methods define its proposition and its message.

That, sum and substance, is the argument of this book, a simple and straightforward account of the first, and, in fact, the sole enduringly definitive, theology of the Judaism of the Dual Torah. That theology defines the point at which Judaism completed its formation: method, message, medium alike. The Torah having been set forth, all the rest would be commentary. Admittedly, it would become a formidable commentary, with many subtexts; but there was, and would be for all time, only one text, the Torah as the Talmud re-presented it.

Since the focus of this book is the statement of the theology of Judaism, I realize, people ordinarily expect, when theology is at issue at all, four further kinds of discourse, none of which they will find here. These are constructive or systematic theology, philosophy of religion, sociology of religion, and theological apologetics, all of which in contemporary writing on theology figure prominently. These take up such questions as why a religion's theological statements transcend that religion and give (or do not give) evidence about the character of God in general, who accepts that theology, and why people should concur in that theology. But what readers may well anticipate they will not find in this book, which in no way takes up the problems of constructive or even systematic theology and apologetics let alone sociology or philosophy of religion. It is important to distinguish these entirely valid approaches to theological writing from the approach followed here, so that readers do not expect what I do not promise to provide.

Commonly but erroneously associated with any discussion of theology are sustained treatments of, first, one's "own" theological system, second, philosophy of religion (is it true by neutral reason and this-worldly rationality, the universal criteria of truth), third, the sociology of religion (who actually believed it all), and fourth, apologetics (why readers should be persuaded to believe). I offer a work of analysis of a particular Judaic system, a description of the unfolding of its ideas through the character of successive documents, an interpretation of the phenomenon of this formative history. I cannot promise to pay attention to other questions entirely, though in their own contexts they are entirely legitimate: philosophy, sociology, and theological apologetics. Let me review these matters and spell out why they are not addressed here.

Theology concerns the knowledge of God that, in accord with the view of a given religion, God affords to us. In the case of Judaism all the knowledge of God that Judaism alleges God has given to humanity is contained in the Torah. That is what theology proposes to describe and explain: the rational principles that govern knowledge in general applied to knowledge of God through the designated source in particular. So theology simply is not to be confused with either philosophy, the sources of which are not revealed truth but demonstrated facts, or sociology, which in the study of religion tells us what people think they know about God and how they conduct themselves on that account. Let me dwell on these matters, so as to highlight the carefully defined program of this book and eliminate the possibility of misinterpreting what I undertake to explain in these pages and how I do the work.

CONSTRUCTIVE OR SYSTEMATIC THEOLOGY: How may we today carry out the same task that (I maintain) "our sages of blessed memory" accomplished through the Talmud's theologization of the received religion? Some readers may look for a model for contemporary theological constructions, including the formation of a systematic theology of Judaism, to the Bavli. I think it entirely appropriate that they do so. The Talmud remains, after all, the single most successful theological document in the history of any Judaism. Its success is attested by its power to define the faith and to compel through persuasion the assent of most practicing Jews. So anyone who today wants to construct a theology of Judaism will find in these pages guidelines on how success was achieved by the Talmud. Not only so, but the Talmud formed one of the few truly systematic theological presentations in the history of its, or any other, Judaism. However, readers who expect me to join description of how a theological presentation came to expression and its principal points of concern to normative formulations for contemporary Judaic theological discourse will find in these pages only disappointment. I am no theologian, though I greatly admire the craft of those who conduct the venture well, as, in the past, some manifestly have done, and, even today, some continue to do. I do allege, however, that no one who wishes to engage in the constructive or systematic theology of Judaism will learn from the Talmud precisely how to do so. The right way is, study a text – but I digress.

PHILOSOPHY OF RELIGION: Is it true? Is it true in general? I deal with specificities, not the rules that govern or describe throughout; of such, philosophy of religion is not made. The evidence upon the basis of which description is undertaken, the rules of argument and the criteria for proof – all are particular to the Torah. None of those stated in this context has any bearing upon religious truth in general, which philosophers analyze, but historians of religions do not address at all. So I offer not generalizations about religion and its truth, but a descriptive, analytical, and interpretative account of the historical formation of Judaism as revealed by the progression of its writings in their own time and place.

The specificities of the history of religions – here, the history of a Judaism – may to be sure provide data for the generalizations of philosophy of religion. For those generalizations of general intelligibility properly mean to explain and analyze not one case but all, not the rule for a single case but the rule governing every case – and do not make possible the philosophical inquiry. I am no philosopher but a historian of religion. Some may take for granted that, when theology is the subject, general statements verified through universally pertinent data and neutral arguments, universally pertinent, about the nature of God in general or of religion wherever it may be found form the object.[3] But a case is not a rule, and a series does not end with one example. Here I offer a case and an example of a sequence, nothing more. So I do not

---

[3]That accounts for the field I think particular to Judaic discourse, "philosophy of Judaism." That field shades over into studies of "ideology," as in "Jewish ideology." "Ideology," of course, is a term with its own history, having no place at all in the discussion of religion. By contrast, there is not so much "philosophy of Christianity" (though there are Christian philosophies) as theology of Christianity. "Philosophies" of Judaism ordinarily appeal to general arguments in the analysis of data particular to Judaism; or they introduce data that are both general and also specific to Judaism, so confusing the distinctive issues of the religious norms of the religion, Judaism, and those that apply to everyone in general; or they ask the generalizations that pertain to religions to validate the particular claims of Judaism in its own terms. These rather confused modes of religious thinking in contemporary Judaism need not detain us, but they do make it necessary to spell out what, when we describe theology, we do not thereby also describe, which is, philosophy of religion or "philosophy of Judaism." I think the Mishnah sets forth a Judaic philosophy, by which I mean, Judaism as a philosophical structure. But that is not the same thing.

propose to generalize in a philosophical way, even about theological statements that are set forth within a philosophical discipline, such as Judaism did make in the writings I treat here.

It follows that I do not offer propositions about knowledge of God attained through rational inquiry that sustain analysis in the framework of philosophy of religion. While the methods of theology as I find them in the Talmud are philosophical, adhering to the rules commonly governing general intelligibility and broadly shared rational inquiry, the sources of propositions and criteria for truth are particular and distinctive – hence by definition, not philosophical. It is one thing to set forth a description that is accessible to any reasonable reader. That I claim to do. It is another to subject to the judgment as to what is true in general the claims of particular truth that this theology formulates. That I do not think should be done at all.

In the program of this book I do not repeat the common error in contemporary Judaic religious discourse (one cannot call it theological in any rigorous sense), which is to confuse philosophy of religion and theology; the mixture of sources, natural and supernatural, and kinds of arguments, some internal to the faith, others subject to generalization and application to any religion. That confusion of philosophy with theology ignores the difference in the sources of philosophy, which are the world at large, reason in the aggregate, and those of theology, which are, as is clear, particular to a single religion and its canon. Not only so, but I am no philosopher, and certainly no philosopher of religion; I claim to write the history of a religion and to participate in the history of religion; these are distinct from philosophical ventures.

SOCIOLOGY OF RELIGION: Who believed these things? Who did not? How to explain the difference? It should be self-evident even at the outset that a study of the theology of Judaism set forth in the first and the definitive of its canonical writings, called, all together, the Torah, in no way concerns what "the Jews" believe or have believed at some determinate time or particular place. A description, analysis, and interpretation of the theology of Judaism finds the sources of that theology, for purposes of description, in what Judaism itself identifies as those sources. These comprise, of course, all writings that enjoy the status of Torah, all norms that define how things are to be done and to be believed: *halakhah, aggadah.* Studies of how, in times past or today, diverse Jews define their personal belief or behavior have no bearing upon the description of the theology of Judaism. The distinction between the religion set forth in books and the religion practiced by the people addressed by those books is familiar; religious elite or virtuosi make proposals, everybody else disposes of them.

The sociology of religion describes everybody else; for my part, I have already outlined and proposed to account for the contrast, for contemporary Jewish behavior in the USA, between norms and actual conduct in *What the Books Say, What the People Do: The Puzzle of Contemporary Religion, Illustrated by Judaism in North America.*[4] For the Jews of Babylonia as portrayed in the Talmud and related writings as well as in archaeological remains, I have done the same in my *History of the Jews in Babylonia,*[5] each volume of which devotes ample attention to the contrast between what the books or the sages said and what the same sources allege people did and proposes to explain where and how the sages could require conformity to their theology and its practiced norms. None of this has any bearing upon theology, nor, truth be told, does theology pertain to popular belief and behavior, except to establish a theoretical norm, of interest to those whom norms interest.

For the formative age in the history of Judaism, sociology of religion provides a picture quite distinct from that of the writings that yield the philosophy, religion, and theology I describe. As a matter of fact, the evidence points to a single conclusion. Most of the stories in the Talmud about what people said, did, and believed contrast actual conduct with norms of *halakhah* or *aggadah*, behavior or belief, that the theology of Judaism set forth in that very document defined. No account of the history of any Judaism, including the paramount one, is going to ignore the issue of the belief and behavior of the people identified with the holy community of Israel.

But theology speaks of knowledge of God, such as God affords through self-manifestation, in the case of this Judaism, in the Torah, and describing that theology hardly demands attention to who acknowledged that knowledge, where or when or why it was accepted, or what people did with it. These are topics of concern to the sociology, not the theology, of Judaism; both sociology and theology, of course, contribute to the history of Judaism. But here, the description of that history focuses upon the unfolding of its structure and system, not their effects upon the society of Israel.

THEOLOGICAL APOLOGETICS: Why should you believe these things? Though, as it happens, I am not only a historian of religion but also a practicing Judaist and Jew, here I describe, analyze, and interpret, but do not advocate. The work of description affords no space for apologetics, which is irrelevant and would distort analysis and corrupt interpretation. An attitude of apologetics and advocacy furthermore would exclude those (many) readers, who want to know about how an

---

[4](Minneapolis, 1994: Fortress Press).
[5](Leiden, 1965-1970: E.J. Brill), I-V.

important religion took shape without assessing the truth or personal relevance (if any) of that religion. Not only so, but advocacy of a religious system in its theological formulation of fourteen centuries ago in any event would vastly distort the system and its theology as these flourish – in perfect continuity to be sure with the authoritative statement examined here – in our own times. Such advocacy of a theological system as it was set forth at a single moment in its unfolding – albeit the defining moment – would prove monumentally beside the point of contemporary religious faith, even if the formation of that present faith for the here and now were at issue here; but of course it is not.

Merely because theology forms the topic, that does not mean the goal must be advocacy of that theology. One need not even admire it; maintain it served some socially beneficial purpose; sustained the group that held it; or otherwise should enjoy our appreciation of its this-worldly uses, let alone its other-worldly appeal. Apologetics simply never has been, and now is not, pertinent to this work of mine, which has for three decades now formed a labor of historical description of the unfolding of a religious system. An apologetic subtext becomes blatant in any text, as historians of Judaism in this period for generations have proven; the museum of discarded theories, rich in curiosities of the nineteenth and twentieth centuries from Zunz and Geiger (for Reform Judaism) to Finkelstein, Zeitlin, Urbach, and Lieberman (for whatever they defined as their orthodoxy) contains ample warning.

If history sets the wrong venue for apologetics, that does not mean the work has no place at all. On the contrary, apologetics defines an honorable task in theology, and other writings of mine, addressed to the community of Judaism, contain a serious effort at theological apologetics in behalf of Judaism. Moreover, theologians of Judaism, past and present, also have carried out their responsibilities as apologists, framing their theology in terms, language, and arguments calculated to invoke belief in what is said, not merely assent for the rationality of what is expounded. But here that is not my intent, and no reader, believer or otherwise, Jew or gentile, should be left out of the discourse set forth in this book by reason of my laying out a special program of pleading aimed at only some readers. I mean solely to expound and explain a theological system in its historical context: how it came to expression, what it proposed to accomplish. I should be less than candid, however, if I did not state at the outset my intense admiration for the religious system at hand, my entire commitment to the theological statement of it that I define here, and my wholehearted admiration for "our sages of blessed memory," who, in making up the Talmud, showed a unique medium for theology and through that stated a compelling message for holy Israel.

But admiration and appreciation do not require advocacy, and, accordingly, this description, analysis, and interpretation of the theology of Judaism in its definitive canonical writings cannot also address the also legitimate, and certainly more urgent, task of theological apologetics. This book simply ignores all issues of apologetics, in no way proposing to persuade readers to adopt the convictions described here, or to explain their plausibility, or to set forth compelling reasons for identifying the knowledge of God afforded by the theology of Judaism with, for example, principles of how God can and should be defined by philosophy of religion.

1

Completing the Formation of Judaism

The history of the formation of Judaism tells the story of how [1] philosophy became [2] religion, which was then re-presented as [3] theology. The medium of theological re-presentation was hermeneutics, so that, when we know how the Torah is properly read, we discern the theology of Judaism.

Before proceeding, I hasten to give a simple definition of hermeneutics, that of Wilhelm Dilthey, since the rest of this book depends upon my claim that in its hermeneutics, the Talmud re-presents the Torah: "The methodological understanding of permanently fixed life-expressions we call explication...culminates in the interpretation of the written records of human existence....The science of this art is hermeneutics."[1] When we know the rules of explication that instruct us on how to interpret the Torah, we gain access to the theology that governs the presentation of the religion Judaism.

The priority of hermeneutics in the theological venture is not difficult to explain. We deal with a Judaism that affords religious experience – knowledge of God, meeting with God – in particular in books. While that same Judaism, like any other religious system, also meets God in prayer, obedience to the covenant, and right conduct, and expresses the sense of the knowledge of God in music and in art, in pilgrimage and in dance, in rite and in cult, and in most of the ways that religions in general celebrate God, what makes this Judaic system distinctive is its insistence that God is made manifest in, and therefore known through, documents, which preserve and contain the encounter with God that in secular language we call "religious experience." Just as, if the principal

---

[1]Cited by K.M. Newton, *Interpreting the Text. A Critical Introduction to the Theory and Practice of Literary Interpretation* (New York, 1990: Harvester/Wheatsheaf), p. 42, further discussed in Chapter Two.

medium for meeting God were theater or music, we should search for theology in aesthetics, so since the principal meeting or encounter with God is the Torah, and the Torah is given in writing and oral formulation as well, this Judaism promises knowledge of God through the documents of the Torah, and its theological medium will be hermeneutics (as much as philosophy).

The character of the evidence therefore governs. Because the formation of (this particular) Judaism as a religious system is fully exposed in its successive documents, the history of that Judaism's formative age – the first six centuries of the Common Era – comes to us in the right reading of the Torah. In this Judaism, the Torah comprises the holy documents and persons – written and oral documents, and the person of "our sages of blessed memory"; the deeds and teachings of sages take the form of stories and statements preserved in the same documents. Not only so, but because the medium for theology in this Judaism was a fully exposed hermeneutics, the message was conveyed through unarticulated but ubiquitious initiatives of a hermeneutical character. Then theological method consisted in constantly and ubiquitously showing the same few things through that hermeneutics, worked out in the Talmuds for the Oral Torah, and in the Midrash compilations for the Written Torah. But, as we shall see at the end, matters ended up in hardly so simple a way, for the profound hermeneutical problem will emerge only at the end, in the documentary re-presentation of the Torah accomplished by the Talmud of Babylonia, and its hermeneutics is not one of words, phrases, or sentences, but connections and continuities: identifying the questions. The answers flow, once we know what to ask.

Stated in documentary terms, the formative history of Judaism tells a story in three sentences. It shows, first, how the Judaic system emerged in the Mishnah, ca. 200 C.E., and its associated Midrash compilations, ca. 200-300 C.E., as [1] a philosophical structure comprising a politics, philosophy, and economics. These categories were defined as philosophers in general understood them: a theory of legitimate violence, an account of knowledge gained through the methods of natural history, and a theory of the rational disposition (and increase) of scarce resources.

This philosophical system then was turned by the Talmud of the Land of Israel and related Midrash compilations, ca. 400-500 C.E., into [2] a religious system. The system was effected through the formation of counterpart categories: an anti-politics of weakness, an anti-economics of the rational utilization of an infinitely renewable resource, a philosophy of truth revealed rather than rules discovered.[2]

Then, finally, the religious system was restated by the Talmud of Babylonia and its companions of Midrash collection, ca. 500-600 C.E. In those writings it was given [3] theological re-presentation through the recovery of philosophical method for the formulation of religious conceptions. In the great tradition, we may say, the formation of Judaism took place through [3] the final synthesis of [1] the initial thesis and [2] the consequent antithesis.

Theology is the science of the reasoned knowledge of God, in the case of a Judaism made possible by God's self-manifestation in the Torah.[3] Seen in its whole re-presentation in the Talmud of Babylonia, the theology of Judaism sets forth knowledge of God. This is in two ways. The first (as I just said) is to know God through God's self-revelation in the Torah. This requires that we know what the Torah is, or what torah is (in a generic sense, which can pertain to either message or media or modes of thought). Then, knowing how to define and understand the Torah affords access to God's self-revelation. The second is to know through that same self-revelation what God wants of Israel and how God responds to Israel and humanity at large.[4] That specific, propositional knowledge comes through reasoned reading of the Torah, Oral and Written, the Mishnah and Scripture, represented by the Talmuds and Midrash compilations, respectively.[5] The hermeneutics governing these documents encapsulate that knowledge of reasoned explication.

---

[2]The characterization of the first two stages in the formation of Judaism is contained within these books of mine: *The Economics of the Mishnah* (Chicago, 1989: University of Chicago Press); *Rabbinic Political Theory: Religion and Politics in the Mishnah* (Chicago, 1991: University of Chicago Press); *Judaism as Philosophy. The Method and Message of the Mishnah* (Columbia, 1991: University of South Carolina Press); and *The Transformation of Judaism. From Philosophy to Religion* (Champaign, 1992: University of Illinois Press).

[3]I elaborate on that definition in Chapter Four.

[4]I paraphrase Ingolf Dalferth, "The Stuff of Revelation: Austin Farrer's Doctrine of Inspired Images," in Ann Loades and Michael McLain, eds., *Hermeneutics, the Bible, and Literary Criticism* (London, 1992: MacMillan), p. 71. Dalferth was my colleague when I was Buber Professor of Judaic Studies at the University of Frankfurt, and it was in reading his writing that I began to think along the lines that come to fruition in this book; his influence is fully spelled-out in Chapter Three and brought to concrete realization in Chapter Four. Other definitions and premises will yield other ways of reading the theology of the Judaism of the Dual Torah.

[5]And that explains why we still will have to undertake a separate account of the theology yielded by the hermeneutics of the Midrash compilations (not only, or mainly, specific words or phrases or sentences found hither and yon in "The Midrash," as the ignorant conduct the inquiry). The characterization of the

The priority of hermeneutics in the theological inquiry in a religion expressed through documents (more than, for example, through creeds, institutions, persons, dancing, singing, acting, or laughing, crying, eating, starving, and the like, all of which, as a matter of fact, convey the systemic statement of this Judaism, too) is then self-evident. Through defining the hermeneutics of the Torah, we learn how the theology of Judaism explains what it means to reason about the Torah, showing how this is to be done in quest of truth about Israel's right action and conviction. The explanation is set forth in the hermeneutics of the Torah, spelled out in the two Talmuds to the Mishnah, and the several Midrash compilations to Scripture. All together, these writings expound the Torah and exemplify the correct hermeneutics for understanding the Torah. The task of describing theology of Judaism therefore is to identify the correct hermeneutics; and the work of framing statements of normative theology requires proper hermeneutics in the analysis of the Talmud's re-presentation of the Torah: the rules of explication, in Dilthey's definition.

The schematic classifications of the successive, related Judaic systems as philosophical, religious, and theological therefore derive from the character of the successive documents, the Mishnah, Yerushalmi, and Bavli.[6] What makes all the difference in the second Talmud's re-presentation of the Judaic religious system therefore is the character of that Talmud itself. Through analysis of the hermeneutics that conveys the intellectual program of that medium, I show, in particular, how a religion rich in miscellaneous but generally congruent norms of behavior and endowed with a vast store of varied and episodic but occasionally contradictory ideas was turned into a proportioned and harmonious theology.[7] Chapter Twelve gives a single, but I think stunning, example of what it means to identify theology through hermeneutics, specifically, the illustrative case of that sentence of the theological ethics of Judaism that sets cause and blame into relationship to right and wrong.

---

hermeneutics of Midrash compilations, early, middle, and late, will stand side by side with the work set forth here. But I cannot conceive of doing the work in a single volume, because the analytical problems of Talmuds and Midrash compilations really are distinct from one another.

[6]That is within the qualification that the Yerushalmi did part of the work of theologizing the Mishnah, the work of showing its proportion, composition, harmony, and coherence. The second Talmud did this work, but it also accomplished the far more sophisticated intellectual tasks.

[7]But as the table of contents has already signaled, I maintain that an important part of the theological work was undertaken by the first of the two Talmuds, which means the differentiation between the two Talmuds provides the key, in literary analysis, to the hermeneutical priority of the second of the two.

Having laid heavy emphasis on the priority of the Bavli, I hasten to qualify matters. As a matter of fact, I show in detail that the process of theological re-presentation went forward in two stages. In the first, in the Talmud of the Land of Israel, the philosophical document that stated that system gained both a vast amplification, in which the categories and methods of the original statement were amplified and instantiated, and also a remarkable reformulation in counterpart categories. Of the three traits of "tradition," for example, as defined in the tractate Avot in its apologia for the Mishnah – harmony, linearity, and unity – the first of the two Talmuds systematically demonstrated the presence of two: harmony and linearity. The second undertook to demonstrate all three, all together and all at once and everywhere, that is to say, the law behind the laws, meaning, the unity, the integrity of truth. That shown, we know the mind of God, the character of truth.

Viewed as a whole, the result is then to be classified as not philosophical but religious in character and theological in re-presentation. Alongside, earlier Midrash compilations undertook the task of showing the relationship between the two media of the Torah, the oral and the written, by insisting that the Mishnah rested on Scripture. The goal was to show linearity and, of course, harmony. They furthermore began the definition of the Torah – in our terms, the reading of Scripture – by systematizing and generalizing the episodic cases of Scripture. The goal was to demonstrate the comprehensiveness of the Torah: its cases were meant to yield governing rules. The later Midrash compilations continued that reading of Scripture by formulating syllogistic propositions out of the occasional data of Scripture.[8]

The religious writings that formed the second stage in the unfolding of Judaism, the Talmud of the Land of Israel, Sifra and the two Sifrés somewhat before, Genesis Rabbah and Leviticus Rabbah somewhat afterward, finally were succeeded – and replaced – by the Talmud of Babylonia and related Midrash compilations, particularly Song of Songs

---

[8]I eliminated from the final draft of this book the chapters I had written on the coherence – hermeneutical, therefore also theological – of the Midrash compilations, earlier, middle, and later, with the Talmuds that these compilations accompany. The reason is that the results struck me as, while relevant, somewhat prolix; only Sifra's embodiment of theology in hermeneutics, and only in hermeneutics, persuaded me that it was essential to the argument of this book. It suffices simply to observe that the companion collections of the Talmuds make their contribution, through hermeneutics, to theology. In the planned work on the unity of the Torah, in its written, oral, and personal re-presentations, I shall spell out this point in its correct context. But I plan to write the companion to this work, that is, "the Midrashic re-presentation," which will take the form of an anthology.

Rabbah, Lamentations Rabbah, and Ruth Rabbah. These were documents that restated in rigorous, theological ways the same religious convictions, so providing that Judaism or Judaic system with its theological statement. In these writings, the religious system was restated in a rigorous and philosophical way. The associated Midrash compilations succeeded in making a single, encompassing statement out of the data of the several books of Scripture they presented.[9]

The re-presentation of the religious system in the disciplined thought of theology took the form of rules of reading the Torah – Oral and Written – and through those rules exposing the character of the intellectual activity of thinking like God, that is, thinking about the world in the way God thinks. The theology of Judaism – reasoned knowledge of God[10] and God's will afforded by God's self-manifestation in the Torah[11] – affords access in particular to the mind of God, revealed in God's words and wording of the Torah. Through the Torah, Oral and Written, we work our way back to the intellect of God who gives the Torah. Thus through learning in the Torah in accord with the lessons of the Talmuds and associated Midrash compilations, humanity knows what God personally has made manifest about mind, that intellect in particular in which "in our image, after our likeness" we, too, are made. That defines the theology of the Judaism of the Dual Torah and in particular forms the upshot of the Talmud's re-presentation of that theology.

Reading the Mishnah together with one or the other of its Talmudic amplifications, the Talmud of the Land of Israel or the Talmud of Babylonia, or Scripture together with any of the Midrash compilations, on the surface does not convey such an account. The canonical writings – the Mishnah and Talmud of the Land of Israel or the Mishnah and Talmud of Babylonia and their associated Midrash collections – portray not successive stages of the formation of a system but rather a single, continuous Judaism, which everywhere is read as unitary and uniform. Not only so, but in the persons and teachings of sages that same Torah makes part of its statement. But, when examined as single documents, one by one, in the sequence of their closure, to the contrary, matters look otherwise. Each writing then may be characterized on its own, rather than in the continuous context defined by the canon of which it forms a principal part.

---

[9]The point of the foregoing note pertains here as well.

[10]That is a standard definition of theology, as I shall show in Chapter Three.

[11]That is my restatement of a standard definition of theology to state what I mean by theology of Judaism.

Then the formation of Judaism, correctly described, may be stated in a single sentence. [1] The Mishnah, then [2] the first Talmud, then [3] the second Talmud, together with their respective sets of associated Midrash compilations, yield the history of a three-stage formation.

The first tells how the document that set forth the first Judaic system formed a philosophy, utilizing philosophical categories and philosophical modes of thought (philosophy, politics, economics, for categories, Aristotelian methods of hierarchical classification).

The second explains how the categorical formation was recast into religious classifications, from philosophy to Torah, from a politics of legitimate power to an anti-politics of weakness, from an economics of scarce resources to an anti-economics of the abundant resource of Torah learning.

The third then spells out how the received categorical system and structure was restated in its main points in such a way as to hold together the philosophical method and the religious message through a hermeneutical medium. Here I specify the character of that medium and its content. As I have already indicated, I once more stress, less I be misunderstood, that this division between the second and the third should be shaded somewhat, since, as I shall show, by the operative definition of theology here, part of the theological work was carried on in the second – the Yerushalmi's – stage, part in the third. But, withal, the Bavli formed the summa, holding the whole together and making its own supreme and unique statement.

I have used the terms "philosophy" and "religion" and suggested they be treated as distinct categories of thought. Let me now spell out what I mean by "philosophy" and "religion," with the systematic definition of theology to be given in the shank of the book, at Chapter Three. By "philosophy" I refer to the category formation, inclusive of categorical definitions, put forth by philosophy in ancient times. By "religion" I refer to the category formation put forth on a wholly other-than-philosophical basis in that same period. The one is secular and worldly in its data, utilizing the methods of natural history for its analytical work; the other is transcendental, finding its data in revelation, utilizing the methods of the exegesis of revelation for its systematic work. Both are exercises of sustained rationality, in the case of this Judaism, of applied reason and practical logic. But the one begins in this world and its facts, which are analyzed and categorized through the traits inherent in them, and the other commences in the world above and its truths, which are analyzed and categorized by the categories of revelation. The one yields philosophy of religion, the other, religious statements, attitudes, convictions, rules of life; the one represents one way of knowing God, specifically, the way through the data of this world, the other, a different way to God altogether, the way opened by God's revelation and self-manifestation, whether through nature or beyond. Let me now spell this distinction out with reference to the systemic results of a reading of the Mishnah and the Yerushalmi.

The Mishnah set forth in the form of a law code a highly philosophical account of the world ("worldview"), a pattern for everyday and material activities and relationships ("way of life"), and a definition of the social entity ("nation," "people," "us" as against "outsiders," "Israel") that realized that way of life and explained it by appeal to that worldview. We have no difficulty in calling this account of a way of life an economics, because the account of material reality provided by the Mishnah corresponds, point for point, with that given in Aristotle's counterpart. The Mishnah moreover sets forth a politics by dealing with the same questions, about the permanent and legitimate institutions that inflict sanctions, that occupy Greek and Roman political thinkers. There is no economics of another-than-this-worldly character, no politics of an inner "kingdom of God." All is straightforward, worldly, material, and consequential for the everyday world. Then the successor documents, closed roughly two centuries later, addressed the Mishnah's system and recast its categories into a connected, but also quite revised, one. The character of their reception of the received categories and of their own category formation, emerging in the contrast between one set of documents and another, justifies invoking the term, "transformation," that is, of one thing into something else. That something else was a religious, as distinct from a philosophical, category formation.

The first Talmud and associated Midrash compilations attest to a system that did more than merely extend and recast the categorical structure of the system for which the Mishnah stands. They took over the way of life, worldview, and social entity, defined in the Mishnah's system. And while they rather systematically amplified details, framed a program of exegesis around the requirements of clerks engaged in enforcing the rules of the Mishnah, they built their own system. For at the same time they formed categories corresponding to those of the Mishnah, a politics, a philosophy, an economics. But these categories proved so utterly contrary in their structure and definition to those of the Mishnah that they presented mirror images of the received categories.

The politics, philosophy, and economics of the Mishnah were joined by the Yerushalmi to an anti-politics, an anti-economics, and an utterly transformed mode of learning. In the hands of the later sages, the new mode of Torah study – the definition of what was at stake in studying the Torah – redefined altogether the issues of the intellect. Natural history as the method of classification gave way to a different mode of thought altogether. As a matter of fact the successor system recast not the issues so much as the very stakes of philosophy or science. The reception of the Mishnah's category formations and their transformation therefore stands for the movement from a philosophical to a religious mode of thinking. For the system to which the Mishnah as a document attests is essentially philosophical in its rhetorical, logical, and topical program; the successor system, fundamentally religious in these same principal and indicative traits of medium of intellect and mentality.

Given the definitions with which I began, how do I know whether a system is philosophical or religious? The answer is not subjective, nor the criteria, private or idiosyncratic. The indicative traits in both instances, to begin with, derive from and are displayed by documents, for – I take it as axiomatic – the mode of the writing down of any system attests to both the method and the message that sustain that system. From how people express themselves, we work our way backward to their modes of thought: the classification of perceived data, the making of connections between fact and fact, the drawing of conclusions from those connections, and, finally, the representation of conclusions in cogent compositions. All of these traits of mind are to be discerned in the character of those compositions, in the rhetoric that conveys messages in proportion and appropriate aesthetics, in the logic that imparts self-evidence to the making of connections, the drawing of conclusions, and in the representation of sets of conclusions as cogent and intelligible, characteristic of writing and expressed in writing.

In the Yerushalmi (and the Bavli later on) scarce resources, so far as these are of a material order of being, for example, wealth as defined by the Mishnah and Aristotle, are systemically neutral. A definition of scarce resources emerges that explicitly involves a symbolic transformation, with the material definition of scarce resources set into contradiction with an other-than-material one. So we find side by side clarification of the details of the received category and adumbration of a symbolic revision and hence a categorical transformation in the successor writings. The representation of the political structure of the Mishnah undergoes clarification, but alongside, a quite separate and very different structure also is portrayed. The received structure presents three political classes, ordered in a hierarchy; the successor structure, a single political class, corresponding on earth to a counterpart in Heaven. Here, too, a symbolic transaction has taken place, in which one set of symbols is replicated but also reversed, and a second set of symbols given instead.

The Mishnah's structure comprising a hierarchical composition of foci of power in the Yerushalmi gives way to a structure centered upon a single focus of power. That single focus, moreover, now draws boundaries between legitimate and illegitimate violence, boundaries not conceived in the initial system. So in all three components of the account of the social order the philosophical system gives way to another. The worldview comes to expression in modes of thought and expression – the logic of making connections and drawing conclusions – that are different from the philosophical ones of the Mishnah. The way of life appeals to value expressed in other symbols than those of economics in the philosophical mode. The theory of the social entity comes to concrete expression in sanctions legitimately administered by a single class of persons (institution), rather than by a proportionate and balanced set of classes of persons in hierarchical order, and, moreover, that same theory recognizes and defines both legitimate and also illegitimate violence, something beyond the ken of the initial system. So, it is clear, another system is adumbrated and attested in the successor writings.

The categorical transformation that was underway in the Yerushalmi, signaling the movement from philosophy to religion, comes to the surface when we ask a simple question. Precisely what do the authorships of the successor documents, speaking not about the Mishnah but on their own account, mean by economics, politics, and philosophy? That is to say, to what kinds of data do they refer when they speak of scarce resources and legitimate violence, and exactly how – as to the received philosophical method – do they define correct modes of thought and expression, logic and rhetoric, and even the topical program worthy of sustained inquiry? The components of the initial formation of categories were examined thoughtfully and carefully, paraphrased and augmented and clarified. But the received categories were not continued, not expanded, and not renewed. Preserved merely intact, as they had been handed on, the received categories hardly serve to encompass all of the points of emphasis and sustained development that characterize the successor documents – or, as a matter of fact, any of them. On the contrary, when the framers of the Yerushalmi, for one example, moved out from the exegesis of Mishnah passages, they also left behind the topics of paramount interest in the Mishnah and developed other categories altogether. Here the framers of the successor system defined their own counterparts.

These counterpart categories, moreover, redefined matters, following the main outlines of the structure of the social order manifest in the initial system. The counterpart categories set forth an account of the social order just as did the ones of the Mishnah's framers. But they defined the social order in very different terms altogether. In that redefinition we discern the transformation of the received system, and the traits of the new one fall into the classification of not philosophy but religion. For what the successor thinkers did was not continue and expand the categorical repertoire but set forth a categorically fresh vision of the social order – a way of life, worldview, and definition of the social entity – with appropriate counterpart categories. And what is decisive is that these served as did the initial categories within the generative categorical structure definitive for all Judaic systems. So there was a category corresponding to the generative component of worldview, but it was not philosophical; another corresponding to the required component setting forth a way of life, but in the conventional and accepted definition of economics it was not an economics; and, finally, a category to define the social entity, "Israel," that any Judaic system must explain, but in the accepted sense of a politics it was not politics.

What is the difference between the philosophical and the religious systems? What philosophy kept distinct, religion joined together: that defines the transformation of Judaism from philosophy to religion. The received system was a religious system of a philosophical character; this-worldly data are classified according to rules that apply consistently throughout, so that we may always predict with a fair degree of accuracy what will happen and why. And a philosophical system of religion then systematically demonstrates out of the data of the world order of nature and society the governance of God in nature and supernature: this world's data pointing toward God above and beyond. The God of the philosophical Judaism then sat enthroned at the apex of all things, all being hierarchically classified. Just as philosophy seeks the explanation of things, so a philosophy of religion (in the context at hand) will propose orderly explanations in accord with prevailing and cogent rules. The profoundly philosophical character of the Mishnah has already provided ample evidence of the shape, structure, and character of that philosophical system in the Judaic context. The rule-seeking character of Mishnaic discourse marks it as a philosophical system of religion. But, we shall now see, the successor system saw the world differently. It follows that a philosophical system forms its learning inductively and syllogistically, by appeal to the neutral evidence of the rules shown to apply to all things by the observation of the order of universally accessible nature and society.

A religious system frames its propositions deductively and exegetically by appeal to the privileged evidence of a corpus of truths deemed revealed by God. The difference pertains not to detail but to the fundamental facts deemed to matter. Some of those facts lie at the very surface, in the nature of the writings that express the system. These writings were not free-standing but contingent, and that in two ways. First, they served as commentaries to prior documents, the Mishnah and Scripture, for the Talmud and Midrash compilations, respectively. Second, and more consequential, the authorships insisted upon citing Scripture passages or Mishnah sentences as the centerpiece of proof, on

the one side, and program of discourse, on the other. But the differences
that prove indicative are not merely formal. More to the point, while the
Mishnah's system is steady state and ahistorical, admitting no movement
or change, the successor system of the Yerushalmi and Midrash
compilations tells tales, speaks of change, accommodates and responds
to historical moments. It formulates a theory of continuity within
change, of the moral connections between generations, of the way in
which one's deeds shape one's destiny – and that of the future as well. If
what the framers of the Mishnah want more than anything else is to
explain the order and structure of being, then their successors have
rejected their generative concern. For what they, for their part, intensely
desire to sort out is the currents and streams of time and change, as these
flow toward an unknown ocean.

The shift from the philosophical to the religious modes of thought
and media of expression – logical and rhetorical indicators, respectively –
comes to realization in the recasting of the generative categories of the
system as well. These categories are transformed, and the transformation
proved so thoroughgoing as to validate the characterization of the
change as "counterpart categories." The result of the formation of such
counterpart categories in the aggregate was to encompass not only the
natural but also the supernatural realms of the social order. That is how
philosophical thinking gave way to religious. The religious system of the
Yerushalmi and associated documents sets forth the category formation
that produced in place of an economics based on prime value assigned to
real wealth one that now encompassed wealth of an intangible,
impalpable, and supernatural order, but a valued resource nonetheless.
It points toward the replacement of a politics formerly serving to
legitimate and hierarchize power and differentiate among sanctions by
appeal to fixed principles by one that now introduced the variable of
God's valuation of the victim and the anti-political conception of the
illegitimacy of worldly power.

This counterpart politics then formed the opposite of the Mishnah's
this-worldly political system altogether. In all three ways the upshot is
the same: the social system, in the theory of its framers, now extends its
boundaries upward to Heaven, drawing into a whole the formerly
distinct, if counterpoised, realms of Israel on earth and the heavenly
court above. So if I had to specify the fundamental difference between
the philosophical and the religious versions of the social order, it would
fall, quite specifically – to state with emphasis – *upon the broadening of the
systemic boundaries to encompass Heaven.* The formation of counterpart
categories therefore signals not a reformation of the received system but
the formation of an essentially new one.

The first fundamental point of reversal, uniting what had been divided, is the joining of economics and politics into a political economy, through the conception of *zekhut*, a term defined presently. The other point at which what the one system treated as distinct the next and connected system chose to address as one and whole is less easily discerned, since to do so we have to ask a question the framers of the Mishnah did not raise in the Mishnah at all. That concerns the character and source of virtue, specifically, the effect, upon the individual, of knowledge, specifically, knowledge of the Torah or Torah study. To frame the question very simply, if we ask ourselves, what happens to me if I study the Torah, the answer, for the Mishnah, predictably is, my standing and status change. Torah study and its effects form a principal systemic indicator in matters of hierarchical classification, joining the *mamzer* disciple of sages in a mixture of opposites, for one self-evident example.

But am I changed within? In vain we look in the hundreds of chapters of the Mishnah for an answer to that question. Virtue and learning form distinct categories, a point I shall underline in the pertinent chapter, which follows, and, overall, I am not changed as to my virtue, my character and conscience, by my mastery of the Torah. And still more strikingly, if we ask, does my Torah study affect my fate in this world and in the life to come, the Mishnah's authorship is strikingly silent about that matter, too. Specifically, we find in the pages of that document no claim that studying the Torah either changes me or assures my salvation. But the separation of knowledge and the human condition is set aside, and studying the Torah deemed the source of salvation, in the successor system. The philosophical system, with its interest in *homo hierarchicus*, proved remarkably silent about the effect of the Torah upon the inner man. The upshot is at the critical points of bonding, the received system proved flawed, in its separation of learning from virtue and legitimate power from valued resources. Why virtue joins knowledge (I call this "the gnostic Torah"), politics links to economics, in the religious system but not in the philosophical one is of course obvious. Philosophy differentiates, seeking the rules that join diverse data; religion integrates, proposing to see the whole all together and all at once, thus (for an anthropology, for example) seeing humanity whole: "in our image, after our likeness." Religion by its nature asks the questions of integration, such as the theory intended to hold together within a single boundary earth and Heaven, this world and the other, should lead us to anticipate.

The second systemic innovation is the formation of an integrated category of political economy, framed in such a way that at stake in politics and economics alike were value and resource in no way subject to order and rule, but in all ways formed out of the unpredictable resource of *zekhut*, sometimes translated as "merit," but, being a matter of not obligation but supererogatory free will, should be portrayed, I think, as "the heritage of virtue and its consequent entitlements." Between those two conceptions – the Torah as a medium of transformation, the heritage of virtue and its consequent entitlements, which can be gained for oneself and also received from one's ancestors – the received system's this-worldly boundaries were transcended, and the new system encompassed within its framework a supernatural life on earth. And appealing to these two statements of worldview, way of life, and social entity, we may as a matter of fact compose a complete description of the definitive traits and indicative systemic concerns of the successor Judaism. It remains to observe very simply: The Bavli in no way innovated in the category formation set forth by the Yerushalmi, and, it follows, no important component of the Bavli's theological statement would have surprised the framers of the Yerushalmi's compositions and compilers of its composites.

My account of the formation of Judaism therefore may be stated in these simple stages, involving method, message, and medium:

[1]   THE METHOD OF PHILOSOPHY: The initial statement of the Judaism of the Dual Torah took the form of a philosophical law code and set forth a philosophical system of monotheism, providing an economics, politics, and philosophy that philosophers in the Aristotelian and Middle- or Neo-Platonic traditions could have understood as philosophical (if they grasped the idiom in which the philosophical system was expressed). That is the point of my *The Economics of the Mishnah;*[12] *Rabbinic Political Theory: Religion and Politics in the Mishnah;*[13] and *Judaism as Philosophy. The Method and Message of the Mishnah.*[14]

[2]   THE MESSAGE OF RELIGION: Through the formation of counterpart categories to economics, politics, and

[12](Chicago, 1989: University of Chicago Press).

[13](Chicago, 1991: University of Chicago Press).

[14](Columbia, 1991: University of South Carolina Press). See also *The Making of the Mind of Judaism* (Atlanta, 1987: Scholars Press for Brown Judaic Studies), and also *The Formation of the Jewish Intellect. Making Connections and Drawing Conclusions in the Traditional System of Judaism* (Atlanta, 1988: Scholars Press for Brown Judaic Studies); and *The Philosophical Mishnah* (Atlanta, 1989: Scholars Press for Brown Judaic Studies). I. *The Initial Probe;* II. *The Tractates' Agenda. From Abodah Zarah to Moed Qatan;* III. *The Tractates' Agenda. From Nazir to Zebahim;* and IV. *The Repertoire.*

philosophy, the successor system, which came to expression in the Talmud of the Land of Israel and associated Midrash compilations, set forth a religious system and statement of the same Judaism of the Dual Torah. That is the point of my *The Transformation of Judaism. From Philosophy to Religion.*[15]

[3]   THE MEDIUM OF THEOLOGY, MELDING METHOD AND MESSAGE: Taking over that system and reviewing its main points, the final Talmud then restated the received body of religion as theology. That then is the point of this book, which explains how Judaism came to completion in its definitive statement when [1] the disciplines of philosophy were used to set forth the message of [2] religion so that Judaism stated [3] its theology. The Talmud that represented the Judaism of the Dual Torah by joining the method of philosophy to the message of religion.

---

[15](Champaign-Urbana, 1992: University of Illinois Press).

2

Judaism States Its Theology

Theology is not philosophy, and philosophy is not a substitute for religious convictions. But whereas religion can exist without philosophy, and philosophy without religion, theology cannot exist without recourse to each of the other two. It rationally reflects on questions arising in pre-theological religious experience and the discourse of faith; and it is the rationality of its reflective labor in the process of faith seeking understanding which inseparably links it with philosophy. For philosophy is essentially concerned with argument and the attempt to solve conceptual problems, and conceptual problems face theology in all areas of its reflective labors.

Ingolf U. Dalferth, *Theology and Philosophy*[1]

Theology philosophically sets forth religion.[2] The final chapter of the formative history of Judaism recorded the formulation of religion in, and as, theology. That is, theology by the definition of theology that is before us: systematic and rigorous reflection on religious questions; faith seeking understanding through processes of rationality; sustained and vigorous argument concerning the solution of conceptual problems of a religious character. The historical formation of Judaism reached completion when [1] a philosophical system having been transformed into [2] a religious one, the religious system through the disciplines of philosophy was re-presented [3] as a theology.

So – stated schematically – the story of the formation of Judaism tells how Judaism progressed in its formation from philosophy through religion to theology. For that Judaism in its fullness, [1] philosophy provided the method, [2] religion, the message, and [3] theology, the

---

[1]Ingolf U. Dalferth, *Theology and Philosophy* (Oxford, 1988: Basil Blackwell Ltd.), p. vii. Chapters Two and Three bring us back to his formulations.
[2]Chapter Three defines theology in relationship to religion and philosophy. Here it suffices simply to introduce the operative terms and categories of the book.

medium of persuasive re-presentation. Theology thus formed out of the received method of the first phase and the message of the second a wholly fresh and compelling statement.

As a religious system – an account of the social order comprising a worldview, ethos, way of life, ethics, and theory of the social entity that realizes the ethos and ethics, the ethnos – wholly spelled out in documents, the entire expression of theology took the form of hermeneutics. Documents correctly subjected to the proper interrogation, a rightly conducted process of interlocution of sacred writings – these made it possible to reenact the theological message in a sustained exercise of applied reason and practical logic applied to conduct and conviction in the common life. So Judaism became lived theology, re-forming the here and now in full accord with the reasoned knowledge of God's will as God has made that will known in the Torah.[3] Then the key to understanding the theology of Judaism lay in the rules by which the Torah was defined and read: hermeneutics in the richest sense.

The method of that theology of Judaism was to speak by indirection, through hermeneutics – the hermeneutics never articulated but everywhere instantiated in the Midrash compilations and the two Talmuds, but the second one in particular – to convey reasoned and coherent knowledge of God. The first principle then was, God is made manifest in the Torah. Then what is the Torah and how is it to be read? The Talmudic re-presentation of that principle takes place, then, in the hermeneutics of pure rationality that guide the right reading of the Torah, Written and Oral, Scripture and the Mishnah in concrete terms. So to restate the proposition of this book: In the literary terms of formative Judaism, the theology set forth by the Talmud of Babylonia at the completion of the formation of Judaism in its paramount and normative system employs and reshapes the philosophical principles of the Mishnah to re-present the religious convictions of the Talmud of the Land of Israel.

To understand the claim of this book, a clear definition of theology is required at the very outset. For that purpose I reverse the elements of the definition provided by Dalferth at the head of this chapter. The predicate becomes the subject in this way:

---

[3]The word choices, "Judaism" and "Torah," are worked out in Chapter Four. These of course correspond, "Judaism" being the secular, academic word for the religious, theological word, "Torah." It is exceedingly important to preserve the distinction between the native categories of a religion and the imposed ones; using only the former, we paraphrase; using only the later, we distort.

[2]   *Where* we have rational reflection on questions arising in religious experience and the discourse of faith,

[1]   *there* we have theology.

When we find reflective labor on the rationality – the cogency, harmony, proposition, coherence, balance, order, and proper composition – of statements of religious truth, for example, truth revealed by God, then we have identified a theological writing.   And, as a matter of acknowledged fact, the Talmud forms the sustained, rigorous, open-ended activity of rational reflection on the sense and near-at-hand significance of the Torah.

Concern with argument, the attempt to solve conceptual problems – these characterize that writing.   By themselves, of course, they do not mark a writing as theological.   Argument concerning conceptual problems yields theology when the argument deals with religion, the conceptual problems derive from revelation.   Only the source of the givens of the writing – revelation, not merely reasoned analysis of this world's givens – distinguishes theology from philosophy, including, as a matter of fact, philosophy of religion. But that suffices. Take for example that splendid formulation of religion as philosophy, the Mishnah.   The Mishnah states its principles through method of natural history, sifting the traits of this-worldly things, demonstrating philosophical truth – the unity of one and unique God at the apex of the natural world – by showing on the basis of the evidence of this world, universally accessible, the hierarchical classification of being.   That is a philosophical demonstration of religious truth.   The Talmud of Babylonia states its principles through right reasoning about revealed truth, the Torah.   The Torah (Written, or Oral) properly read teaches the theological truth that God is one, at the apex of the hierarchy of all being. That is a theological re-presentation of (the same) religious truth.   But that re-presentation in the two Talmuds (and in the Midrash compilations, not treated here) also exhibits the traits of philosophical thinking: rigor, concern for harmonies, unities, consistencies, points of cogency, sustained argument and counter argument, appeal to persuasion through reason, not coercion through revelation.

That explains how and why, for Judaism in its classical, Talmudic statement, the methods of philosophy applied to the data of religious belief and behavior produced theology.   By these criteria deriving from propositions of general intelligibility, I maintain that the second of the two Talmuds, the Talmud of Babylonia, formed a massive and sustained work of theology, in which, as I said, the method of philosophy shapes the message of religion into a restatement characterized by rationality and entire integrity.   Through that second Talmud in particular Judaism states its theology. Because of the distinctive character of that Talmud, the power of its modes of analytical inquiry, that theology defined the intellect of Judaism, which is to say, the Torah, for generations to come.

Let me explain the specific historical and literary terms that have just now been used. We start with the end product, which is, the Torah as defined at the end of the formation of Judaism.[4] That Torah, called in due course "the one whole Torah of Moses, our rabbi," was formulated and transmitted by God to Moses in two media, each defining one of the components, written and oral. The written is Scripture as we know it, encompassing the Pentateuch, Prophets, and Writings. The oral part of the Torah came to be written down in a variety of works, beginning with the Mishnah, ca. 200 C.E. The canon of the Judaism the theology of which is described here is made up of extensions and amplifications of these two parts of the Torah. The written part is carried forward through collections of readings of verses of Scripture called Midrash compilations. The oral part is extended through two sustained, selective commentaries and expansions, called talmuds, the Talmud of the Land of Israel, a.k.a. the Yerushalmi (ca. 400 C.E.), and the Talmud of Babylonia, a.k.a. the Bavli (ca. 600 C.E.).

In literary terms, then, the formation of Judaism reached its fruition in extensions of the Oral Torah and the Written Torah. For the Oral Torah, the formative age came to its conclusion when the Talmud of Babylonia set forth the theological statement of Judaism by expressing the religious convictions of the Talmud of the Land of Israel in accord with a profound reconsideration of the philosophical norms of the Mishnah, ca. 200 C.E. Joining the method of the Mishnah to the messages of the prior Talmud, the framers of the second Talmud thereby defined the theological, including the legal, norms of Judaism. For the Written Torah, the Midrash compilations of the successive ages, corresponding to the two Talmuds and associated with them, carry forward the same modes of discourse and express in their ways the same hermeneutics.

This somewhat schematic account should not be permitted to obscure the continuities that join the two Talmuds, on the one side, and distinguish both of them from the Mishnah, on the other. The second Talmud said little that the framers of the prior Talmud would have found surprising. The form of discourse of the second Talmud,

---

[4]By "Judaism" I mean one Judaic system in particular, the Judaism of the Dual Torah, Oral and Written. The canon of that Judaism is what is described in this and following paragraphs. Other Judaic systems have flourished and do today. Here I focus upon the system that predominated and now continues, in a variety of modulations, to define Judaism for most practitioners of (a) Judaism, and to provide a principal source for all the others. That operative definition is descriptive, of course.

moreover, on the surface closely resembles that of the first one.[5] And a fair part of the program of the second Talmud simply recapitulates the goals, though not the details, of the first.[6] But as I shall show, the second Talmud so radically reframed the received media of thought and modes of discourse that what emerged became the principal and authoritative statement of Judaism.

This it did through a set of analytical initiatives rare in the first Talmud[7] but commonplace in the second and definitive of its structure and program. These initiatives take the form of a hermeneutics, guiding the way in which the Mishnah and other received, definitive traditions are to be read and analyzed. While the first Talmud had undertaken some of the principal tasks of systematic exegesis, reasoned reading of the received oral part of the Torah, the second formulated an utterly fresh and governing mode of accomplishing the same goal. While, therefore, much we find in the second Talmud appears to recapitulate, if not the results, then the methods of the first, in fact the Bavli stands by itself and speaks for itself.

Its distinctive hermeneutics, which I maintain contains within itself the theology of the Judaism of the Dual Torah, is exposed not in so many words but in page-by-page repetition; it is not articulated but constantly (even tediously) instantiated; we are then supposed to draw our own conclusions. The unique voice of the Talmud,[8] which bears that hermeneutics, speaks with full confidence of being heard and understood; and that voice is right; we never can miss the point. For the hermeneutics itself – insistence on the presence of philosophy behind jurisprudence, law behind laws, total harmony among premises of

---

[5]That is the point of Chapter Five.

[6]That is spelled out in my presentation of the commonalities of the two Talmuds in Chapter Five. I do maintain that the Bavli is unique and scarcely intersects with the Yerushalmi at its critical initiatives; but I do not represent the Bavli as totally unlike the Yerushalmi; the opposite is the fact. The first Talmud accomplished several goals I regard as theological in its rigorous exposition of the Mishnah. But the second Talmud did the main work, as I explain in Chapters Eight through Ten.

[7]Appropriate caution attends the claim that the initiatives I shall identify in Chapters Nine and Ten are characteristic of the Bavli but only "rare" in the Yerushalmi. I think they are virtually unknown in the prior Talmud, but even though I have translated both Talmuds, I still find that it is easier to say what is in the Talmuds than what is not there. Hence I speak only of a preponderance of data, not the definitive character of the data. But my differentiation between the two Talmuds is definitive, and I do maintain that the Bavli is unique in its context (and not only there) in its mode of making its statement.

[8]That characterization of the Talmud as a coherent voice, speaking everywhere in the same well-modulated way, is spelled out in Chapter Eight.

discrete and diverse cases pointing to the unique and harmonious character of all existence, social and natural – properly understood, bears the theological message: the unity of intellect, the integrity of truth.

As the Mishnah had demonstrated the hierarchical classification of all natural being, pointing at the apex to the One above, so the second Talmud demonstrated the unity of the principles of being set forth in the Torah. The upshot is that Judaism would set forth the religion that defined how humanity was formed "in our image, after our likeness," not to begin with but day by day: in the rules of intellect, the character of mind. We can be like God because we can think the way God thinks, and the natural powers of reason carry us upward to the supernatural origin of the integrity of truth – that sentence sums up what I conceive to be the theological consequence of the Talmud's hermeneutics. Then the principal task of this book, in its critical chapters, requires that I reframe the literary hermeneutics into its theological premises. If the formulation proves more plausible, it is to spell out the theological implications of the second Talmud's analytical program.

The Talmud of Babylonia therefore forms the pinnacle and the summa – what we mean when we speak of "Judaism"[9] – because from the time of its closure to the present day it defined not only Judaic dogma and its theological formulation but also Judaic discourse that carried that dogma through to formulation in compelling form. Not only so, but the entire documentary heritage of the first six centuries of the Common Era was recast in that Talmud. And that body of writing was itself a recapitulation of important elements of the Hebrew Scriptures and in its basic views indistinguishable in theological and legal character from elements of the Pentateuch's and Prophets' convictions and requirements.[10] Scripture itself ("the Written Torah") would reach coming generations not only as read in the synagogue on the Sabbath and festivals, but also, and especially, as recast and expounded in the Talmud in the schoolhouses and courts of the community of Judaism.

Other received documents that had reached closure during that long period of time – the Mishnah, the Tosefta, the Talmud of the Land of Israel itself, the score of Midrash compilations – furthermore flowed into

---

[9]That is the point of Chapter Four.

[10]That is the point of my planned work of constructive theology, *From Texts to Theological Matrix: The Torah, One, Entire, and Whole [2] Written and Oral*, which concerns itself with the unity of the two components of the Torah. Scarcely a line of the two Talmuds and the entire corpus of Midrash compilations fails to make that point, through incessant allusions to or citations of texts of the Written Torah, for example. The unity of the two parts of the Torah forms the Judaic equivalent to the conception of "the Bible," made up of "Old Testament" and "New Testament."

the Talmud of Babylonia. So each prior writing found its proper position, in due proportion, within the composite of the Bavli. And the Bavli made of the entire heritage of the revealed Torah, Oral and Written, not a composite but a composition, whole, proportioned, coherent. That is what I mean by, "the Talmudic re-presentation," that is, the second Talmud's re-presentation of the Torah given by God to our rabbi, Moses, at Mount Sinai.

That re-presentation was accomplished through one medium: a governing, definitive hermeneutics, the result of applied logic and practical reason when framed in terms of the rules of reading a received and holy book. I need not hide my conviction that the persuasive power of the Talmud's hermeneutics explains the Talmud's success in taking the primary position in the canon of Judaism. That conviction admittedly is subjective, resting as it does on the unprovable premise that ideas and attitudes account for conduct and social policy. But it is the indubitable fact that the second Talmud effected the re-presentation of all that had gone before. Given the Talmud's priority of place among all Judaic writings, before and since for all time, I set forth an objective fact when I maintain that the Talmud also stated in its distinctive way, through its particular hermeneutics, the authoritative theology of the Judaism for which it formed the summa. Religious belief and right behavior to express that belief – both would find definition in its pages, exposition and exegesis in accord with its modes of analytical thought. With the Bavli, the theological text had been inscribed; all the rest was commentary.[11] The commentary would flourish from then to now; the exegesis of that exegesis would define the future history of Judaism.

For the later history of Judaism, from late antiquity to the present day, theology would take a distinctive, and I think, unique form. It provoked rigorous argument,[12] rather than merely laying out well-

---

[11]We of course should not ignore the fact that that labor of extension, amplification, application, and commentary in the richest sense went forward, and now goes forward, in a variety of directions. But no contemporary Judaic system takes its leave from the Talmud and the oral part of the Torah represented by it. In the seminaries of all Judaic systems, and in the synagogues of all contemporary Judaisms, the Torah is presented in both the written and the oral components, though, I hasten to add, different Judaisms take up their own position on what fits into that entire Torah and how the Torah is to be received and re-presented.

[12]In today's yeshiva world, that argument exhibits a certain ritualized character, e.g., the ritual of study of Torah involves heated argument, shading over into rudeness and abuse, and that mode of argument in its secular form has characterized sectors of not only Judaic studies – the religious study of the Torah, the secular study of the religion – but the rest of Jewish studies – the ethnic

defined propositions. In this way it guided the conduct of theological
thought, rather than merely defining its propositions and syllogistic
goals.[13] When the sages of Judaism chose to make their statements of

---

studies of the Jews as an ethnic entity. So the ritual persists when the myth has
been abandoned.

[13]But I do not for one minute suggest that the theology of Judaism involves
process but not proposition, or mainly is a matter of process – not at all. I
characterize hermeneutics as the medium for the message, not the message. This
is by contrast to the proposal of David Kraemer's *The Mind of the Talmud: An
Intellectual History of the Bavli* (New York, 1990: Oxford University Press).
Because of the argument I set out here, let me spell out what Kraemer has
proposed and why I maintain he has misunderstood the character of the Bavli.
Claiming to "trace the development of the literary forms and conventions of the
Babylonian Talmud and analyze those forms as expressions of emergent rabbinic
ideology," which expresses the conviction of "the inaccessibility of perfect truth,"
and concluding that [not the determination, but the mere] "pursuit of
truth...becomes the ultimate act of rabbinic piety," Kraemer spells out his
program in these terms: "[The book is]...a literary history. It traces the
development of the literary forms and conventions by which rabbinic
sages...recorded their opinions and rulings. What motivates this examination is
the assumption...that literary conventions are reflections of ideological choices
and that by tracing the history of literary developments we can say something of
the history of ideas. This is also, therefore, intended as an intellectual history of
the Jews who produced the Bavli." Kraemer adduces in evidence of his claim
that the document concerns itself with argument, not decision, a variety of
specific traits characteristic of what he calls the anonymous layer of the writing.
He finds, for instance, that the redactor will "extend the range of the original
argumentation" (p. 80). "The authors of the gemara also saw fit to create
argumentation out of amoraic sources that were originally not argumentational"
(p. 84). They created "fictional argumentation" (p. 87), "argumentation for its
own sake" (p. 90). He then claims to have illustrated the point that "the
Babylonian gemara is, at the level of its anonymous composition, an
uncompromisingly deliberative/ argumentational text." He properly compares
this Talmud to the other one, the Talmud of the Land of Israel (a.k.a. the
Yerushalmi) and finds that a principal difference is that the Yerushalmi reaches
conclusions, the Bavli does not. From Kraemer's description of the Bavli, we
should hardly know the simple fact that, while cogent and coherent as he claims,
the rhetorical focus of coherence is upon a prior document, the Mishnah. Further,
from Kraemer's description, we should hardly have realized that the Bavli does
set forth a highly propositional program, which it repeats time and again
throughout. The allegation that the purpose of the document is to represent
argument, not conclusion, contradicts that fact, spelled out in my *The Bavli's One
Statement. The Metapropositional Program of Babylonian Talmud Tractate Zebahim
Chapters One and Five* (Atlanta, 1991: Scholars Press for South Florida Studies in
the History of Judaism). In other words, it is difficult for me to identify, in the
terms of Kraemer's description, the paramount literary and propositional
program of the Bavli, as sustained and not merely episodic and exemplary
analysis has shown it to be. So not only is his proposition on the indeterminacy
of truth on the face of it implausible, his characterization of the document as a

matter of fact simply fails to encompass the document's fundamental and indicative traits, since he has not bothered to tell us what he thinks the Bavli is. Kraemer appears not to have read and understood my *The Making of the Mind of Judaism* (Atlanta, 1987: Scholars Press for Brown Judaic Studies) and *The Formation of the Jewish Intellect. Making Connections and Drawing Conclusions in the Traditional System of Judaism* (Atlanta, 1988: Scholars Press for Brown Judaic Studies). In these two works I formulated precisely the same question that Kraemer's book asks; but I framed it in terms and categories quite different from his. The results were what led me precisely to the results, as to the overall characteristics of the writing, set forth just now: we deal with a sustained and systematic commentary to the Mishnah, and the problem of the intellectual history of the document is to be defined in the framework of a writing in exegetical form, but with a well-framed propositional program. Of all of this Kraemer knows nothing. A brief account of how I have defined the task will explain why I think the flaws in his description are formidable. In the former work I describe the distinctive modes of thought that produced a kind of writing in Judaism quite different in the basic structure of its mentality and interior traits of logic and, especially, the formation of large-scale structures of knowledge, from the kind of writing carried out by contemporary Christian theologians – even on the same questions. I then described and analyzed, in the context of the concrete expression of mind provided by principal canonical writings, the four critical processes of thought, which I call logics, as I see them, three being propositional logics, the philosophical, teleological, and metaproposition, and one a nonpropositional logic, the logic of fixed association. In this description of the modes of coherent thought and cogent argument, I was able to characterize precisely what Kraemer claims to describe, namely, the intellectual traits of the writing. I cannot point to a single passage in his book in which he tells us about not "truth" (e.g., "truth in the classical philosophical tradition" [p. 175]) but logic in the framework of intelligible thought. Telling about "truth" leads us to attend to mere propositions, e.g., this is so, that is not so. But a description of the intellectual processes of a piece of writing should tell us about modes of thought: what is plausible and why, what is found cogent, how are connections made, for instance. In the latter work, turning to the larger tasks of comparison and contrast of documents, where reliable intellectual history *is* possible (as what I call "the documentary history of ideas"), I claimed to account for how Judaic system builders framed their systems by comparison to the modes of cogent discourse characteristic of prior ones, beginning with the pentateuchal system of Judaism. "The formation of the Jewish intellect" interprets the word "formation" in two senses. The first is "formation" as the ways in which that intellect formed a Judaic system, and the second is "formation" as an account also concerning the structure of that intellect, that is, of what modes of thought that intellect was formed. First I set forth the order, proportion, structure, and composition of a Judaic system, that is, a worldview and way of life addressed to a defined social entity called (an) "Israel." Second, I explained how framers of such a system made connections and drew conclusions in the setting up of their system. The order was deliberate. *For the order of the formation of the intellect is from the whole to the parts.* The reason is that it is the systemic statement that to begin with defines the logic needed to make that statement. The manner of making connections and drawing conclusions – the true life of intellect – does not percolate upward into the framing of the systemic statement. What Kraemer has said about the traits of norms, they began in the Talmud, worked within its categories, framed their ideas in accord with its intellectual discipline, and spoke in its language about its problems. They did so in the (descriptively valid) conviction that the Talmud had made the full and authoritative statement of the Torah of Sinai, Oral, covering the Mishnah and Midrash compilations, and Written, covering Scripture, as well. That is why everything to come would validate itself as a commentary to the text set forth by the Talmud out of all the prior texts that all together comprised the Torah.

It follows that the power of the Talmud of Babylonia to govern the long future flowed from its capacity to recapitulate, in its own way, the mentality, the intellectual vitality, the qualities of mind, of each of the writings of the Torah. And its own way was, to form of them all a single, astonishingly coherent and harmonious statement. But coherence and harmony themselves form traits of a deeper intellectual conviction, which is, the truth is one, possessed of integrity, capacious and whole, holding all truths together. The Bavli formed truth out of truths, and that is its singular theology: the intellectual form of the deepest conviction of monotheism, one God, one Torah, one whole and harmonious truth, to all Israel.

Since the Talmud sets forth its entire composition as a commentary to the Mishnah, and since the Mishnah itself is a philosophical law code, the vast legal system of the Judaism of the Dual Torah served as the theological statement of Judaism. All contemporary expositions of the theology of the Judaism of the Dual Torah recapitulate that fact, insisting that it is in the Talmud that theological norms, extending not only to right thought but also right action and therefore to matters of law or *halakhah* as much as of faith or *aggadah*, come to full expression. The *halakhah*, the faith lived in deeds, as much as the *aggadah*, the faith expressed in attitudes and sentiments and conveyed by words, began in the Talmud and appealed to the Talmud. For the most part, therefore, the systematic and cogent statement that Judaism would make would take a form scarcely accessible to those to whom the Talmud was alien, since the modes of thought and the media of discourse – dialectical, analytical argument concerning the harmonization of discrete principles

---

the Bavli therefore is not only dubious as a characterization of the writing as a whole. It is also monumentally beside the point, if the issue is the intellectual structure (if not history) of the Bavli. In this rather facile, shallow, and private work, therefore, Kraemer has presented an intellectual history which is neither historical, nor intellectual, since what he describes as the indicative intellectual traits of the document prove in fact to be subordinate and contingent, not systemic, not typical, and not determinative.

– rested upon, and constantly referred to, the norms already set forth in the Talmud.

Expressing its theology only in the adumbration of hermeneutics, Judaism did not put forth theological statements in the idiom and media familiar to its monotheist companions, Christianity and Islam. That mode of expression had the advantage of allowing the faithful to draw their own conclusions through their own intellects; they could not err or fall into schism or heresy, since they read the Torah as the Talmud defined the Torah and they explicated the Torah following the signals given by the Talmud for the reconstitution (re-presentation) of the reading and interpretation of the Torah. But it had the disadvantage of not bringing to clear and articulated propositional formulation the truths of the Torah; too much was left unsaid.

The problem was not that Judaism lacked systematization and philosophical grounding of its religious convictions, such as theology in propositional form as well as in argument provides for Islam and Christianity. The Talmud provides such a systematization and philosophical grounding: that on every page defined its authors' purpose, and that is what they accomplished. It was that the modes of theological discourse proved particular and did not correspond to the more accessible ones familiar in the other two heirs of the Greco-Roman intellectual traditions. All three drew upon the received philosophical heritage of the Greco-Roman tradition, whether Aristotelian or Platonic. But while Christianity and Islam adhered to the categorical structure of the received philosophy and explicitly accommodated themselves to its method and discipline, the Judaic heirs spoke in an idiom quite alien to the generalizing language of philosophy, even while exploring profoundly philosophical issues.[14]

As a result, the philosophical character of the Mishnah's program does not enjoy the recognition that the counterpart thought and expression in Christian and Muslim theology do.[15] And discourse in an

---

[14]A case in point is the problem of the nature of mixtures, which interested Stoic physics, as shown by S. Sambursky, *Stoic Physics* (Jerusalem, 1955). Precisely the same classification of types of mixtures comes to expression, with precisely the same consequences, in the analysis of the consequences of mixtures of the several types in Mishnah-tractate Tohorot (among kindred tractates, e.g., Hullin, Abodah Zarah). If one knows the Stoic theory of mixtures, then the detailed law of those tractates forms an exposition of the same principles; if not, then the laws appear to be discrete, episodic, and fundamentally capricious. In more general terms, I show these same facts in *Judaism as Philosophy. The Method and Message of the Mishnah* (Columbia, 1991: Carolina Press) and further works, cited below.

[15]Even Maimonides did not grasp the profoundly Aristotelian position of the Mishnah's economics and politics, though that position as to economics simply is

openly and blatantly philosophical mode – that is, free-standing, not exegetical in form; generalizing, not particular to cases, yielding unarticulated principles of a philosophical character in agenda – would not enter into the theology of Judaism for centuries after the formation of the Talmud. Because of the nature of revelation in Judaism – the Torah alone and unique and final – theology in Judaism would insist for a very long time upon exegetical form, on the one side, and hermeneutical character of expression, on the other: always cases, rarely generalizations, and never articulated abstract principles, except, of course, when right thinking produced knowledge of precisely those principles of high abstraction that conveyed the integrity of truth.

What accounts for the particularity of the medium chosen by the theology of Judaism? The answer is clear from what has already been said. Since, for Judaism, the task of theology was to define and explain the Torah, because God was made manifest solely in the Torah by God's own action, hermeneutics formed the correct medium of expression. It was through guiding the reading of the Torah, beginning with the definition of canon (in secular language) that reasoned inquiry into faith would go forward, and that was at the first (but only at the first) step a hermeneutical task. By contrast, Christianity knew God through the person of Jesus Christ, God incarnate. The Bible recorded the faith, but is to be distinguished, in its place and function in Christianity (of all kinds), from the Torah; the Torah dictated by God to Moses at Sinai formed the sole and exhaustive account of everything that God wished to tell humanity. True, the person of the sage as much as the oral and written components of the Torah formed the medium of conveying the whole Torah of Sinai. But that is a generic claim concerning the sage, not the specific claim concerning Jesus Christ that the Church put forth. So while alike, the media prove profoundly different in conception and expression. The person of Christ, not the Bible, formed the counterpart. So the Church, the living body of Christ, and the tradition that it preserved, as much as the Bible, carried the burden of the faith. The Bible did not, and could not, be represented as the sole and exhaustive account of Christ. Other media for theological discourse stood side by side with the exegetical ones, and hermeneutics formed the child of theology, not its father, as was the case for Judaism.

People therefore have recognized that while, of course, the Judaic system expressed in the Mishnah and related writings put forward religious convictions ("dogmas"), for example, God is one, the Torah is revealed by God, all Israel has a portion in the world to come, God wants

---

indistinguishable in principle and in detail from Aristotle's, and, as to politics, more than episodically congruent.

Israel to live by the covenant by observing the laws of the Torah and affirming its truths ("covenantal nomism"), they have not understood a simple fact. It is that that same system also came to highly disciplined and rigorous re-presentation in a theological formulation. But, as we see in these pages, just as the philosophical character of the Mishnah was hidden within a morass of detailed rules, so the theological character of the second Talmud – theological by definitions that apply perfectly naturally to Christianity and derive from an account of Dalferth's theory of theology in Christianity – remains to be identified and articulated. In this Judaism we have a religion that speaks in cases and requires the faithful to draw their own, right conclusions from those cases.[16]

For when we understand how the second and definitive Talmud received and recast the vast received heritage of religious conviction – the norms of behavior and belief, the messages of myth and symbol, the entirety of Scripture and the written down, but earlier oral elements of the Torah as well – we shall understand not only the method, but also the system and cogency of the simple message, of the Judaic theological statement. That is contained within the Talmud's re-presentation which became the norm for time to come. It finds its articulation, in particular, in the Talmud's recurrent analytical program, the part that is particular, and even unique, to itself; it is a theology that relies for its full expression upon not propositional discourse and argument but rather hermeneutics, a theology that is conveyed by that hermeneutics. So while the Mishnah hid its philosophical program within details of rules and laws about very humble, everyday things, the Talmud concealed its theological program within its unique hermeneutics.[17]

---

[16]The Mishnah showed the way, by saying everything but the main thing, leaving that for the reader to perceive, and by providing its own best commentary within the very structure of its formulation. I have spelled these matters out in my *A History of the Mishnaic Law of Purities* (Leiden, 1977: E.J. Brill). XXI. *The Redaction and Formulation of the Order of Purities in the Mishnah and Tosefta.*

[17]I use the word "unique" to convey the fact that the modes of analytical exegesis I shall discuss occur commonly in the second Talmud and rarely, if ever, in the first. Where an analytical initiative is common to both Talmuds, I do not address to it the questions that govern in these pages. Having translated both Talmuds (*The Talmud of the Land of Israel. A Preliminary Translation* [Chicago, 1984-1993], I-XXXV, and *The Talmud of Babylonia. An American Translation* [Atlanta, 1984-1993], I-XXXVI) and systematically compared the two (*The Talmud's Unique Voice* [Atlanta, 1993], I-VII), I am now ready to draw conclusions for these systematic presentations and comparisons. I may observe, however, that a counterpart to the Bavli's mode of presenting the law and theology of (its) Judaism is exceedingly difficult to identify, and I know of none. I compare this way of presenting a tradition with Zoroastrian counterparts in *Judaism and Zoroastrianism at the Dusk of Late Antiquity. How Two Ancient Faiths Wrote Down Their Great Traditions*, submitted to Athlone Press, London.

I therefore describe that re-presentation: Of precisely what elements
– thought and expression alike – did it consist? Where and how do we
identify its principal formulation? And what is the theological statement
made through the hermeneutics at hand? We know the answers to those
questions, because a close and accurate reading of the sources reveals it
with great clarity. Readers will review samples of each of the types of
analysis I identify as systematically emblematic and judge for themselves
my interpretation of what I maintain is at stake in them. I have tried to
select typical examples of each hermeneutical phenomenon of
consequence, also to abbreviate the abstracts; but there is no entry into
the theological statement of Judaism that the Bavli makes without a
direct and detailed encounter with the way in which that statement was
made, in its exact words. Here I spell out those answers, with ample
attention to an exposition of where in the sources I find them and how I
understand them.

The upshot is simple. In these pages we investigate the way in
which a religious system was "theologized." By "theologization," as
suggested at the outset, I mean, how diverse, varied, and often
contradictory sayings, stories, rules, beliefs, opinions, exemplifications of
virtue, principles of conduct and conviction – the detritus of a vast realm
of religious belief and behavior – were formulated in a systematic,
unitary, coherent, rigorously consistent, proportioned way, each element
fitting together with all others, the whole bearing the weight and the
power of compelling reason. Theology imparted to tradition the traits of
harmony, linearity, and unity – back to Sinai, meaning, upward to
Heaven. Harmony and linearity came first, in the first of the two
Talmuds; unity, in the second of them. Discourse that transformed the
Torah from discrete cases to cogent statements of harmony and
proportion began in the first of the two Talmuds and reached fruition in
the second. At this point it suffices to say very simply that with the first
of the two Talmuds (and its associated Midrash compilations), the
received Torah, Oral and Written, was ordered: the components were
brought into relationship, on the one side, the details made to form
propositions, on the other. With the second of the two Talmuds (and its
companions of Midrash collection), these propositions were cast into a
few large and simple statements, the law behind the laws, on the one
side, and shown through sustained argument to be reasonable and
rigorously demonstrable, on the other.

While the received religious categories and convictions (merely)
came to restatement, in the theological formulation of the religion, the
whole changed in character, focus, and effect. To explain what changes
with theology, it suffices to make an obvious observation. The same
thought or principle (for example, God loves us, or life is unfair, or

beauty is evanescent but precious, or wisdom is futile) not only looks different but *is* different when expressed in the media of poetry, on the one side, prose on the second, fiction on the third, philosophy on the fourth, syllogistic argument on the fifth, music on the sixth, physicalized expression in ballet on the seventh, drama on the eighth, architecture on the ninth, even in athletics on the tenth – and on and on for the many, many sides of human expression of attitude, feeling, and thought. In our case, the religious system's theologization produced a re-presentation of remarkably persuasive power. By consequence, for age succeeding age, holy Israel found it possible through initiation in the original re-presentation to join in the very process of theological thinking about belief and behavior, themselves reproducing through their wit, perspicacity, and acuity, those very processes of intellect that to begin with produced the initial re-presentation.

Understanding the theology of Judaism as the Talmud defined that theology as a matter of fact accounts for the character of nearly all Judaisms from then to now, which have looked to the Talmud for the definition of norms of conduct, conscience, character, and conviction. The principal document, the Talmud of Babylonia, formed the curriculum for Judaic education: the formation of the personality and intellect of Israel "in our image, after our likeness."[18] I thus appeal to the character of the Talmud and associated writings to interpret the final and definitive stage in the formation of Judaism as a fundamentally theological re-presentation of a religious system. In this way then I make sense of the structure and system of that same Judaism for all time, to the present, and for all circumstances in which the Judaism flourishes that appeals to that Talmud as its summa. Today, most Judaisms do, so at stake in the history of the formation of Judaism is an explanation of not only past and received, but also acutely contemporary Judaic systems, too.

Critical to my reading of matters is the conception of hermeneutics, which requires brief definition as well. A reliable definition comes from K.M. Newton:

> The central concern of hermeneutics as it relates to the study of literature is the problem created by the fact that texts written in the past continue to exist and to be read while their authors and the historical context which produced them have passed away in time. Reading such texts, therefore, becomes inseparable from the question of interpretation. Before the modern period hermeneutics was concerned primarily with how scriptural texts such as the Bible should be read. Should the Bible, for example, be seen as a text which exists in its own terms and read

---

[18]The Midrash compilations, often refracted through the choices of those who restated their main results, guided the reading of the Written Torah.

accordingly or should any understanding of it be mediated by an acceptance of the doctrines of the church?[19]

It follows that, by hermeneutics is meant "the rules of reading a text and interpreting it." Then precisely what constitutes the understanding of a text, which is what I mean by, the rules for defining and reading a document – text, context, matrix of meaning? Newton cites Wilhelm Dilthey's dictum, "an act of understanding constitutes what he called a 'lived experience.'" Dilthey states:

> The methodological understanding of permanently fixed life expressions we call explication. As the life of the mind only finds its complete, exhaustive, and therefore, objectively comprehensible expression in language, explication culminates in the interpretation of the written records of human existence. This art is the basis of philology. The science of this art is hermeneutics.[20]

Now, as we shall see, the second Talmud forms a coherent hermeneutics, because it provides a systematic, coherent account of how to read the language of the Torah, Scripture but especially the Mishnah, and makes possible the uniform interpretation of the records of the Torah. The basis for this work, when fully exposed, turns out to comprise certain quite specific doctrines about the character of the Torah and the quality of mind – the mentality – required to understand the Torah. Those doctrines constitute the theological statement of Judaism. The reason is that, from them, we learn how to think, and knowing how, we always know what to think; comprehension then follows, and all things become clear and certain. We work back then from the language to the rules of defining the text and reading it, from the identification of the text and understanding it to the rules of comprehension and full understanding, and these govern thought. In Chapter Two I shall explain how we move from the Torah's words to its rules of reading – text and world alike – which reveal God's way of thinking, as surely as our sentences yield access to our manner of crafting them, our minds.

A crafted text exhibits its hermeneutics in every line, and, among the documents of Judaism in its formative age, the Mishnah, the two Talmuds, and most Midrash compilations were very carefully crafted indeed; we have no difficulty at all identifying the rhetorical, logical, and topical program of the various writings, respectively, and we can generally explain how the parts express the program of the whole, and

---

[19]K.M. Newton, *Interpreting the Text. A Critical Introduction to the Theory and Practice of Literary Interpretation* (New York, 1990: Harvester/Wheatsheaf), pp. 40-41.
[20]Cited by K.M. Newton, *Interpreting the Text*, p. 42.

how the whole has governed the formulation of the parts.[21] That fact is not surprising; by definition, our sages of blessed memory were highly educated men, who thought in sophisticated ways about the urgent issues of intellect. The rules for the interpretation of literary texts in ancient times drew attention to formal analysis of structure and style, composition, how the parts hold together, how the whole is expressed in the parts. In modern times close attention is paid to philology as well. Hermeneutics in this context furthermore refers to a certain way of asking questions, the presence of an agenda of issues that tell us what we wish to know and why it matters. And that points toward a way rich in presuppositions, in the language of Bultmann, "it is always guided by a preunderstanding of the subject matter about which it questions the text. Only on the basis of such a preunderstanding is a way of asking questions and an interpretation at all possible."[22]

That formulation of matters explains the prominence assigned here to the matter of hermeneutics, for, as I show in Parts Two and Three, a coherent set of questions guide the reading of the Mishnah and other Tannaite materials, and these questions result from a set of doctrines that are everywhere implicit and normative. When therefore I maintain that the theology of Judaism comes to expression in hermeneutics, I speak of how convictions formed prior to the encounter with the text provoke one set of questions, rather than some other – with a coherent result in detail, attesting to a cogent doctrine in general.

Once we recognize that a set of questions guides the reading of the received scriptural or Tannaite texts, of course, we identify in the premises of those questions the theology that the questions embody in

---

[21]My entire corpus of form analysis, from the Mishnah through the Talmuds to the Midrash compilations, simply applies with appropriate accommodation to the character of the evidence the criteria of rhetoric, logic of coherent discourse, and topic. I do maintain that nearly all canonical documents exhibit the marks of a well-conceived and unitary program that links rhetoric, logic, and topic, in such a way as to form a balanced and coherent whole, and I have demonstrated that fact by defining, document by document, precisely how these are matched and why I maintain all three work together to make the statement that a given document is meant by its writers to make. There are exceptions to the rule that rabbinic documents express hermeneutical policy; the Tosefta, on the one side, and (as I read it), Mekhilta Attributed to R. Ishmael, on the other, seem to me scrapbooks, not well-crafted documents that make statements in a coherent way, through rhetorical, logical, and topical correspondence and coherence. The Mishnah and Sifra are the best examples of the opposite kind of document, for Tannaite writings, and the Bavli, for Amoraic ones.

[22]Rudolf Bultmann, *New Testament and Mythology. And Other Basic Writings*, selected, edited, and translated by Schubert M. Ogden (Philadelphia, 1984: Fortress Press), p. 72.

guides to interpreting the Torah. But identifying the hermeneutic medium and its theological message involves a denser discourse still.[23] For at issue in the Talmuds and Midrash compilations is a vast labor of not merely commentary but translation, and hermeneutics involves not only the rules for explication of a text, but also the principles for the re-presentation of a text. And that re-presentation must be understood as translation, for, if the original form and language define the text's presentation, then the recasting of the text for analysis provides its re-presentation. To put matters very simply, our sages of blessed memory, in both the Talmuds and the Midrash compilations, engage in a vast labor of re-presentation; they do not simply present the texts in situ and paraphrase or amplify them; they recast the texts altogether. To state matters bluntly, the Midrash compilations write with Scripture, meaning, they translate Scripture for purposes of a discourse of their own fabrication, and the Talmuds write with the Mishnah, meaning, they translate the Mishnah into a framework of thought of their own invention.

We deal in the Talmuds and Midrash with a work of translation, for the Mishnah is not copied in the Talmuds, it is subjected to a process of selection, arrangement, recasting, analysis and synthesis, dissection and reconstitution. The Talmuds address bits and pieces; they ignore entire divisions; they take up a sentence here and set it side by side with a sentence there. The Mishnah does not emerge in the Talmuds except through a work of reconstitution for a discourse other than that of the Mishnah itself (clarified and extended, for example); the Mishnah is used for purposes defined by the authors of the compositions and composites of which the Talmuds are composed. This is not a process of presentation or even, in any narrow sense, re-presentation; it is a process of translation: of writing with the Mishnah in a language other than that of the Mishnah, in accord with rules of grammar that are not those of the Mishnah, to express thoughts that are of an order different from that of the Mishnah. The same of course is true of the way in which the authors of Midrash compositions and compilers of Midrash compilations write with Scripture.[24]

Now here, too, the issue of hermeneutics enters in, so that the very character of the re-presentation of Scripture and the Mishnah in the Talmuds and Midrash compilations forms a systematic expression, in the

---

[23]As though the identification of the generative questions and the demonstration of their premises were thin!

[24]This is explained in detail in *Writing with Scripture: The Authority and Uses of the Hebrew Bible in the Torah of Formative Judaism* (Philadelphia, 1989: Fortress Press) (with William Scott Green).

rules of translation, of a prior theology. In Bultmann's language: "To translate means to make understandable, and this presupposes an understanding."[25] Before our sages of blessed memory in the Talmuds could have undertaken the re-presentation of the Mishnah in the way in which they chose to do the work, that is, in phrases and perhaps sentences but not in the Mishnah's own, large sense units, they had to have in mind principles that would guide how the work was to be done, a picture of not the Mishnah or the Tannaite sayings, but of the Torah and its dimensions; an account of not accurate knowledge of opinion of this authority or that, but a large theory of authority, of the sage in relationship to Heaven (to mention only two among the many theological convictions given literary expression in the Talmud in accord with sages' hermeneutics of Talmud making).

Clearly, sages know how one thing connects to some other, and, since they are not bound by the formulation of the Mishnah as they, and we, know it, they had some other conception of connection than that of the Mishnah's authorship.[26] Then a conception of making connections and (thereby) drawing conclusions – in the nature of things, other conclusions than those that flow from the Mishnah's or Scripture's ways of making connections and drawing conclusions – has to have governed; and that conception, when identified,[27] will lead us deep into the primary convictions, the theological norms, revealed in the work of translation, on the one side, and making connections between one matter and some other, on the other side. In this connection, Bultmann's language provides a fine formulation of the issue: "The forces that are effective in connecting phenomena are understandable only if the phenomena themselves, which are connected thereby, are also understood."[28] In context, then, I should paraphrase in my own terms Bultmann's language:

---

[25]Op. cit., p. 148.

[26]In Chapter Eight I make much of the matter of connection, moving beyond the hermeneutics of the Mishnah – far beyond. But at this point, it is necessary to remain in bounds.

[27]And we stand some distance from identifying it; our task now is only to describe the problems created for us but solved for themselves by those who connected things in one way, rather than in some other.

[28]Op. cit., p. 149. But I am not drawn to his concern with history as a means of explaining connection, as he says in the next sentence: "This means that an understanding of the subject matter itself belongs to historical understanding." I should claim precisely the opposite; we can see the problems to which I point in Chapter Eight entirely outside the framework of history, meaning, specific context at one point in time. In this same context Bultmann states, "One cannot understand the decisions of persons who act in history if one does not understand human beings and their possibilities...." That may be so, but one can

Historical understanding presupposes an understanding of the subject
matter of history itself and of the men and women who act in history.
This is to say, however, that historical understanding always
presupposes that the interpreter has a relation to the subject matter that
is (directly or indirectly) expressed in the text.

In the context of the hermeneutics of the Torah and its theology, I should
recast that formulation, eliminating history and introducing God: a
correct theological understanding presupposes that the interpreter has a
relationship to the God that is expressed in the Torah. That somewhat
obscure formulation means simply: [1] our sages of blessed memory
stand in relationship to Sinai, as part of the chain of tradition; [2] their
hermeneutics of the Torah presupposes a theology of the Torah that they
maintain is expressed in the text of the Torah. Working back from who
they thought they were and how they read the Torah (defined the Torah,
determined its qualities and its properties, for example, harmony, unity,
perfection, and demonstrated the character of its propositions, that is,
their integrity), we find ourselves confronting their theology. To give
Bultmann his well-deserved last word: "A particular understanding of
the subject matter of the text, grounded in a life relation to it, is always
presupposed by exegesis, and to this extent no exegesis is without
presuppositions."[29] In the Talmuds, for the Mishnah, and the Midrash
compilations, for Scripture, we have the full account of our sages,
"particular understanding of the subject matter of the text"; that is what
the Talmuds and Midrash compilations mean to provide. The "life
relationship" of course is defined to begin with: our sages' standing in
relationship of tradition to Sinai. We further have full evidence of the
exegesis; that is what the Talmuds and Midrash compilations do provide.
Our work, then, is to identify the theological presuppositions and
premises of the hermeneutics that provoke the exegesis in our hands.

The hermeneutics that conveyed the rules of proper reading of the
Talmud thus formed of occasional rules and conceptions a single,
demonstrably cogent statement, one of entire integrity. And to do this, I
am required to speak in very specific terms indeed: this recurrent
formulation, that persistent point of inquiry, the other ubiquitous
question. The Mishnah, Yerushalmi, and Bavli repeat themselves
endlessly, because they say the same thing (respectively) about many
things. It is that same thing that in the Mishnah sets forth one set of
categories, in the Yerushalmi, an altogether different set of categories,

---

very well understand the decisions of sages of the Torah if one does understand
their conception of the Torah and of themselves as sages, on the one side, and
their processes of analytical thought, on the other – and that is entirely outside of
the framework of this morning's headlines, or history.
[29]Op. cit., p. 149.

and categories of a religious, not a philosophical, classification, and, in the Bavli, re-presents the received categorical structure and system in a theological formulation.

In so expressing matters, moreover, that statement not only re-presented the received traditions as a unitary tradition; it also redefined what is meant by tradition, thereby opening the way for generations to come to gain access thereto. Tradition in general had meant, and elsewhere would continue to mean, the truth, linear, harmonious, and incremental, that had come from some one point, for example, out of the past, from Sinai. The truth is one, whole, integrated; the result of a unitary, harmonious, and linear process of transmission. That is the conventional picture of "tradition," and forms, of course, a commonplace apologetic. But the Bavli recast the Torah to encompass not only the result of thought (God's thought) but also the modes of thought that produced those results: the sustained, dialectical arguments that pursued practical reason and applied logic to their necessary conclusion. How, not only what, people thought formed a part of tradition, for, after all, argument appealed to the Torah (Oral, Written), and how God through the Torah set forth the results of thought.

In the Bavli, therefore, tradition would emerge no longer as wholly, or mainly, propositional; the deepest layers of mind, most profound structures of intellect, the unity of premises, the law behind laws – all these evidences of the cogency of world order would be exposed through sustained, systematic demonstration of harmony, unity, and order. Consequently, educated in the discipline of rigorous demonstration, for all time to come, minds could be so formed as themselves to enter into the work: method, message, medium shown to come together in mind, tradition became a thing of intellect, not of fact or even truth alone.

So in my analysis of the unfolding of how people wrote down in the Talmud not only what but how they thought, I set forth the way in which the chaotic congeries of attitudes, beliefs, symbols, stories, rules and norms compiled by – and in some measure clarified in – the Talmud of the Land of Israel and related Midrash compilations were reshaped into a coherent, theological system. By that it is now clear that I mean, a cogent and compelling religious statement, one that accorded with the rules of philosophical inquiry in its order, rigor, insistence upon harmony and coherent principles of generalization (in contemporary language: "generalizability"). That restatement was accomplished mainly by the framers of the Talmud of Babylonia and associated Midrash collections, who – as is now clear – used the intellectual methods of the Mishnah to set forth the religious system of the Talmud of the Land of Israel. What the earlier of the two Talmuds had collected and explained, the later of them restated in a proportioned, balanced, harmonious whole, a statement possessed of integrity and unity. In the Bavli we learn the rules of theological discourse and the results thereof. So we are taught to join in the argument, which is to say, how to make such a statement (too).

Part One

DEFINING THEOLOGY IN THE CONTEXT OF RELIGION,
AND, IN PARTICULAR, OF JUDAISM

3

Philosophy, Religion, and Theology: The Differences and Why They Matter

The three terms before us, philosophy, religion, and theology, characterize the three phases in the formation of Judaism. Since the synthesizing characteristics of that medium, theology, in particular defined the third and final phase in Judaism's formative history, I have therefore to state precisely what traits of intellect formed out of religion a theological structure and system. The stakes in this explanation prove formidable, for this Judaism predominated, and its theology's definitive traits framed the thought of that Judaism. From that second Talmud, the Talmud of Babylonia or Bavli – hereinafter: *the Talmud,* par excellence – forward, norms of both belief and behavior appealed to the Talmud; innovations legitimated themselves by its criteria; new writings claimed descent, either in authorship or in tradition or in principle, from therein.

Most important, the definitive modes of thought that characterized most authorities of Judaism, the attitudes of mind and the rules of intellect, found definition in the matrix of the Talmud. Clearly, the theological medium defined future discourse, providing its focus. That fact explains why we now ask, precisely what, in general terms, do we mean by "theology" and how did that theology come to full expression? The answers to begin with require specifying what theology does, and how theology differs from philosophy, on the one side, and religion, on the other.

Theology employs the methods of philosophy for the reasoned inquiry into religion's revealed truth. And that is precisely how – as the documentary progression shows us – theology came into the Judaism of the Dual Torah.[1] The two Talmuds use and even refine the methods of

---

[1]Indeed, there can be no theology without religion, on the one side, and philosophy, on the other, as my exposition of definitions will show. So the logic

the Mishnah, which are profoundly philosophical, being the methods of hierarchical classification standard in philosophy from Aristotle's time. The first of the two systematizes, clarifies, and refines. The second composes arguments of a dialectical character, which are made to serve for the analytical re-presentation of the doctrines of the Torah, that is to say, the truths of religion. These two statements – the philosophical, in religion, and the theological – may well say the same thing, the one in general, the other in particular terms. Indeed, in time to come, much work would go into proving that, in concrete terms, they did and do say the same thing.

But as to the origin and reliability of truth, they differ profoundly, the one being focused upon the factors revealed through analysis of this world and its data, the other upon truths revealed by God (in the case of Judaism, in the Torah). Philosophy finds truth in ordinary things and their traits, laws, for instance, in the points in common among items on a common list. The Torah, by contrast, finds truth in what God has given ("manifested," "revealed"). Philosophy analyzes the truth of common things in this world, finding the logic that makes them cohere; the Torah properly studied yields its truths through a logic of cogency as well.

So the difference between philosophy and theology comes about not from the diversity of the propositions put forth by each, the hierarchical classification of all things to show God at the apex being a philosophical demonstration of monotheism, for example. The difference between the two derives, rather, from the distinct sources of truth to which each appeals, and the commonalities, from the shared modes of thought that define rationality or logic. Philosophy appeals to facts, the texts, of nature, history, society, alike.[2] Theology by contrast calls upon only its one, revealed text: "Philosophy is not related...to a set of foundation documents"[3] in the way in which theology, and, in the case of Judaism, the Torah is. For the counterpart text for theology of Christianity, the Bible, in the case of the theology of Judaism is the Torah, inclusive of all of its components. It follows that there can be, and has been, philosophy addressed to the generality of reasonable people put forth by Judaism, Christianity, or Islam. But while there is a generic, theology, there has been only a theology of Judaism addressed to holy Israel (and its Christian and Muslim counterparts). And the difference between

---

of the language at hand corresponds to the character of the documents that form the systemic statement.

[2] I paraphrase Basil Mitchell, "Philosophy and Theology," in Gerard J. Hughes, ed., *The Philosophical Assessment of Theology* (Tunbridge Wells and Washington, 1987: Search Press and Georgetown University Press), p. 4.

[3] Ibid.

philosophy of religion, or religious philosophy, and theology of Judaism (or of Christianity or of Islam) flows from the source of truth, rather than specific allegations concerning what is true; and, by reason of the character of that source, also from the methods of establishing truth and the media for the expression of truth.

Then how can I maintain that religion becomes theology when it adopts the rigorous discipline of philosophy? Because it is only when religion formulates a statement that is coherent, proportioned, cogent, subject to sustained analysis for imperfections of disharmony with good result – only when religion says some one thing in many ways, exceedingly persuasively, that religion becomes fully intelligible, wholly accessible to reasoned comprehension. And the analytical process, identifying disharmony and disproportion, pointing out contradictions in principle or in the premises of principle, reconstructing harmony and proportion and the unity of premises and consequently principles and cases, makes religion comprehensible. The process of reason therefore finds its definition in philosophy and its problem in religion; allowed to run its course, that process defines theology.

Take for example the matter of God. Obviously, for ordinary rationality, which chokes on the union of opposites, one God cannot be both material and immaterial, omnipotent and weak, transcendent and immanent, able to govern history and also subject to rules beyond divine authority, and so on and so forth. The premise of monotheism certainly excludes the possibility of contradictions of such an order. Both merciful and just, perhaps, but never both strong and weak, or one and many, or unique and wholly other and also immanent and consubstantial with this world![4]

But for Judaism one source of knowledge of God, the Written Torah, represents God through each trait and its opposite. And the other source of knowledge of God, the Oral Torah in its various written versions, assigns to one and the same God a mass of traits of varying consequence and proportion, allowing no guidance as to the composition of the whole into a single cogent account. Or – to move to metaphysical principles important in any account of created reality – take the principle that we treat what is potential as though it already had come into being, because it is (surely) going to come into being. Becoming may be treated as tantamount to being, with diverse, concrete results for law, or it may be treated as not tantamount to being, with opposite results. But it cannot

---

[4]Except by choice, e.g., for Christianity, in God incarnate, the union of opposites and the point of the unique statement that holds the whole together; for the Judaism of the Dual Torah there are counterparts whenever we find uniqueness as a definitive trait, e.g., with respect to Israel.

be both. And the problem of alleging about God everything and its opposite forms only one difficulty; another is reckoning with truth in right proportion, what is more important, what less; and still another, the balance and order of truths, how they form, all together, a coherent and also elegant statement. These, too, form tasks to be taken up by religious thinkers who call upon the methods of philosophy, which concern generalization and therefore take up contradiction, uniformity, balance, order, and harmony, and therefore rigorously form judgments upon issues of proportion and composition of thought.

Now, as a matter of fact, were philosophy to be asked to form an account of God or metaphysics, beginning with first principles and fundamental definitions, philosophy's God would surely exhibit none of the contradictions and disharmonies that the Torah's account of God reveals. And its metaphysics would set forth principles of metaphysics – being, becoming, actual, potential, and the like – only in entire harmony and full resolution. But the nature of the revelation that contains the data of God and metaphysics confronting Judaic system framers, by contrast, does not permit the orderly progression from the observation of the facts of nature upward to the systematic construction of a well-composed world.

There is no need to belabor the point. The sources of truth differ, with intellectually paralyzing results for religion. That is why Aristotle can offer a wholly coherent account, then, for example, assign to the gods activities in accord with the premise that they must be blessed and happy.[5] The revealed Torah – God's self-manifestation – yields no such systematic formulation, from premise to principle to fact. To the contrary, what is revealed, on the surface, is a mass of facts, some coherent, some contradictory; some fitting together (coherent or otherwise) into a picture of what kind, some forming a picture of a different kind altogether; some making much of one thing, some of another.

Theology heals the paralysis.[6] For, while religion formulates the revealed truth, theology asks philosophy's questions in re-presenting that same truth in accord with philosophy's principles of what is reasonable. This it does by moving from the surface to the depths, reversing the process that (at the end product) philosophy claims for the origin of its system: premise to principle to coherent propositions. Those

---

[5]D.W. Hamlyn, "Aristotle's God," in Hughes, op. cit., p. 23.
[6]I underline that the task of the theological medium at this time was not to harmonize Aristotle and the Torah; that would be addressed only many centuries later. And then it was through philosophy, not theology, that the great systems of union of Aristotle and the Torah were worked out.

building blocks of philosophy (of religion) serve at the foundations. The raw materials of theology lie at the very surface of things. The philosopher takes the perspective of the architect, with a plan in hand at the outset of the building; the theologian discovers the perspective of the building only from inspection of the finished edifice. God is portrayed as the first theologian, looking into the Torah and creating the world; but God also is the first philosopher, with the Torah in hand as his plan for the world:

1.   A.   "In the beginning God created" (Gen. 1:1):
      B.   R. Oshaia commenced [discourse by citing the following verse]: "'Then I was beside him like a little child, and I was daily his delight [rejoicing before him always, rejoicing in his inhabited world, and delighting in the sons of men]' (Prov. 8:30-31).
      C.   "The word for 'child' uses consonants that may also stand for 'teacher,' 'covered over,' and 'hidden away.'..."
2.   A.   Another matter:
      B.   The word means "workman."
      C.   [In the cited verse] the Torah speaks, "I was the work plan of the Holy One, blessed be He."
      D.   In the accepted practice of the world, when a mortal king builds a palace, he does not build it out of his own head, but he follows a work plan.
      E.   And [the one who supplies] the work plan does not build out of his own head, but he has designs and diagrams, so as to know how to situate the rooms and the doorways.
      F.   Thus the Holy One, blessed be He, consulted the Torah when he created the world.
      G.   So the Torah stated, "By means of 'the beginning' [that is to say, the Torah] did God create..." (Gen. 1:1).
      H.   And the word for "beginning" refers only to the Torah, as Scripture says, "The Lord made me as the beginning of his way" (Prov. 8:22).

Genesis Rabbah I:I.1-2

The Torah was the plan, fully in hand; so God created the way a philosopher or architect does, consulting the principles in laying out the lines of the building. But all that humanity now has for understanding the world is the Torah; in creating the Torah, God worked as a theologian, and, through study of the Torah, the sage can uncover, out of the details, the plan of the whole – so doing the work of the theologian. Working back from the details of the Torah, we gain access to the plan that guides God: what is in God's own mind, how God's intellect does its work.

Let us now take up a concrete definition of theology that stands independent of the sources and task at hand and set forth the criteria by which I shall have to demonstrate the theological character of the

Talmud's re-presentation of Judaism. Let me repeat the definition of Ingolf U. Dalferth, with which I began Chapter Two:

> Theology is not philosophy, and philosophy is not a substitute for religious convictions. But whereas religion can exist without philosophy, and philosophy without religion, theology cannot exist without recourse to each of the other two. It rationally reflects on questions arising in pre-theological religious experience and the discourse of faith; and it is the rationality of its reflective labor in the process of faith seeking understanding which inseparably links it with philosophy. For philosophy is essentially concerned with argument and the attempt to solve conceptual problems, and conceptual problems face theology in all areas of its reflective labors.[7]

Dalferth's definition admirably fits the labor of the Talmud, which uniquely takes as its task the exposition of argument and the spelling out of solutions to conceptual problems. The argument concerns the revealed law of the Torah. The conceptual problems address the deepest layers of the premises, at the most abstract, that underlie principles, at the most general, that come to expression in cases, in the most concrete formulation. That is not to suggest theology merely exposes processes of thought, for that is not true. Theology in Judaism sets forth revealed truth, specifically by showing how we know what is so. That means, how we know what the Torah is, and how we know how to learn what the Torah says: hermeneutics.

But the formulation of revelation in the second Talmud's re-presentation of the whole of the Oral Torah shifts from the narrative, encompassing rules of the covenant, characteristic of the Written Torah, to the argumentative. The basis for truth in that powerful restatement of matters extends from God's word alone, such as the Written Torah and much of the Oral Torah conveys, to the very processes of thought by which God, and therefore humanity in God's image, reach that one and the same conclusion that God reveals in bald, naked truth in the Torah. Dalferth expresses this conception in neutral terms in the following language:

> Unlike faith theology is a rational enterprise – not because it unfailingly pronounces the truth but because it proceeds by argument. It presents reasoned beliefs, not non-debatable dogmas for the faithful to believe and the godless to ignore; and although it aims at truth, its reasoning...is not invariably valid or sound...theology is rational, if and when it argues, for it is the idea of reasons, not of true reasons, which is

---

[7]Ingolf U. Dalferth, *Theology and Philosophy* (Oxford, 1988: Basil Blackwell Ltd.), p. vii.

central to rationality....There are many rudimentary forms of rationality, but it can flourish only in an atmosphere of argument.[8]

As we shall see, those statements could well have been formulated as a description of the Talmud – but the Talmud alone – in neutral and abstract terms. Is that to claim that, wherever we have reasoned argument, we find theology? Obviously not. In most cases, what we find is philosophy in one or another of its permutations. But wherever, in matters of truth that comes through revelation – God's self-manifestation, that is, in the Torah for Judaism – we have reasoned argument, there we have theology: the religious permutation of philosophy. That is what theology is: reasoned argument about revealed truth. And, as we shall see in Chapter Four, theology in Judaism in particular tells the revealed truth about God. That is, in particular, what God has made manifest through the Torah: God's words, God's way of forming sentences, God's manner of making the world, and the rules of life that have been formulated in God's own mind – all fully exposed, for those who know how to read the language of intellect.

Now, as a matter of fact, theology may serve more than a single purpose. Ordinarily, when people work on theological problems, they may do so for one of two equally valid reasons: to construct a theology (meaning, a theological system) or to reconstruct the theology that inheres in religious reflection (broadly construed: attitudes, ideas, myths, symbols, rules, writings, and rituals). Speaking of this dual program, Dalferth states in Christian terms:

> Christian theology is the intellectual quest for clarity about faith in Christ and its view of reality in the internal perspective of Faith. It is a permanent process of 'faith seeking understanding' faced with two major hermeneutical problems. First, it has to understand the Christian faith and its manifestations in the Christian community which logically, factually and historically precede theological reflection; this is the reconstructive task of theology. Second, it has to understand the whole of reality in the light of (its reconstruction of) faith; this is the constructive task of theology. Accordingly, the interpretative process of theology involves both explication and elucidation. It seeks to understand faith through the reflective explication and conceptual reconstruction of its data in systems of Christian doctrine; and it seeks to understand reality through its reflective elucidation and conceptual construction in the light of faith and its doctrinal reconstructions.[9]

Dalferth's definitions may be recast in neutral language, if we simply define the reconstructive task of theology as an effort to understand the diverse manifestations of a religious system.

---

[8]Ibid., p. viii.
[9]Op. cit, p. 152.

Required, then, is a work of explication and elucidation of facts, aimed at showing how diverse facts hold together, make sense, form a cogent statement, speak in behalf of a system that compels assent through the power of reason. Since contradiction challenges reason, harmonization establishes it; since disproportion creates chaos, proportion brings order; since disconnected detail produces confusion, the search for connections establishes order; theology then proposes to uncover and demonstrate the wholeness and self-evident truth of a composition. In these neutral terms, I define that reconstructive task of theology that I impute to the Talmud.

Now what shall we say of a document that so re-presents the principal received documents of the long and old tradition, Scripture (with its exegetical companions) and the Mishnah (with its complementary traditions), to demonstrate systematically that cases rest on premises, which point toward principles? The answer is simple. We classify as theological the program of writers who demonstrate on every page of their writing that principles carry us to other premises; these in turn yield other cases; and diverse cases, their premises and their principles. For the purpose is rigorously to demonstrate that the whole coalesces in, if not harmonious statements, then statements of fixed and few differences at the level of high abstraction. Harmony, linearity, uniformity – these form the character of the writings; proportion, composition, coherence – these define the character of the system. Dialectical, analytical argument, applied reason, and practical logic – these form the qualities of the intellectual work to be done. Hermeneutics never spelled out but tediously instantiated – that forms the theological medium for the theological method revealed when the work is fully exposed. And the exposure of the whole by the Talmud of Babylonia constituted the re-presentation as theology of the religious system of the Talmud of the Land of Israel and related writings. As ballet is music "physicalized," so theology is religion philosophized. The counterpart then to the notes for the music is the hermeneutics for the text: what is the Torah? how do we read it properly?

These writers propose to reduce the range of diversity to a few differences; demonstrate the harmony of discrete rules; show the operation of some few laws, so moving jurisprudence upward to the level of philosophy. Of such writers and their book, I can find no more appropriate language than that used by Dalferth: "The theology of Judaism is the intellectual quest for clarity about the Torah and its view of reality in the eternal perspective of the Torah." What requires clarification, in particular, has to be named: it is the way in which things connect and hold together, the systemic cogency of the system. In the Talmud I find that matter of clarification to come to expression in the sustained concern – the obsession, really – with the harmony of laws in law.

Precisely how does that concern come to expression? The idiom chosen by the Torah rarely speaks about abstract things in abstract ways. Rather, it prefers to speak through cases and examples. When the Written Torah generalizes, it immediately becomes concrete: "And the Lord said to Moses, Say to all the congregation of the people of Israel, You shall be holy, for I the Lord your God am holy. Every one of you shall revere his mother and his father, and you shall keep my sabbaths; I am the Lord your God. Do not turn to idols or make for yourselves molten gods; I am the Lord your God" (Lev. 19:1-4). People are not left in doubt about that of which "holiness" consists. So, too, the Mishnah rarely speaks in generalities, but invariably sets forth the governing rules. It is through the making of lists of things with common traits that follow the same rule that the Mishnah makes its point about the governing rule. The first Talmud never says, "The Mishnah is a work of perfection," but it repeatedly shows that the Mishnah does not repeat itself. It never says, "The Mishnah forms part of the Torah, making its statements on the foundations of verses of Scripture," but it shows over and over again that the Mishnah's rules give concrete expression to the laws of the Torah. So the Torah speaks to humanity in humanity's way, by case and example. But the Torah lays down the laws of life.

So, too, the second Talmud (like every other canonical writing of Judaism in its formative age) speaks in concrete terms about abstract things, rarely using abstract language but always relying on the masters and disciples to see the point of matters. Hence, here as throughout this book, we take up details but determine to identify what is at stake. In the present case, I offer as an example of my generalization about the Talmud's search for the main point beneath detail the Talmud's insistence on showing how contending authorities (meaning, of course, positions in conflict) in fact harmonize, saying the same thing in different ways, for example, or differing about points that are, in fact, distinct. That persistent interest in limiting difference and extending consensus forms a principal plank in the document's program.

Let us now turn from generalizations to some concrete illustrations. My illustrative case, meant only to clarify the meaning of the characterization of the Talmud as a sustained effort at reconstruction through elucidation of the fundamental unities of the Torah's laws, takes up the Bavli's persistent interest in showing that a variety of named authorities can concur on a single, unattributed rule. What is at issue is an interest in showing the fundamental unity of the law, and of sages' discrete opinions on the law. The thesis of this book requires that I take the route of comparing the two Talmuds. For I maintain that the second, but not the first, Talmud made the theological re-presentation of Judaism (in language the sense of which becomes clear in Chapter Four: the second Talmud presented the one whole Torah of Moses, our rabbi). Hence critical to all exposition is the work of the comparison of the two Talmuds, showing that the second of the two, but not the first, accomplished that work of rigorous analytical demonstration of the integrity of the truth that constituted the statement of the theology of Judaism, the character of the whole Torah, Oral and Written.

To show that this trait is distinctive to the second Talmud and rarely generates the formation of large-scale compositions in the first Talmud, I compare the two Talmuds' treatment of the same matter. What we see is that while the Yerushalmi is satisfied to lay out differences of opinion, as a matter of information, the Bavli wishes to analyze for the possibility of concurrence among superficially differing opinions. That is not a mere hermeneutical preference. It is critical to the Bavli's most profound quest, which is for the point in its search for the abstraction at which discrete principles come together in shared premises, and premises in a point common to them all.

In the following instance, the Yerushalmi declares flatly that our unattributed Mishnah accords with a position assigned to Judah. The Bavli asks the same question – who is the authority behind the anonymous, therefore authoritative, rule – but then adduces evidence to support the view that all concerned authorities, not only Judah, concur. At stake, then, is to demonstrate the consensus of opinion, the probability that all authorities concur, so the law does not attest to schism. There is no more solid demonstration of the unity of the law than that. This venture requires us to reread the language at hand, on the one side, and then to draw a distinction on some other basis. But the payoff is that we can demonstrate that the law accords with all authorities, not a schismatic opinion, and if the authors of the Bavli's compositions of this type can accomplish such a demonstration, they always will do so. Laying out the texts side by side underscores the contrast. The citation of the Mishnah passage to which allusion is made is in boldface type, and, for the Talmud of Babylonia, Aramaic is in italics, Hebrew in plain type.

The Talmud of the Land of Israel	**The Talmud of the Land of Babylonia**
[IX.A] He who says, "As the vows of the respectable folk," has said nothing whatsoever [M. 1:1H].	II.1 A. **[He who says,] "As the vows of the suitable folk," has said nothing whatsoever. "As their [suitable folks'] freewill-offerings," ...he has made a**
[B] Is that to say that people who take oaths	

are respectable?

[C] Once he has taken a vow, he is no longer regarded as a suitable person.

[D] The Mishnah passage before us accords with the view of R. Judah. It has been taught in the name of R. Judah:

[E] "The pious men of old used to want to bring a sin-offering. But the space on the altar was not sufficient for the bringing in their behalf of offerings in expiation of inadvertent sins. So they would offer Nazirite vows as freewill-offerings, so that they might bring a sin-offering."

[F] Rabban Simeon b. Gamaliel says, "They were sinners, for they would take a vow as a Nazir, as it is said 'And he shall make atonement for him, because he sinned against the soul' (Num. 6:11)" [T. Ned. 1:1H-P].

[G] This sin, to which reference is made, against his soul, is that he has kept himself from drinking wine.

B. binding vow in the case of a Nazir or in the case of [bringing] an offering:

B. *Who is the Tannaite authority who distinguishes between a vow and a pledge of a freewill-offering? Might one say it is not in accord with R. Meir or with R. Judah? For it has been taught on Tannaite authority:* "'It is better not to vow than take a vow and not pay' (Qoh. 5:4) — best of all is not taking a vow at all," *the words of R. Meir. R. Judah says, "Best of all is to vow and carry out the vow."* [Thus neither authority distinguishes between a vow and a freewill-offering.]

C. *You may even say that it is R. Meir who draws that distinction. When* [9B] *R. Meir made his statement, it was with reference to a vow, but he did not make reference at all to a freewill-offering!*

D. *But lo, the Mishnah states explicitly:* "As their [suitable folks'] freewill-offerings," ... he has made a binding vow in the case of a Nazir or in the case of [bringing] an offering!

E. *Repeat the passage in this manner:* He has made a binding vow for a freewill-offering in respect to a Nazirite and a sacrifice.

II.2   A.   *Then what differentiates the case of the one who takes a vow [*"**As the vows of the suitable folk**"*], that he is not subject to the same rule?*

B.   *He may stumble [and not carry out the vow].*

C.   *So in regard to one who vows a freewill-offering, won't he face the possibility also of stumbling?*

D.   *It is like Hillel the Elder, for it has been taught on Tannaite authority:* They said concerning Hillel the Elder that during all his lifetime no one ever committed sacrilege through an animal designated in advance as a burnt-offering. He would bring the animal as yet unconsecrated to the Temple courtyard and there he would declare it to be sanctified for the stated purpose and put his hands on it and then slaughter it.

E.   *Well, that solves the problem in regard to a freewill-offering in the classification of ordinary sacrifices, but what about the freewill-offering presented in the context of the Nazirite vow* [Freedman: since the possibility of violating one of the laws of the Nazirite may also form a stumbling block]?

F.   *The operative theory is that of Simeon the Righteous, for it has been taught on Tannaite authority....*

The Bavli's consistent polemic in favor of a unanimous sponsorship of what can be read as a schismatic but anonymous and therefore consensual position is what differentiates the two readings of the same Mishnah rule.

This same quest for consensus explains why the issue of "who stands behind an unassigned rule" will attract close scrutiny in the Bavli, but uncommonly in the Yerushalmi. That fact shows that the second Talmud is different from the first and pursues a program we may characterize as other than the exegetical one that the first of the two Talmuds carries out. My example derives from M. Nedarim 1:2 at B. II.1, where we see how the Bavli – as is very commonly the case – introduces compositions that raise theoretical questions, worked out on the basis of established facts, this, if X, then what about Y? That persistent drive toward new principles, generated through syllogistic reasoning, in general characterizes the Bavli, not the Yerushalmi:

[Q] "Like the sheds" – "Like the sheds for wood," "Like the sheds for offerings."	**III.1 A.** [If he said, "May it be to me] like the lamb [of the daily whole-offering]," "...like the [Temple] sheds":
[R] "Like the wood" – "Like two bundles of wood."	**B.** *A Tannaite statement:* **If he said, "A lamb, for a lamb, as a lamb; sheds, for sheds, as sheds; wood, for wood, as wood; fire, for fire, as fire; the altar, for the altar, as the altar; the Temple, for the Temple, as the Temple; Jerusalem, for Jerusalem, as Jerusalem" – in all cases adding, "Be anything that I eat with you," he is bound; "Be anything that I don't eat with you," he is permitted [T. Ned. 1:3A-D].**
[S] "Like the fires" – "Like the flame of the fires."	
[T] "Like the altar" – "Like the offerings of the altar."	
[U] "Like the sanctuary" – "Like the offerings of the sanctuary."	
[V] "Like Jerusalem" – "Like the offerings of Jerusalem."	
	C. *Now what Tannaite authority has let us know that there is no point of differentiation among the language usages,* **a lamb, for a lamb, as a lamb?** *It is R. Meir [by*

contrast to Judah: **He who says, "Jerusalem," has said nothing]**. *So then notice what is going to come:* **"Be anything that I don't eat with you," he is permitted.** *But we have learned in the Mishnah:* **[If he says,] "For a qorban shall be what I eat with you," R. Meir declares him bound [M. 1:4I-J]**! And R. Abba said in that connection, "He is treated as though he had said, 'For an offering will it be, therefore I shall not eat with you.'"

D.   *There is no contradiction, in the one case he said, "Not for a lamb," in the other, "Not-for a lamb."*

The Bavli seeks to draw conclusions, to ask about authorities behind unnamed rules, to identify operative principles and unarticulated premises. The Yerushalmi cites a passage that is left inert.

The quest for consensus should not be misconstrued as merely political, far from it. It is an interest in the unity, at deep layers of thought, of diverse and discrete truth. This concern for uncovering the unity of principle and premise that units discrete topics and verses of Scripture surfaces even in the inquiry into the scriptural foundations for a Mishnah rule. If we ask ourselves, what could possibly link one such problem to another, the answer becomes obvious: at the level of hermeneutics. And so, at M. Makkot 2:1A-L we find an interesting contrast. Both Talmuds wish to find a scriptural basis for the Mishnah's rulings. But while the Yerushalmi suffices with a simple statement of its facts, the Bavli digs deeper and discovers the hermeneutical foundations for the dispute. In that way, a considerable number of unrelated disputes on Scripture are brought into a single framework.

[I.A] What is the scriptural basis for the position of Rabbi [at M. 2:2D-E]?

[B] Here it is stated, "...[and the head] slips [from the handle and strikes his neighbor so that he dies...]" (Deut. 19:5).

[C] And later on, the same verb root is used: "[...for your olives] shall drop off..." (Deut. 28:40).

[D] Just as the verb root used later means "dropping off," so here it means "dropping off."

[E] What is the scriptural basis for the position of the rabbis [at M. 2:2F]?

[F] Here the verb root "slipping" is used.

[G] And later on elsewhere we have the following: "...and clears away many nations before you..." (Deut. 7:1).

[H] Just as the verb root "clearing away" refers to an [active] blow there, so here, too, it speaks of an [active] blow [by an object which strikes something, for example, the ax, not chips of wood].

I.1 A. *It has been taught on Tannaite authority:*

B. Said Rabbi to sages, "But is it stated, 'And the iron slips from its wood' (Deut. 19:5)? What it says is, 'from the tree.' And 'tree' appears twice, just as in the first instance, the reference is to the tree that is being cut down, so in the second case, it is to the tree that is being cut down."

2. A. Said R. Hiyya bar Ashi said Rab, "And both parties interpret the same verse of Scripture, namely, 'And the iron slips from the tree' (Deut. 19:5).

B. *"Rabbi maintains that the unvocalized letters of the text are deter-*

minative, *so we may read the word as* 'and was hurled away,' *and rabbis hold that* the vocalization of the letters of the text is determinative, *so we can only read* 'and slipped.'"

C.   *But does Rabbi really maintain that the unvocalized letters of the text are determinative?* [8A] *And has not R. Isaac b. R. Joseph said R. Yohanan said, "Rabbi, R. Judah b. Roes, the House of Shammai, R. Simeon, and R. Aqiba all take the view that we read Scripture in the way in which the supplied vowels direct it to be read"?*

D.   *Well, that is quite right, and that is why he gave them an additional argument.*

The important difference is at B.'s No. 2. The question produces an answer that allows us to move far afield; our rule becomes a case, for testing against other cases. Once again, if the Bavli is a talmud, the Yerushalmi is something else. This juxtaposition of quite various compositions of the Bavli's yields a single proposition, which is, at their profound levels, in their most abstract statements, the laws yield law — and law means something other than laws.

The characterization of the second Talmud in particular as a theological writing, aimed at setting forth a theological system, of course requires substantial analysis of texts to be examined later on (at Chapters Ten through Eleven). But at the outset, the point of that analysis has to be stated. It is not merely that the Talmud raises questions and answers them; that important trait of philosophical discourse is necessary but not sufficient evidence, since, after all, the question-and-answer form is routine in a variety of religious writings, not all of them theological by any means, as any reading of the book of Job will suggest. Nor is it the equally important fact that the Talmud's principal discourses are dialectical, for even though that trait is definitive for the Talmud, by itself it indicates only a remarkable intellectual rigor.

What qualifies the Talmud's entire program as distinctively, particularly, properly theological is its persistent effort to understand the received facts of faith through a process of systematic reflective explication and conceptual reconstruction. This was a process worked out through practical reason and applied logic, so that all details are made to make a single statement, everything in its place, in proper proportion and perspective. It was a process repeated from one page to the next, with a few set consequences, always guided by a few rules of reading. All of the Talmud's secondary devices of testing an allegation – a close reading of the formulation of the Mishnah, an appeal to the false conclusion such a close reading, absent a given formulation, might have yielded, to take the examples before us – serve that primary goal.

What makes these traits of mind, these hermeneutical principles, theological and not merely philosophical or jurisprudential is a simple fact, with which we began: "our sages of blessed memory" appeal to the Torah and to the authority of sages who stand in a direct line of tradition to Sinai, and the entire purpose of their work is to show the unity of the Torah, its coherence and cogency. Since, it hardly needs saying, the Torah comes from God, and, when we speak of truth, we mean, God's truth, the sole issue of the Talmud is theological, and in the service of theology, philosophy and jurisprudence are called to make their contribution. "Theology" here, in the context of Judaism, is not generic but specific to the components of the word itself: the logic of God. What is revealed in the Torah is God: God's intellect and consequent intention. The theology of Judaism consists in the knowledge of God that God has made manifest, and the task of theology is to identify of what that knowledge consists. No more essentially theological definition of thought is possible.

The Bavli's framers find themselves constantly drawn toward questions of generalization and abstraction (once more: the law behind the laws), moving from case to principle to new case to new principle, then asking whether the substrate of principles forms a single, tight fabric. What gives the Bavli its compelling, ineluctable power to persuade, the source of the Bavli's intellectual force, is that thrust for abstraction and orderly reflection, transforming religious facts into theological propositions, truths into truth, laws into law, evidences for God's will into a statement of God's purpose. This is accomplished through generalization (and in that order, generalization, toward abstraction). To spell out in very simple terms what I conceive to be at issue: The way that the law behind the laws emerges is, first, generalization of a case into a principle, then, the recasting of the principle into an abstraction encompassing a variety of otherwise free-standing principles. To state the theological formulation of the religion, Judaism, I make two statements that will take some time to unpack.

First the Mishnah's cases time and again point toward a single abstraction, the hierarchical order of all being, the unstated conclusion being: one God governs the world.

Second, the counterpart and completion of the Mishnah's deepest layer of thought are formed by the Talmud's method: the intellectual medium to match the philosophical message.

In due course, therefore, we shall have to specify not only what is unique to the Talmud's hermeneutical method, but also, what (I conceive) the theological message is that inheres in that method. For the task is not merely to show that the Talmud presents theology. It is to specify of what that theology consists.[10] The upshot is clear. The theology of Judaism may then be defined as "intellectual quest for clarity about the Torah and its view of reality in the perspective of the Torah."[11] It is time to define Judaism. Specifically, what is the sense of the term "Judaism" as the canonical writings treated here permit us to use that term? What is the meaning of the term "theology" in the particular setting of that same Judaism, as these same writings permit us to speak, also, of theology as has now been defined?

---

[10]An interesting essay in comparative theology would take up Dalferth's chapter, "Revelational Theology" (op. cit., pp. 188-203), with the theology of revelation proceeding from a specific text and its hermeneutics, such as I mean to present here.

[11]I paraphrase Dalferth, p. 151, cited above.

4

Knowing God through the Torah: The Theological Paradigm of Judaism

Defining the term, "Judaism," we start with two categories, the native and (equally legitimate, but different) neutral ones. Two sentences that say the same thing show what is at stake in the distinction:

[1]   In the secular, descriptive terms defined in Chapter Three, rigorous, sustained reflection upon revelation forms the theology of Judaism.

[2]   In the native language of Judaism, we say the same thing in these words: study of the Torah as the Talmud presents the Torah teaches us the will of God.

The native category, or name, of "Judaism" in the Judaism set forth by "our sages of blessed memory" in "the Torah, Written and Oral," is "the Torah." When, in ordinary speech in the West, we want to speak of the religion set forth by the Torah, we call it "Judaism." So the two terms stand for two distinct, but comparable, categories, each in its own language world: the whole, complete, authoritative, fully composed religion, with its system comprising a way of life, worldview, and theory of the social entity, Israel, is Judaism (for the secular language of the West) or is what the Torah presents (for the theological language of the faith).

The formulation, quite routine and immediately clear, in Western languages, "Judaism says" or "teaches," finds its counterpart, in the language of the Judaic canon in two usages. For the Written Torah the native idiom uses "the Torah says" or its many equivalents, for example, "as it is said," or "as it is written." For the Oral Torah, "Rabbi X says," or "it is written," or a simple, declarative statement of a rule in Mishnaic Hebrew (whether in the Mishnah, Tosefta, Talmuds, or other compilations) equally suffices. So the contemporary, secular formulation, "Judaism teaches," "believes," "maintains," and the like, serves in both its elements, subject ("Judaism") and verb ("teaches," "believes," "maintains," and other such verbs of ratiocination) as a formulation yielding as its counterpart "the Torah" and "says," or other references to the propaedeutic, pedagogical actions undertaken by a component of the one whole Torah, Written and Oral, of Moses our rabbi. Use of that language signals authoritative, reliable teaching, just as "Judaism maintains" or "believes" does in more descriptive and less mythic wording. Not only so, but appearance of an unassigned statement in a document of the Oral Torah, for example, the statement of the consensus of sages, all the more so bears authoritative standing and forms a statement of the Torah. In our secular languages, too, we should call that statement an equivalent to one using the formula, "Judaism says...."

How then differentiate native from secular and descriptive categories? The native category "Torah" formulates truth in a mythic framework, the Western one, "Judaism," portrays in a neutral way facts or propositions in a philosophical setting of description. The appearance of the "-ism" (or -ity) then for secular discourse signifies order, system, generalization and abstraction; the operative verbs, "teaches," or "maintains," and the like, bear the same message of generalization and principled conviction.

The use of "Torah" by contrast appeals to a text and to revelation, and the use of "says" or "as it is said" or "as it is written" with reference to the media of Torah, the sage or Scripture, respectively, appeals for sense to the act of speech, which, in context, is the medium of authority attained through not reason and persuasion but revelation. It follows that "the Torah says" and "Judaism teaches" or "believes" really do not correspond, the native category referring to revelation, the academic one, reasoned sorting out of data.

And yet, the two distinct ways of referring to the same thing – the position of the religious system, Judaism/the Torah – do bear a single purpose. It is to state the sum of all the many cases, the rule, the conclusion, the authoritative principle. Whether the language is liturgical,[1] "Hear O Israel, the Lord our God, the Lord is one," or "Judaism is the religion of ethical monotheism," whether it is "You shall

---

[1]And nearly all dogmas of this Judaism come to authoritative expression liturgically; the liturgy forms the medium for the dogma and creedal formulation of Judaism, as in the cases given here. Public prayer then forms a rehearsal in theatrical and choreographic terms of the theological convictions of the faith: theology sung, theology acted out (as in the display of the Torah scroll), and theology (when liturgy is rightly carried out) danced in procession.

be holy, for I the Lord your God am holy," or "Judaism is a religion of covenantal nomism," the intent and effect are the same. So, too, the generic, torah, is defined not only in the character of writings and their contents, for example, "Moses received Torah at Sinai," but in the liturgical formulas that begin and conclude the proclamation of the Torah in synagogue worship: "Blessed...who has chosen us from among all the nations by giving us the Torah...blessed...who gives the Torah," and "Blessed...who has given us the authentic Torah and thereby planted within us eternal life...blessed...who gives the Torah." Another way of saying the same dogma is: [1] Israel is elect by reason of the Torah; [2] eternal life comes to us through the Torah; [3] God gives the Torah, present tense, meaning, here and now; and here and now, we receive the Torah.

The importance of recognizing the distinction between native and academic categories is in two aspects. First, we must permit "Judaism" to speak in its own terms, that is to say, as "the Torah." But, second, we must insist that "the Torah" also speak to us in language we can grasp – albeit in its native categories, idiom, and language (though in English) – meaning, formulate its positions or principles in terms and categories that we also may understand: describe, analyze, and interpret.

Mine is the work of mediation, like the bilingual translator. But as translation begins with native speech, which dictates the task of the translator into some other language, so the native category defines the starting point. That is to say, we accomplish this account of mine into what I conceive as the "theologization" of a religious system by close attention specifically to the Torah and its purpose and definition, its expression and the definition and character of its texts, and only then proceed to interrogate the Torah about its theological program, traits, and categories. The Torah, once defined, will inform us about that program and its traits of message and method alike.

It follows that, Torah being the native category, understanding "the theology of Judaism" as that theology came to full and systematic expression in its authoritative document requires an inquiry into the nature and structure of the Torah: the media designated with the status of Torah, the persons, books, gestures, hierarchical authority in the social order, modes of thought and expression, that fall into the category, Torah, and require orderly systematization as a single, coherent statement. Indeed, that statement – the theology of Judaism comes to realization in the Torah – self-evidently forms a redundancy, since, as I just said, "theology of Judaism" in one language of thought is the same as "the Torah" in the other.

I have maintained that it is through the Torah that God is made manifest, and, specifically, it is through the intellection exemplifed in the

Torah that we know the mind of God. That means, what defines humanity and what defines God, in rationality, is the same thing: we are consubstantial in mind. I therefore allege that, first, the category, "Torah," defines the theology of Judaism, and, second, knowledge of the Torah tells us how God thinks. Let me now demonstrate that these allegations are natural to the sources with which I deal.

Lest readers suppose, first, I have exaggerated my contention that the category, "Torah," defines the focus of theology, so that the documentary representation of the Torah forms the presentation, or re-presentation, of that theology, let me give a concrete example of the extent to which that single category overspreads the social order – intellect and hierarchy alike – governing conduct and conviction in all details. There are, then, usages that show how correct conduct and conviction form "torah" – authoritative propositions and governing rules – and come to formulation in The Torah. These dictate correct usage, right action and doctrine, matters of status, position, the arrangement of the social order, and on upward to who may marry whom. Proper speech and proper conduct find entire definition in the Torah, and errors in the one or the other indicate one is not a master of the Torah and so is not reliable. The following story shows us the range of what is at issue when we speak of torah or The Torah:

5. A. *There was a man from Nehardea who went into a butcher shop in Pumbedita. He said to them, "Give me meat."*

    B. *They said to him, "Wait until the servant of R. Judah bar Ezekiel gets his, and then we'll give to you."*

    C. *He said, "So who is this Judah bar Sheviskel who comes before me to get served before me?"*

    D. *They went and told R. Judah.*

    E. *He excommunicated him.*

    F. *They said, "He is in the habit of calling people slaves."*

    G. *He proclaimed concerning him, "He is a slave."*

    H. *The other party went and sued him in court before R. Nahman.*

    I. *When the summons came, R. Judah went to R. Huna, he said to him, "Should I go, or shouldn't I go?"*

    J. *He said to him, "In point of fact, you really don't have to go, because you are an eminent authority. But on account of the honor owing to the household of the patriarch [of the Babylonian Jews], get up and go."*

    K. *He came. He found him making a parapet.*

    L. *He said to him, "Doesn't the master concur with what R. Huna bar Idi said Samuel said, 'Once a man is appointed administrator of the community, it is forbidden for him to do servile labor before three persons'?"*

    M. *He said to him, "I'm just making a little piece of the balustrade."*

    N. *He said to him, "So what's so bad about the word 'parapet,' that the Torah uses, or the word 'partition,' that rabbis use?"*

    O. *He said to him, "Will the master sit down on a seat?"*

P.   *He said to him, "So what's so bad about 'chair,' which rabbis use, or the word 'stool,' which people generally use?"*

Q.   *He said to him, "Will the master eat a piece of citron fruit?"*

R.   *He said to him, "This is what Samuel said, 'Whoever uses the word "citron fruit" is a third puffed up with pride.'* It should be called either etrog, as the rabbis do, or 'lemony thing,' as people do."

S.   *He said to him, "Would the master like to drink a goblet of wine?"*

T.   *He said to him, "So what's so bad about the word 'wine glass,' as rabbis say, or 'a drink,' as people say?"*

U.   *He said to him, "Let my daughter Dunag bring something to drink?"*

V.   *He said to him, "This is what Samuel said, 'People are not to make use of a woman.'"*

W.   *"But she's only a minor!"*

X.   *"In so many words said Samuel, 'People are not to make use of a woman in any manner, whether adult or minor.'"*

Y.   *"Would the master care to send a greeting to my wife, Yalta?"*

Z.   *He said to him, "This is what Samuel said, 'Even the sound of a woman's voice is [forbidden as] lustful.'"*

AA. *"Maybe through a messenger?"*

BB. *He said to him, "This is what Samuel said, [70B] 'People are not to inquire after a woman's health.'"*

CC. *"Through her husband?!"*

DD. *He said to him, "This is what Samuel said, 'People are not to inquire after a woman's health in any way, shape, or form.'"*

EE. *His wife sent word to him, "Settle the man's case for him, so that he not make you like any other fool."*

FF. *He said to him, "So what brings you here?"*

GG. *He said to him, "You sent me a subpoena." He said to him, "Now if even the language of the master I don't know, how in the world could I have sent you a subpoena?!"*

HH. *He produced the summons from his bosom and showed it to him: "Here is the man, here is the subpoena!"*

II. *He said to him, "Well, anyhow, since the master has come here, let's discuss the matter, so people should not say that rabbis are showing favoritism to one another."*

JJ. *He said to him, "How come the master has excommunicated that man?" "He harassed a messenger of the rabbis."*

KK. *"So why didn't the master flog him, for Rab would flog someone who harassed a messenger of the rabbis."*

LL. *"I did worse to him."*

MM. *"How come the master declared to the man that he was a slave?"*

NN. *"Because he went around calling other people slaves, and there is a Tannaite statement:* Whoever alleges that others are genealogically invalid is himself invalid and never says a good thing about other people. And said Samuel, 'By reference to a flaw in himself he invalidates others.'"

OO. *"Well, I can concede that Samuel said to suspect such a man of such a genealogy, but did he really say to make a public declaration to that effect?"...*

B. Qiddushin 70A-B

The category, "Torah," enters this story at a number of distinct points. First of all, the master of Torah is accorded authority and honor; when not, he will exclude the other party from "Israel," placing him into ostracism ("excommunication") or assigning him to a social status, as a slave, that prevents him from marrying into "Israel." Second, the master of Torah conducts himself in a proper way. He signifies his status by using one word, rather than some other word, for common objects. He accomplishes the same goal, also, by the manner of his conduct with women. It goes without saying that sages not only act impartially but make certain they are seen to act impartially. It follows that, if we wish to know how this religious system speaks and what it wishes to say, we have to listen to what it says in the Torah and how it makes that statement.

Before we can approach the more profound issue, how the Torah gives us access to God's rationality, we have to take a roundabout route. First, to speak intelligibly, we have to utilize our categories, so that defining the task in overlapping languages – the secular languages of Western learning, the religious language of "Judaism" or "the Torah" – is required. That is for a simple reason. It is the only way in which we can formulate what is required to accomplish our task of theological description, analysis, and interpretation in a determinate historical setting. So both languages – the language of the academy, speaking of "Judaism" or "theology," and the language of the native category, speaking of "torah" and "the Torah" – are necessary. The language of the academy of the West shapes our intellect and forms our organizing categories; that language forms our analytical tool; without it, all we do is paraphrase our sources. The language of the academy of Judaism, the yeshiva, provides access to our sources and defines the subject and system that we study; without it, we generalize without data, describe what we have not, in fact, examined at all.

A restatement of matters using the two functionally equivalent word formations ("Judaism" or "Torah") defines our work by showing what is at stake. Since (in the authentic speech of Judaism) "the Torah is given by God to Moses at Sinai" – a statement of not historical but theological consequence – it must follow that any grasp of (in the intelligible speech of our own modes of thought and expression) the theology of Judaism must begin with an understanding of (in language suitable to both Judaism and contemporary sensibility) how the Torah is mediated and comes to mature expression. So speaking our language, [1] we invoke the category, "the theology of Judaism," and speaking also the language of the faith, [2] we talk about torah (status, method, authority) and the Torah (substance, message, truth) in the language of the documents of the Torah, which is to say, the canonical writings of the Judaism of the

Dual Torah, Written and Oral (Scripture, the Mishnah, Midrash, and Talmud).

To accomplish the purpose of definition announced at the end of Chapter Three, therefore, let me now state matters in the two languages at once: [1] Judaism states its theology through [2] the language and in the propositions of the Torah. Since Judaism is classified as a religion among religions, that statement ("Judaism states its theology") addresses to begin with the matter of what we know of God and how we know it. The reason is that at stake in the Torah – for the religion of the Torah that is called Judaism – is knowledge of God. Then the entire theology of Judaism may be expressed in the language of the Torah in a formulation that accommodates both Western, academic language and the forms of speech of the Torah: it is through the Torah – God's own manifestation to Moses and holy Israel, and God's self-manifestation – that faithful Israel knows God.

Now let me state the theology of Judaism in the language of the Torah, once more joining the two categories, native and secular: The Torah is the sole medium of God's revelation; it bears the unique message of God; and (as I argue in this book) the Torah also conveys the correct method for the inquiry into the medium in quest of the truthful message: all three. Through learning in the Torah – singing its melody, in its words, in its rhythms, so making its natural sounds – we know God.

These statements, setting forth as generalizations of a descriptive character the generative convictions of the Torah, that is "Judaism," are unique to Judaism. The reason is not only the "context-specific" usage, "the Torah." It is more general: no other religion can make them. That is because these authoritative statements of the Torah/Judaism exclude much else that in other religions is commonly thought to afford knowledge of God, the two most common and paramount being knowledge of God through nature and history, for instance. In the Torah God is made known not through nature on its own, nor through history uninterpreted, but through nature set forth by the Torah as God's creation ("In the beginning God created...," "The heavens declare the glory of God"), through history as explained through the Torah as a work of God's will ("You have seen how I..."). So we recover our starting point to define the term, "theology": knowing God defines the work of the theology of Judaism, or, to phrase matters in the native category and its language once more, through the Torah Israel meets God.

We may then identify the theology of this Judaism – that is to say, the truth of the Torah – with the following formulation: "All our knowledge of divine truth...depends on God's prior self-manifestation;

there is no knowledge of God unless he reveals and we reason."[2] That formulation of contemporary philosophical theology in correct, academic language accurately and completely describes the entire program of the theology of Judaism. It is hardly necessary once more to translate into the language of Judaism, but an appropriate counterpart language for the same position may be identified in the liturgical setting when the Torah is proclaimed to faithful Israel at worship: "Blessed are you, Lord, our God, who has chosen us from among all nations by giving us the Torah. Blessed are you, who gives the Torah," and, at the end, "Blessed are you, Lord, our God, who has given us the true Torah and so planted within us life eternal. Blessed are you, who gives the Torah." When we know how through the Torah Israel knows God, we know the theology of Judaism. And then, about God there is nothing more to be known.

Now this brings us to the second point I promised to instantiate earlier, namely, how the Torah reveals God's intellect and ours as well. What, exactly, is to be known about God in the theology of Judaism, or, phrasing the question in the native category: "What does the Torah say about the Holy One, blessed be He?" Obviously its messages are many, from an account of attributes ("The Lord, the Lord is merciful and long-suffering"), to the story of immediate encounter ("You shall not see my face...," "...the thin voice of silence"), and, above all, to the detailed and insistent account of what God commands Israel and covenants himself to do in regard to Israel. That, after all, is the principal message of the Torah par excellence, which is the Pentateuch. But the Torah not only sets forth propositions – things God is, has done, or wants of us. Our sages of blessed memory notice that the Torah also lays out sentences God has said. Since through language we reveal not only what is on and in our minds, but also the very working of our minds, through the language of the Torah we gain access to God's mind.

Since this representation of the Talmud's re-presentation of the Torah lays claims that may prove unfamiliar and might even appear egregious, let me pause once more and turn to a text, to show that that view comes to expression, not only implicitly, on every line of the Torah. It is stated in so many words in a story embedded in the Talmud itself, one that says quite explicitly that in Heaven the Torah is studied in accord with the same rules of rationality as on earth, so that in Heaven, as much as on earth, the intervention of the sage is required. God is bound by the same rules of reasoning as the sage; a common rationality governs; the Torah contains that truth of utter integrity. It is the fact that that conviction is

---

[2]Ingolf Dalferth, "The Stuff of Revelation: Austin Farrer's Doctrine of Inspired Images," in Ann Loades and Michael McLain, eds., *Hermeneutics, the Bible, and Literary Criticism* (London, 1992: MacMillan), p. 71.

made articulate that entirely validates my representation of matters. The italics represent Aramaic, boldface type, a citation of a Mishnah passage, regular type, Hebrew. I give the bulk of the story, to show the broader context in which, it is taken for granted, God and the sage think in the same way about the same things. Not only so, but the same rules that govern on earth dictate right thinking in Heaven as well, and God is bound by those rules. That is because God made them to begin with, and made humanity in conformity with them. First, that God and the sage think in the same way about the same things:

A. *Said R. Kahana, "R. Hama, son of the daughter of Hassa, told me that Rabbah b. Nahmani died in a persecution. [And here is the story:]"*

B. *Snitches squealed on him to the government, saying, "There is a man among the Jews who keeps twelve thousand Israelites from paying the royal poll tax for a month in the summer and for a month in the winter."* [This Rabbah did by conducting huge public lectures, keeping people away from home, where they were counted for the poll tax.]

C. *They sent a royal investigator [parastak] for him but he did not find him. He fled, going from Pumbedita to Aqra, from Aqra to Agma, from Agma to Shehin, from Shehin to Seripa, from Seripa to Ena Damim, from Ena Damim back to Pumbedita. In Pumbedita he found him.*

D. *The royal investigator happened by the inn where Rabbah was located. They brought him two glasses of liquor and then took away the tray [and this excited the ill will of demons]. His face was turned backward. They said to him, "What shall we do with him? He is the king's man."*

E. *[Rabbah] said to them, "Bring him the tray again, and let him drink another cup, and then remove the tray, and he will get better."*

F. *They did just that, and he got better.*

G. *He said, "I am sure that the man whom I am hunting is here." He looked for him and found him.*

H. *He said, "I'm leaving here. If I am killed, I won't reveal a thing, but if they torture me, I'm going to squeal."*

I. *They brought him to him and he put him in a room and locked the door on him. But [Rabbah] sought mercy, the wall fell down, and he fled to Agma. He was in session on the trunk of a palm and studying.*

J. *Now in the session in the firmament they were debating the following subject:* **If the bright spot preceded the white hair, he is unclean, and if the white hair preceded the bright spot, he is clean. [The Mishnah paragraph continues: And if it is a matter of doubt, he is unclean. And R. Joshua was in doubt] [M. Neg. 4:11F-H]** –

K. the Holy One, blessed be He, says, "It is clean."

L. *And the entire session in the firmament say,* "Unclean." [We see, therefore, that in Heaven, Mishnah study was going forward, with the Holy One participating and setting forth his ruling, as against the consensus of the other sages of the Torah in Heaven.]

M. *They said, "Who is going to settle the question? It is Rabbah b. Nahmani."*

N.   For said Rabbah b. Nahmani, "I am absolutely unique in my knowledge of the marks of skin disease that is unclean and in the rules of uncleanness having to do with the corpse in the tent."

O.   *They sent an angel for him, but the angel of death could not draw near to him, since his mouth did not desist from repeating his learning. But in the meanwhile a wind blew and caused a rustling in the bushes, so he thought it was a troop of soldiers. He said, "Let me die but not be handed over to the kingdom."*

P.   *When he was dying, he said,* "It is clean, it is clean." *An echo came forth and said,* "Happy are you, Rabbah bar Nahmani, that your body is clean, and your soul has come forth in cleanness." [The body would not putrefy.]

Q.   A note fell down from Heaven in Pumbedita: "Rabbah bar Nahmani has been invited to the session that is on high."

R.   *Abbayye, Raba, and all the rabbis came forth to tend to his corpse, but they did not know where he was located. They went to Agma and saw birds [vultures] hovering over and overshadowing the corpse.* "This proves that he is there."

S.   *They mourned him for three days and three nights. A note fell down:* "Whoever refrains [from the mourning] will be excommunicated." *They mourned for him for seven days. A note fell down:* "Go now to your homes in peace."

T.   *The day on which he died a strong wind lifted a Tai-Arab who was riding on a camel from one side of the Pappa canal and threw him down onto the other side. He said, "What is this?"*

U.   *They told him, "Rabbah bar Nahmani has died."*

V.   *He said before him, "Lord of the world, the whole world is yours, and Rabbah bar Nahmani is yours. You are Rabbah's, and Rabbah is yours. Why are you destroying the world on his account?" The wind subsided.*

Bavli Baba Mesia 86A

The critical point in this story for my argument comes at three points. First, God and the sages in Heaven study the Torah in the same way as the Torah is studied on earth. Second, God is bound by the same rules of rationality as prevail down here. Third, the sage on earth studies the way God does in Heaven, and God calls up to Heaven sages whose exceptional acuity and perspicacity are required on the occasion. It follows that, when I claim our processes of analytical reasoning rightly carried out replicate God's, we can think like God and in that way be holy like God, I merely paraphrase in abstract language precisely the point on which this story and others bearing the same implication rest.

Now to move onward: why the rules reveal the mind of God. That derives from the implicit proposition of the foregoing. It is that God is bound by the same rules of logical analysis and sound discourse that govern sages. But that view is stated explicitly as well. In the following story, also found for the first time in the second Talmud and assuredly speaking for its authorship,[3] we find an explicit affirmation of the priority of reasoned argument over all other forms of discovery of truth:

II.1   A.   *There we have learned:* **If one cut [a clay oven] into parts and put sand between the parts,**

       B.   **R. Eliezer declares the oven broken-down and therefore insusceptible to uncleanness.**

       C.   **And sages declare it susceptible.**

       D.   **And this is what is meant by the oven of Akhnai [M. Kel. 5:10].**

       E.   *Why* [is it called] the oven of Akhnai?

       F.   Said R. Judah said Samuel, "It is because they surrounded it with argument as with a snake and proved it was insusceptible to uncleanness."

III.2   A.   *It has been taught on Tannaite authority:*

       B.   On that day R. Eliezer produced all of the arguments in the world, but they did not accept them from him. So he said to them, "If the law accords with my position, this carob tree will prove it."

       C.   The carob was uprooted from its place by a hundred cubits – and some say, four hundred cubits.

       D.   They said to him, "There is no proof from a carob tree."

       E.   So he went and said to them, "If the law accords with my position, let the stream of water prove it."

       F.   The stream of water reversed flow.

       G.   They said to him, "There is no proof from a stream of water."

       H.   So he went and said to them, "If the law accords with my position, let the walls of the schoolhouse prove it."

       I.   The walls of the schoolhouse tilted toward falling.

       J.   R. Joshua rebuked them, saying to them, "If disciples of sages are contending with one another in matters of law, what business do you have?"

       K.   They did not fall on account of the honor owing to R. Joshua, but they also did not straighten up on account of the honor owing to R. Eliezer, and to this day they are still tilted.

       L.   So he went and said to them, "If the law accords with my position, let the Heaven prove it!"

       M.   An echo came forth, saying, "What business have you with R. Eliezer, for the law accords with his position under all circumstances!"

       N.   R. Joshua stood up on his feet and said, "'It is not in Heaven' (Deut. 30:12)."

III.3   A.   *What is the sense of,* "'It is not in Heaven' (Deut. 30:12)"?

       B.   Said R. Jeremiah, "[The sense of Joshua's statement is this:] For the Torah has already been given from Mount Sinai, so we do not pay

---

[3]We obviously cannot rely on attributions that are beyond verification or falsification. For our characterization of the sequence of ideas and the traits of a given phase in the documentary unfolding of the Torah, all we have is the document and its date. In any event, I claim to describe the qualities of documents, not the history of ideas as they may or may not have been held outside of said documents.

attention to echoes, since you have already written in the Torah at Mount Sinai, 'After the majority you are to incline' (Ex. 23:2)."

III.4   A.   *R. Nathan came upon Elijah and said to him, "What did the Holy One, blessed be He, do at that moment?"*

B.   *He said to him, "He laughed and said, 'My children have overcome me, my children have overcome me!'"*

Bavli Baba Mesia 59A-B

The testimony of nature is null. The (mere) declaration of matters by Heaven is dismissed. The Torah now forms the possession of sages, and sages master the Torah through logical argument, right reasoning, the give and take of proposition and refutation, argument and counter argument, evidence arrayed in accord with the rules of proper analysis. Then the majority will be persuaded, one way or the other, entirely by sound argument; and the majority prevails on that account.

So when Heaven sends for Rabbah, it is because Rabbah stands for a capacity that Heaven as much as sages requires; if God rejoices at the victory, in the give and take of argument, of the sages, it is because God is subject to the same rules of argument and evidence and analysis. Then, as I said, if we want to know God, we shall find God in the Torah: not in what the Torah says alone, but in how the Torah reaches conclusions, meaning, not the process of argument, but the principles of thought. God has revealed these in the Torah, and in them we encounter God's own intellect. That is why I maintain, the theology of Judaism sets forth knowledge of God as God is made known through God's self-revelation in the Torah.

So the Torah reveals not only what God wants of humanity through Israel, but what (humanity can know of what) God is. The being of God that is revealed in the Torah – by the nature of that medium of revelation, the Torah itself, made up of words we know and sentences we can understand and forming connections we can follow and replicate – is God's will and intellect. Within the religion of the Torah called Judaism, therefore, there is ample occasion to take up the labor of learning not only what, but how God thinks. What is at stake in that lesson is how we, too, should conduct intellection. And the upshot will be, if we think the way we should, we may enter deep into the processes of the Torah and so reach propositions in the way in which God has thought things through, too. That is why I maintain, the theology of Judaism provides an account of what it means to know God through the Torah, a sentence that, I should hold, is made up of two equivalent and redundant clauses: [1] theology of Judaism provides... and [2] know God through the Torah. What makes that theology interesting is its special sense of what knowing God through the Torah involves, requires, and affords:

knowing what it means rightly to know. Three steps lead to that simple conclusion.

First, knowing God and striving to be holy like God – "Let us make Man in our image...after our likeness," "You shall be holy, for I the Lord your God am holy" – define the lessons of the Torah or "Judaism."

Second, that knowledge is both unique and also sufficient: it is only through the Torah that knowledge of God comes to humanity. The Torah comes to Israel in particular because of God's decision and choice: God gave the Torah, or, in the language of liturgy, "...who gives the Torah."

Third, knowledge of God depends not only on God's self-revelation through the Torah. It requires also humanity's – therefore, uniquely, Israel's – proper grasp of the Torah. And that requires active engagement: sagacity, wit, erudition and intelligence. Gifts of intellect form instruments of grace: elements of God's self-revelation. The reason is that by thinking about thought as much as thinking thoughts, we ask the deeper question about what we can know about God, which is, God's thoughts in God's words, which, rightly grasped, expose God's thought.

Proper inquiry after God in the Torah therefore requires sound method: right questions, proper modes of analysis, reliable use of probative evidence, compelling reasoning. These are media of revelation accessible to humanity, to which through the Torah (in its oral as much as in its written components) and its everywhere unitary rules of reasoning we gain access. For the Torah comes to Israel in the medium of language – some of it written down right away, at Sinai, some of it orally formulated and transmitted and only later on written down – and Israel knows God. Knowledge of God comes through not the silence of wordless sentiment nor inchoate encounter in unarticulated experience, nor through the thin voice of silence alone, a silence without words. Knowledge of God reaches us solely through the reflection afterward on what has been felt or thought or said by the voice of silence.

Now modes of bringing upward into the form of language knowledge of God begin with the writing down of the Torah itself, which, for Israel, records not only God's will but the actual words God used in stating that will to Moses, our rabbi. Therefore knowledge of the grammar and syntax of God's thought, learned through mastery of how to read the words themselves, which words pertain here, which there, and what conclusions to draw about God, on the one side, and what humanity embodied in Israel, on the other – that knowledge begins in the right reading of the Torah. The authentic theologians of Judaism then are our sages of blessed memory, who know how, and, also, the reason why behind the how.

I said earlier that the religious system reaches its statement, in the case of this Judaism, in documents, even though, as we have already seen in the story about right conduct with women and right word choices, other media besides closed writings serve the same purpose. Still, the principal statement is made by a single, formidable, sustained writing, which – now speaking in description and fact – from the time of its closure to our own day made, now makes, the summary statement of Judaism, and, in centers where people study the Torah, defines the curriculum. That sustained, systematic exposition, through one instance after another, of the right reading of the Torah in both its media comes to Israel now as in the past in a single document, the Talmud of Babylonia, a.k.a. the Bavli, hereinafter simply: the Talmud.

That statement of fact describes the centrality of the Talmud in the curriculum of the Judaic intellect, the priority of the Talmud from the time of its closure in ca. 600 C.E. to the present time. The Talmud is the prism, receiving, refracting all light. Let me first state the proposition in academic language: Into that writing all prior canonical (that is, authoritative) documents flowed; from it, all later canonical writings emerged; to it all appeal is directed; upon it, all conclusions ultimately rest. Now in the language of the Torah itself: Study of the Torah begins, as a matter of simple fact, in the Talmud.

Proof of these simple propositions on the Talmudic re-presentation of the Torah, which is to say, Judaism's statement of its theology, its norms of action and reflection (*halakhah, aggadah* respectively), and of the authority that sustains them and signifies right from wrong, derives from the character of Judaic discourse. In all times, places, and writings, other than those rejected as heretical, from then to now, the Talmud formed the starting point and the ending point, the alpha and omega of truth; justify by appeal to the Talmud, rightly read, persuasively interpreted, and you make your point; disprove a proposition by reference to a statement of the Talmud, and you demolish a counterpoint. In reading the Written Torah itself, the Talmud's exegesis enjoys priority of place. Scripture rightly read reaches Israel in the Talmud (and related writings of Midrash); sound exegesis conforms to the facts of the Talmud (and Midrash) or can be shown to be, at least, not out of line with them. Even greater consequence attaches to action. In all decisions of law that express theology in everyday action, the Talmud forms the final statement of the Torah, mediating Scripture's rules.

Innovation of every kind, whether in the character of the spiritual life or in the practice of the faith in accord with its norms, must find justification in the Talmud, however diverse the means by which validation is accomplished. The schools and courts of the holy community of Israel studied the Torah in the Talmud and applied its laws. The faithful emulated masters of the Torah in the Talmud and accepted their instruction. Even in modern times, when, rejecting the self-segregation of "the people that dwells apart," Judaic systems took shape intending to integrate holy Israel into the common life of the nations where Jews lived, those systems acknowledged the authority of the Talmud, whether by proposing to validate a profound change in the social policy of holy Israel by appeal to its norms or by attempting to invalidate the entire received theory of Israel's society by discrediting the Talmud in some detail or in its entirety. The authority of the document found its most profound recognition in the centrality accorded to it even by those who undertook to overturn that authority.

The premise is then shown to generate yet another principle, reaching upward, at a different terrain altogether, into other cases. Do the cases presuppose contrary principles? Do the principles express conflicting premises? Then the disharmony demands detailed attention, a work of harmonization not of detail nor yet of principle but of the most abstract formulations of premise. Right reasoning and its rules hold the whole together.

To what end? Clearly, knowing how to decipher the signals of dialogue allows us not only to come to conclusions but, more to the point, even to recreate an argument, one that would lead from out here, in the real world of cases and examples, inward, into the profound reaches of the Torah, where at the deepest structure we grasp what we can of God's will and intellect. The Talmud makes it possible to replicate the modes of thought that yielded principles and rules. The Torah then forms the data out of which, in our joining of the issue, we may find at the layers of abstraction and generalization the rules of reasoned reality: the world attests to the intent and mind of its Maker. The integrity of truth, its unity and coherence – these traits of intellect attest to God's mind, from which all things come, to which all things refer. The rules of life therefore came to this-worldly expression within, and to those with wit and patience would be fully exposed in all their unity and integrity by, the Torah.

So the stakes of the second Talmud prove formidable indeed. That is why I maintain, the theology of Judaism (in academic language) forms a statement of what it means to know God; and that theology defines what it means to know God in terms both particular but wholly accessible to the mind of all creation endowed with sensibility. God is wholly other, but God has given the Torah, so revealing to holy Israel both the terms of endearment – what God wants of Israel – and also the terminology thereof: the how and the why behind the what.

The Torah defines above all relationships, how God loves humanity, how humanity is to respond in deed and deliberation. Then the Torah comes to Israel in an encounter ("dialogue"), first between Moses and God, then between the disciple and the master, replicating the relationship between Moses and God. It follows that the critical moment comes at the encounter of master and disciple, where here and now, both enter into the situation of God and Moses.

That conception of relationship reaches definition in three ways, concrete, abstract, and mythic, in the following, first the concrete rule:

I. A. [If he has to choose between seeking] what he has lost and what his father has lost,
    B. his own takes precedence.
II. C. ...what he has lost and what his master has lost,
    D. his own takes precedence.
III. E. ...what his father has lost and what his master has lost,
    F. that of his master takes precedence.
    G. For his father brought him into this world.
    H. But his master, who taught him wisdom, will bring him into the life of the world to come.
    I. But if his father is a sage, that of his father takes precedence.

Mishnah-tractate Baba Mesia 2:11

Now the abstract statement of the theological fact:

A. Moses received the Torah at Sinai and handed it on to Joshua, Joshua to elders, and elders to prophets. And prophets handed it on to the men of the great assembly. They said three things: Be prudent in judgment. Raise up many disciples. Make a fence for the Torah.

Tractate Avot 1:1

Third, the explicit mythic formulation of how the relationship of master to disciple replicates the relationship between God and Moses:

A. *Our rabbis have taught on Tannaite authority:*
B. What is the order of Mishnah teaching? Moses learned it from the mouth of the All-Powerful. Aaron came in, and Moses repeated his chapter to him and Aaron went forth and sat at the left hand of Moses. His sons came in and Moses repeated their chapter to them, and his sons went forth. Eleazar sat at the right of Moses, and Itamar at the left of Aaron.
C. R. Judah says, "At all times Aaron was at the right hand of Moses."
D. Then the elders entered, and Moses repeated for them their Mishnah chapter. The elders went out. Then the whole people came in, and Moses repeated for them their Mishnah chapter. So it came about that Aaron repeated the lesson four times, his sons three times, the elders two times, and all the people once.
E. Then Moses went out, and Aaron repeated his chapter for them. Aaron went out. His sons repeated their chapter. His sons went out. The elders repeated their chapter. So it turned out that everybody repeated the same chapter four times.

We conclude with yet another concrete formulation of the theology in terms of everyday rules of conduct:

> F.   On this basis said R. Eliezer, "A person is liable to repeat the lesson for his disciple four times. And it is an argument a fortiori: If Aaron, who studied from Moses himself, and Moses from the Almighty – so in the case of a common person who is studying with a common person, all the more so!"
>
> G.   R. Aqiba says, "How on the basis of Scripture do we know that a person is obligated to repeat a lesson for his disciple until he learns it [however many times that takes]? As it is said, 'And you teach it to the children of Israel' (Deut. 31:19). And how do we know that that is until it will be well ordered in their mouth? 'Put it in their mouths' (Deut. 31:19). And how on the basis of Scripture do we know that he is liable to explain the various aspects of the matter? 'Now these are the ordinances which you shall put before them' (Ex. 31:1)."

Bavli Erubin 54B

We see, therefore, what is at stake in the Talmud, its study in the right way, its transmission in the proper manner: knowledge of God, such as God makes manifest through the Torah. And that is the only knowledge of God that (this) Judaism maintains we have.

So let me state what I conceive to be the entirety of the theology of Judaism in its documentary presentation, which is to say, how Judaism states its theology as the Talmud re-presents that theology. I use the language of the Torah: Accessible only in the living encounter of master and disciple, never through all of its history, from the seventh century onward, merely "read" or "glanced at," but always, and only, studied aloud in song, word by word and line by line and phrase by phrase in the company of guides of every age, the Talmud set forth the Torah as Israel received – and now receives – it night and morning through all time. What that abstract statement means in concrete terms then is simple. In reconstructing its arguments, analyzing its initiatives of proposition and objection, argument and counter argument, thrust and parry, movement of thought and momentum of mind, the Talmud's disciples formed their minds, framed their modes of thought, in the encounter with the Torah. And, in making up their own statements, the best of them could therefore claim (though none of them ever did, nor should I in their behalf!) to think the way God thought about the things about which God thinks: the rules of life as set forth in the Torah.

I hasten to clarify the context. I speak in fact not of "Judaism" (as though there were ever only one authoritative Judaism) but only this one Judaism. There were others, and today there are others. Here is a representation of the Torah as set forth in only one Judaism, albeit the paramount one. But that is not how the Torah invariably came to definition, nor is the form of sustained, continuous, dialectical argument the sole or primary form by which the Torah came to expression. To the contrary, in the history of all Judaic systems – Judaisms – that appealed to the same Scripture, the Written Torah or Pentateuch or, indeed, the entirety of the Scriptures the generality of people call "the Old Testament," the Talmud of Babylonia is an utterly unique document. The Judaism that found definition in that writing, the system that came to expression therein, has no counterpart in any other of the Judaisms of all times and places.

Take the simple but fundamental matter of how the Torah (that is, "Judaism") is set forth, for example. All other Judaisms made their statement in declarative sentences and defined their systemic messages solely in propositions. This Judaism insisted on exposing the how, not only the what, of thought. Whatever any other Judaism chose to say, its authors spelled out in so many words. This Judaism insists the faithful participate in the discovery of the norm and understand the modes of rationality that come to expression in the norm.

For every other Judaism, as a matter of simple, descriptive fact, the content of the Torah, or of tradition, was wholly doctrinal, rules of belief and behavior bearing the entire message of the Torah. For only one Judaism, the one that made its statement through the Talmud, did, and does, the Torah consist of not only the laws of life – faithful conviction, right conduct – but also the laws of rational thought. The Bavli in particular lays out the how of the Torah, as well as the what: the rules of thought as well as of life, how God thinks as well as what it means to be "holy for I the Lord your God am holy."

And only of that Torah ("Judaism") that the Talmud states may it be rightly and truly said: In this (in descriptive language: our version of the) Torah, we gain access to not only the will of God for us, but the mind of God that formed the will. Rightly read, the Torah teaches not only the various rules that guide, but the principles that generate those rules; the premises that link principle to principle; the deep structure of intellect that comes to the surface in those premises: the structure of mind, the integrity of truth, the oneness of the One who is (for that very reason) the one and sole God. That is the power (and I believe, the glory) of this Judaism, which for a long time, and for the majority of practitioners of Judaism(s) today, defines the normative, the classical, the authentic Torah: Judaism.

That formulation of the theology of Judaism, which is to say, of the Torah, therefore constitutes the Talmud's re-presentation of the Torah. But, such a conception of how to present the Torah – that is, as a statement of humanity's guide to the mind of God, the path to the integrity of truth – did not always characterize the unfolding canon of that very Judaism of the Dual Torah that identifies the Talmud as its summa. All prior writings – the Pentateuch (450 B.C.E.), the Mishnah and Tosefta (200 C.E. and afterward), the Talmud of the Land of Israel (400 C.E.), Sifra (to Leviticus), Sifré to Numbers, Sifré to Deuteronomy (all: ca. 250-300), Genesis Rabbah, Leviticus Rabbah, Pesiqta deRab Kahana (ca. 450-500) – present propositions. Some (the Written Torah, some compositions of aggadic character) appeal to narrative to make their points, some (the Mishnah and the Tosefta) to straightforward demonstration in syllogisms, others still (the Midrash compilations, the Talmud of the Land of Israel) to exegesis of a received text (Scripture, the Mishnah). All of them say in so many words whatever it is that they wish to offer as their statement of the Torah. They make their statement, they spell it out, they clarify it, then they conclude. What makes the second Talmud unique in context is its insistence that, to know the Torah, we have to think in the way in which the Torah teaches us to think – and then it spells out that way, in massive, tedious, repetitive detail, case by case by case.

It follows that for the authors of the compositions collected in all of the prior documents and the compilers of their composites, the Torah comprises its contents, and the purpose of "tradition" is to preserve and hand on propositions. But none of the received documents prior to the Talmud of Babylonia, including the earlier Talmud, shifts the burden of tradition from what God wants alone, as exposed in the Torah, to how God thinks in addition, which also is exposed therein. For the framers of the Bavli, what it means to be "in our image, after our likeness," is not only to act like God ("You shall be holy as I the Lord your God am holy: just as I am merciful and long-suffering, so must you be merciful and long-suffering"; "You shall be holy, for I the Lord your God am holy," that is to say, "If you sanctify yourselves, I shall credit it to you as though you had sanctified me, and if you do not sanctify yourselves, I shall hold that it is as if you have not sanctified me" [Sifra 195:1.3A-B]). To be "in our image" is also to think in full consciousness, in accord with articulated rules of rationality, like God. The Torah teaches how God speaks, therefore how God thinks – but it is only in the Talmud that we find a sustained and articulated effort to show in detail the meaning of that how. What then does the Talmud have to show us?

Part Two

THE FIRST TALMUD:
THE ORDERING OF THE MISHNAH

Prologue

The First Stage in Transforming Religion into Theology

Defining the Torah, Demonstrating the Hermeneutical Medium for the Theological Re-Presentation of the Torah

Since the Judaism of the Dual Torah proposes to offer knowledge of God through the Torah, which is God's self-manifestation, its principal theological task lay in identifying the Torah, meaning, designating precisely what documents (written or oral) comprise the Torah. And, further, since the Torah comprised words, sentences, paragraphs – God having made the divine manifestation in the form of language formed into intelligible thoughts (rules, narratives, declarative propositions of what is and is not, must be and must not be) – the concomitant labor required explaining, in so many words or by way of repeated illustrations, precisely how to understand the Torah. In simple terms, what books? how to read them?

To explain the stress on the theological analysis of writing, my reading of the history of the formation of Judaism focuses upon the character of writings. The reason derives from the premise that how people set down their thoughts, as much as what they said, bears their messages. Then the "how" of thinking (and therefore also writing) bears a greater burden of the systemic character than the "what" – that is, what in particular, is said. That is why, beginning to end, it is by analyzing writings that I describe the formulation of Judaism's theological system.

I therefore speak of documents, and with good reason: God's self-manifestation, the Torah, takes the form of documents. These then serve to set forth Judaic systems and form their principal monument.

The answer to what books? was, one Torah in two media, written and oral, Scripture and the Mishnah. The answer to how to read them? was, the lessons of reading are recorded in the Midrash compilations, for Scripture's part of the Torah, and in the two Talmuds, for the Mishnah's part of the Torah. That statement of literary facts – the Midrash compilations serve Scripture, the two Talmuds explain the Mishnah – corresponds to the theological categories and convictions of a Judaic system that afforded knowledge of God through God's self-manifestation in the Torah.[1]

The theology of Judaism therefore took shape in two parallel formations, writing concerning the Written Torah, writing concerning the Oral Torah. And each formation in the theological re-presentation of the religion is divided into two stages, one at which theological discourse got under way, the second at which theological discourse produced concrete results, statements concerning the Written Torah, re-presentations of the Oral one. The first of the two stages saw the development of those exercises of generalization and abstraction. These in the end would transform the Torah – seen merely as writing – from a compilation of rules and stories (the Written Torah/the Pentateuch) and a collection of topically arranged rules (the Oral Torah/the Mishnah) into a coherent system, cogent and encompassing, accessible in the form of generalizations and propositions, shown linear, unitary, and harmonious, upward to Sinai. At the second phase, the real theological work came to full realization. The first stage is represented by the Talmud of the Land of Israel and related Midrash compilations, fore and aft; the second, by the Talmud of Babylonia and associated Midrash compilations.[2]

From the recognition of the theological structure and its main beams came an account of the principles of order, coherence, composition: the unity of the structure; from the hermeneutical statement of how the Torah would yield its truths came a sustained specification of the truths that given books of the Torah indeed set forth. The first stage in the

---

[1]Asking why the Mishnah in particular draws us to the mode of explanation that appeals to politics, I can think of no other way of explaining the naked facts of choice than to appeal to either coercion and interest (someone chose and made the choice stick) or the inner logic of a coherent, unfolding system; and the latter serves better as a mode of analysis than a medium of explanation of social facts.

[2]I remind the reader that we deal only with the phase of the work undertaken by the Talmuds, but a comparable exercise will produce illuminating results out of the Midrash compilations.

formation of theology out of the Oral Torah is embodied in the Talmud of the Land of Israel; out of the Written, in the Midrash compilations of the late third through fifth centuries, represented here by Sifra. The formulation of propositions out of the cases of Scripture was undertaken by Sifré to Deuteronomy, and the demonstration of syllogisms out of the same materials is exquisitely accomplished by Leviticus Rabbah and its first cousin, Pesiqta deRab Kahana. The second and definitive stage in the formation of theology out of the Oral Torah is realized in the Talmud of Babylonia, and, out of the Written Torah, the late Midrash compilations, Song of Songs Rabbah, Lamentations Rabbati, and Ruth Rabbah.

What the earlier phase contributed to the theologization of the religion were, first, the literary form for the theology of Judaism, which would be, commentaries to the Torah, Oral and Written; second, the hermeneutical medium for the theological message; and, third, the generative conceptions of that message – no mean achievement. Taking the form of commentaries, as, in a religious system appealing to a supernatural source of truth now in writing, was quite natural, these writings accomplished a variety of tasks. Some of them effected the first stage of the theological reformation of the congeries of religious ideas and practices set forth in Scripture and the Mishnah. Specifically, using the medium of rules of reading and interpretation, the framers of the documents began the shaping of the theological system by recognizing the uses of hermeneutics as an ideal mode of theological discourse for a theology built out of a revealed document (oral or written in form). And, finally, given the character of the revelation – in the dual form, oral and writing – the first theological principle requiring attention had to declare the perfection of the one whole Torah but also to explain how the two components of revelation stood in relationship to one another.

How did this take place? The Talmud of the Land of Israel defined as the hermeneutics of the Mishnah two principal issues, which everywhere would define discourse in that Talmud and the next, and both of which formed principal planks in the theological platform of the Judaism that would emerge with the Bavli.

The first, in theological language, maintained the unity of the Torah in its two media, that is to say, in literary-critical language, systematic proof of the derivation of the Oral Torah from Sinai via the Written Torah. The Mishnah then was to be read, first and foremost, in light of the demand: Demonstrate the unity of the Torah.

The second was the perfection of the Oral Torah, shown by the demonstration of the perfect harmony of all of its statements. In literary-critical language, this required sustained efforts to remove the flaws of contradiction, imperfection in wording, unclarity, and the like.

In other contexts, these two tasks – showing the relationship between two documents, examining the flaws of a writing – could have been classified as merely secular, lacking all theological consequence. But in the setting of a system that identified the Torah with God's self-manifestation, and the very writing of one part of the Torah as God's wording of God's will, literary criticism pointed toward a reality in depths way beyond its surface issues.

The first stage in the formation of theology out of the Written Torah addressed issues of method and message, too. The Midrash compilations for their part took up the Written Torah and accomplished two tasks of reading that produced the same effect, namely, recasting religious writings into theologically systemic form. As to method, they demonstrated that the raw facts of Scripture could be shaped into propositions accessible to reasoned inquiry. The stories and rules of Scripture constituted hard facts; we have then to learn how to draw conclusions from those facts. As it happens, all of the conclusions that would be drawn made theological statements – abstract, generalized, reasoned, demonstrated on the basis of right reasoning about solid facts. As to message, a sustained and systematic demonstration of the unity of the two components of the Torah, Oral and Written, would carry a profound critique of the method of the Mishnah and recast that method in the proper way. Sifra shows us how that was done. For the argument set forth here concerning the hermeneutical medium of the theological method, Sifra is a fine example, because the only way to understand Sifra is to recognize its hermeneutics, and, further, because of the blatant character of the theological message in hermeneutical guise.

Clearly, for both parts of the Torah, Written and Oral, the writings of the first stage in the theologization of the Torah accomplished fundamental goals. Both aimed at generalization. In the case of each, generalization took the form of commentary, rather than free-standing, abstract propositions with accompanying arguments, evidence, demonstrations. That is because the form of commentary to a received text impedes the formulation of thought in sustained and systematic generalizations. But, as a matter of fact, there is more than a single way to set forth a generalization, and the way chosen by both the first Talmud and its associated Midrash compilations yielded generalizations as lucidly and effectively stated as if they were presented in well-crafted essays, like the generalizations of a philosophical writer. What the framers of the writings did in each case was again and again to use a single method to make a single point. Through repeated demonstrations, in the same way, of the same point, they managed to make of their commentaries not random collections of one thing and another but sustained demonstrations of some one point.

That explains what I mean when I speak of how hermeneutics formed the medium for the theological message. I refer to the phenomenon exhibited early and late in the formation of Judaism. It was this expression of the main thing through many things, the repetition, to the point of tedium, of a single kind of demonstration, through quite diverse materials, of a matter never spelled out but always self-evident. Theology expressed through hermeneutics had its say, therefore, when, as in Sifra (as we shall see in Chapter Seven), we are shown over and over again the limitations of taxonomy based on the innate traits of things and the absolute necessity of appeal to taxonomy dictated by the categories set forth in the Written Torah. In that way, the theological point is made that all truth derives from the Written Torah and only from there.

The hermeneutical medium for theological discourse is made manifest, also, in the proof that the Torah makes coherent statements, establishes propositions in the manner of philosophy; does not merely tell us things but illuminates the nature of being, both the life of society and the construction of history. The laws of society and history are set forth by the Written Torah, properly read, in the same way as the laws of nature are set forth by the facts of astronomy or botany or zoology, that is, through the medium of natural history: classification of things and identification of the rule that governs them. When we follow this mode of discourse, appealing in its form to the methods of natural history, aimed at establishing theological truths in a philosophical way out of the raw data of the facts of revealed religion, we see a fine example of how philosophy transforms religion into theology.[3]

But the principal writing of the Judaism of the Dual Torah was the genus, talmud, which produced two species, the Talmud of the Land of Israel and the Talmud of Babylonia. In describing the genus and the traits characteristic of both of its species, I shall show how the hermeneutics of the Mishnah affected the literary-critical task of clarification of the received text, but at the same time realized the theological task of framing a systematic and coherent, rigorous, reflected upon, theological statement and made that statement through a single, unitary hermeneutics, everywhere in play. That is the task of the next chapter.

---

[3]For the illustration of that aspect of theological discourse, Sifra suffices; but I could have introduced as well Sifré to Deuteronomy, with its interest in transforming the cases and rules of Deuteronomy into general and encompassing laws; or Leviticus Rabbah, with its interest in syllogistic argument formed out of the facts of Scripture and utilizing the medium of commentary. To keep this presentation within reasonable limits, I take up only one document among a variety of candidates.

5

The Talmuds and the Mishnah

The Talmud of the Land of Israel, like its successor, forms a commentary on the Mishnah. What the framers of the first Talmud accomplished was not the invention of the conception of a talmud, meaning, a sustained, systematic amplification of passages of the Mishnah and other teachings accorded the status of Tannaite authority. That had already been accomplished by whoever compiled the Tosefta, which laid out the Mishnah alongside supplementary teachings that amplified or enlarged its rules.[1] The notion of a talmud as a source of information was thus established; but information was left inert. What the first Talmud contributed was the definition of a talmud in which received facts ("traditions") were treated as active and consequential, requiring analysis and deep thought. And the second Talmud transformed thought into argument, subordinating fact to processes of dialectical argument and reasoning.

The model of the final development of the species, talmud, as we know it, was formed through an active program of supplying not merely information but guidance on its meaning: a program of inquiry, a set of consequential issues, in place of mere information. And that program would be fully realized in the second, and last, of the two Talmuds. But both Talmuds in common undertake the program of harmonizing one rule or principle with another and showing the scriptural foundation of the Mishnah's rules, thus, the sustained demonstration of the theology of the Torah: its perfection, on the one side, its unity (oral and written), on the other. Because of that fact, we may properly speak of "the Talmuds," since both do one thing, though the second does another.

---

[1] See *The Bavli That Might Have Been: The Tosefta's Theory of Mishnah Commentary Compared with That of the Babylonian Talmud* (Atlanta, 1990: Scholars Press for South Florida Studies in the History of Judaism).

That here was a labor of theology, not merely the presentation of religious truth but its reasoned demonstration in accord with rules of proof applicable everywhere – that is, the philosophical re-presentation of religion – is shown by a simple fact. The two philosophical traits of mind we associate with theology characterize the Yerushalmi and its Midrash companions. First, they worked to systematize the received heritage of law and lore; second, they wished to show how a work of generalization and abstraction, moving from cases to principles, was to be undertaken. And this they did in accord with rules of rationality that anyone might replicate. These two projects, subject to processes of public reason, are necessary for theological work to progress, even though they are not sufficient to define the entirety of that work. The first Talmud was necessary, but insufficient.[2]

The contribution to theologization of the religion put forth by the Yerushalmi made its mark not only in defining modes of thought but also in laying out two messages fundamental to the Torah as it would be

---

[2]That is not to suggest the second Talmud took shape in response to the first. It is generally maintained, and I concur, that the framers of the second Talmud did not "know" the first. I would reframe that commonplace: The framers of the compositions that make up the raw material of the Bavli, and the compilers of the composites that make up more of the same, not to mention the editors who established the discourse and context that forms of the compositions and the composites the Talmud as we know it, had no access to the work of their counterparts in the Land of Israel. The formation of compositions and the compilation of composites were entirely localized in the two intellectual provinces of Israel, Babylonia and the Land of Israel. What passed between them were sentences, sayings and opinions and stories; in both Talmuds we have proof of that fact, since the same sentences occur from time to time in both; more to the point, sentences in the names of the same authorities, e.g., Abbahu, Yohanan, Simeon b. Laqish, abound in both. But it is very rare that what was done with the same sentences in both Talmuds produces a writing of the same character and consequence; the opposite is the case. And, so far as I know, not a single large-scale composite that we find in one Talmud occurs also in the other. The Talmuds meet in Scripture, the Mishnah, and the Tosefta. In *The Talmud's Unique Voice*, cited earlier, I have shown that the authors of the second Talmud's compositions and the compilers of its composites, while enjoying access to the teachings of the Land of Israel, including not only Scripture and the Mishnah and the Tosefta but the first Talmud's own authorities, produced the compositions and composites that comprise the Bavli without the slightest contact with the work of the authors of the Yerushalmi's compositions and composites; we deal with the regionalization of the tradition. That the two Talmuds stand fully out of touch with one another does not change the fact that the second Talmud completed what the first Talmud did only in part; except for the general availability of the Written Torah and the Oral one in the Mishnah, on which both sides built, I do not claim an incremental history accounts for the formation of Judaism, first this Talmud, then that; or first this Midrash compilation, then, in response to its lacunae, that one.

defined and to the formation of its hermeneutics as well. First, the Yerushalmi's Mishnah commentary systematically set forth, in grand detail, a statement of the definition of the Torah, which the Bavli later on merely recapitulated. Second, the Yerushalmi's Mishnah commentary undertook the demonstration that the Torah is perfect, and defined as a principal component of the hermeneutics of the Mishnah the work of proving that fact by identifying imperfections and removing them through harmonization. Now, so far as the task of theology in Judaism has been the definition of the Torah and the demonstration of the perfection of the Torah, the Mishnah commentary of both Talmuds demands classification as theology.

In both cases a primary point of interest is the demonstration that the Oral Torah, the Mishnah, rests upon the Written Torah; the two components of the Torah form a single revelation, with the oral part inextricably bound to the written, and that demonstration marks the work of Mishnah commentary as not only theological in general – defining the Torah – but doctrinal in a very particular way. A second theological trait concerns the perfection of the Mishnah and the laws of the Torah contained therein, both Talmuds' writers concurring that inconsistency and disharmony would flaw the Torah and must be shown not to occur therein. Hence the first of the two Talmuds certainly undertook a part of the theological labor, though, as we shall see in due course, the profundities of the theology of Judaism awaited the discovery and exploration of the intellects who produced the second one.[3]

Before proceeding, let me give a single example of the character of Mishnah exegesis found in both Talmuds. My illustration derives from both Talmuds' reading of a brief passage of Mishnah-tractate Makkot. The unity of purpose – Mishnah commentary– and the identity of proposition – the unity of the Torah, its perfection – should not obscure the simple fact that the two Talmuds do not intersect except at the Mishnah and at Scripture. The Talmuds bear each its own message, but both ask the same questions. Mishnah and Tosefta passages in both Talmuds are in boldface, Bavli's use of Aramaic in italics, Hebrew in regular type. We begin with the Yerushalmi:

Y. to Makkot 1:8 = B. to Makkot 1:10

[A] **He whose trial ended and who fled and was brought back before the same court –**

---

[3]In Chapters Eight through Ten, I shall identify what is unique to the Bavli, and at that point we shall not again consider these points, which begin with the Yerushalmi and most certainly represent a theological formation, not merely a religious one; and a theological formation set forth in the same manner as the Bavli's.

[B]   they do not reverse the judgment concerning him [and retry him].

[C]   In any situation in which two get up and say, "We testify concerning Mr. So-and-so that his trial ended in the court of such-and-such, with Mr. So-and-so and Mr. So-and-so as the witnesses against him,"

[D]   lo, this one is put to death.

[E]   [Trial before] a Sanhedrin applies both in the Land and abroad.

[F]   A Sanhedrin which imposes the death penalty once in seven years is called murderous.

[G]   R. Eleazar b. Azariah says, "Once in seventy years."

[H]   R. Tarfon and R. Aqiba say, "If we were on a Sanhedrin, no one would ever be put to death."

[I]   Rabban Simeon b. Gamaliel says, "So they would multiply the number of murderers in Israel."

[I.A]   [Trial before a] Sanhedrin applies both in the Land and abroad [M. 1:8E],

[B]   as it is written, "And these things shall be for a statute and ordinance to you throughout your generations in all your dwellings" (Num. 35:29).

[C]   And why does Scripture say, "You shall appoint judges and officers in all your towns [which the Lord your God gives you]" (Deut. 16:18)?

[D]   The meaning is that in the towns of Israel they set up judges in every town, but abroad they do so only by districts.

[E]   It was taught: R. Dosetai b. R. Yannai says, "It is a religious requirement for each tribe to judge its own tribe, as it is said, 'You shall appoint *judges* and officers in all your towns which the Lord your God gives you, according to your tribes' (Deut. 16:18)."

[II.A]   Rabban Simeon b. Gamaliel taught, "Those declared liable to the death penalty who fled from the Land abroad – they put them to death forthwith [upon recapture].

[B]   "If they fled from abroad to the Land, they do not put them to death forthwith, but they undertake a trial *de novo.*"

The Yerushalmi wants the scriptural proof for the Mishnah's allegation; it then harmonizes the implications at hand. Since the prooftext, I.B, yields results contrary to the assumed implications of that at C, D must indicate otherwise. Unit II is an independent saying, generally relevant to M. 1:8E. It is a simple paraphrase and clarification.

The Bavli does the same thing, but makes its own points. The comparison then is based on the shared program; the contrast, the different results.

Bavli to Mishnah-Tractate Makkot 1:10

A.   He whose trial ended and who fled and was brought back before the same court –

B.   they do not reverse the judgment concerning him [and retry him].

C.   In any situation in which two get up and say, "We testify concerning Mr. So-and-so that his trial ended in the court of such-

and-such, with Mr. So-and-so and Mr. So-and-so as the witnesses against him,"

D. lo, this one is put to death.

E. [Trial before] a Sanhedrin applies both in the Land and abroad.

F. A Sanhedrin which imposes the death penalty once in seven years is called murderous.

G. R. Eleazar b. Azariah says, "Once in seventy years."

H. R. Tarfon and R. Aqiba say, "If we were on a Sanhedrin, no one would ever be put to death."

I. Rabban Simeon b. Gamaliel says, "So they would multiply the number of murderers in Israel."

I.1 A. He whose trial ended and who fled and was brought back before the same court – they do not reverse the judgment concerning him [and retry him]:

B. Before that court in particular the judgment is not reversed, but it may be reversed before some other court! *But then it is taught further on:* In any situation in which two get up and say, "We testify concerning Mr. So-and-so that his trial ended in the court of such-and-such, with Mr. So-and-so and Mr. So-and-so as the witnesses against him," lo, this one is put to death!

C. Said Abbayye, "This is no contradiction. The one statement refers to a court in the Land of Israel, the other, to a court abroad."

D. *For it has been taught on Tannaite authority:*

E. R. Judah b. Dostai says in the name of R. Simeon b. Shatah, "If one fled from the Land to abroad, they do not reverse the verdict pertaining to him. If he fled from abroad to the Land, they do reverse the verdict concerning him, because of the higher priority enjoyed by the Land of Israel" [T. San. 3:11A-B].

II.1 A. [Trial before] a Sanhedrin applies both in the Land and abroad:

B. *What is the source of this rule?*

C. *It is in line with that which our rabbis have taught on Tannaite authority:*

D. "And these things shall be for a statute of judgment to you throughout your generations in all your dwellings" (Num. 35:29) –

E. we learn from that statement that the Sanhedrin operates both in the Land and abroad.

F. If that is so, then why does Scripture state, "Judges and offices you shall make for yourself in all your gates that the Lord God gives you tribe by tribe" (Deut. 16:18) [meaning only in the tribal land, in the Land of Israel]?

G. "In your own gates you set up courts in every district and every town, but outside of the Land of Israel you set up courts in every district but not in every town."

III.1 A. A Sanhedrin which imposes the death penalty once in seven years is called murderous. R. Eleazar b. Azariah says, "Once in seventy years":

B. *The question was raised: Does the statement,* A Sanhedrin which imposes the death penalty once in seven years is called murderous *mean that even one death sentence was enough to mark the Sanhedrin as murderous, or is this merely a description of how things are?*

C. *The question stands.*

IV.1   A.   **R. Tarfon and R. Aqiba say, "If we were on a Sanhedrin, no one would ever be put to death." Rabban Simeon b. Gamaliel says, "So they would multiply the number of murderers in Israel":**

       B.   *So what would they actually do?*

       C.   R. Yohanan and R. Eleazar both say, "Did you see whether or not the victim was already dying from something, or was he whole when he was killed?" [Such a question would provide grounds for dismissing the charge of murder, if the witnesses could not answer properly.]

       D.   *Said R. Ashi, "If they said that he was whole, then, 'Maybe the sword only cut an internal lesion'?"*

       E.   *And in the case of a charge of consanguineous sexual relations, what would they actually do?*

       F.   *Both Abbayye and Raba said, "Did you see the probe in the kohl-flask [actually engaged in sexual relations]?"*

       G.   *And as to rabbis, what would suffice for conviction?*

       H.   The answer accords with Samuel, for said Samuel, "In the case of a charge of adultery, if the couple appeared to be committing adultery [that would be sufficient evidence]."

Bavli to Makkot 1:10/I-IV

Standard Mishnah exegesis in both Talmuds is represented by this brief passage from Bavli Makkot. The counterpart Talmud presents numerous exercises that follow the same program. We start, I, with a challenge to the implications of the stated rule, I.B, yielding a dissonance, which is ironed out by a suitable distinction. We proceed, II, to a scriptural source for the passage at hand. Item III raises a theoretical question meant to clarify the sense of the language before us. Entry IV reverts to the systematic glossing of the language and sense of the Mishnah. There is no kind of comment in this passage that the Yerushalmi does not provide as well; each of these types of inquiry is standard for both Talmuds.

The two Talmuds look alike because both comment on the same prior text, the Mishnah.[4] Both take up a few sentences of that prior text

---

[4]When, in Chapters Eight and Nine, we contrast the two Talmuds, we identify what is distinctive – indeed, unique – about the second of the two. Those points of particularity lead us to the location of the hermeneutics of that Talmud, taken up in Chapter Ten. But before we may contrast, we must compare. The reason for starting with comparison and only then proceeding to contrast is clear. Only when we have shown that things are alike do observations about difference bear consequence. Comparing things that to begin with simply do not relate – apples to atomic bombs – imposes a connection that is not there, with results that are implausible (or merely silly). That is why comparison begins in likeness (apples to apples) and proceeds to difference (Granny apples from Macintosh apples). Conclusions then come to us out of the contrasts of like things. With that simple observation in mind, we have to ask, what validates the comparison of the two Talmuds and the insistence that the second of the two stands apart from all prior

and paraphrase and analyze them. Both ask the same questions, for example, clarifying the language of the Mishnah, identifying the scriptural foundations of the Mishnah's rules, comparing the Mishnah's rules with those of the Tosefta or other Tannaite status. They furthermore compare because they organize their materials in the same way. They moreover take up pretty much the same topical agenda, in common selecting some divisions of the Mishnah and ignoring others, agreeing in particular to treat the Mishnah's divisions of Appointed Times, Women, and Damages. Both documents moreover are made up of already available compositions and composites, which we may identify, in each document, by reference to the same literary traits or indications of completion prior to inclusion in the Talmuds.[5] So they exhibit traits of shared literary policy.

In both, moreover, we find not only the same received document, the Mishnah, but also citations of, and allusions to, the same supplementary collection to the Mishnah, the Tosefta, and also a further kind of saying, one bearing the marks of formalization and memorization that serve to classify it as authoritative ("Tannaite') but external to the composition of the Mishnah and the compilation of the Tosefta. The points of coincidence are more than formal, therefore, since both Talmuds cite the same Mishnah tractates, at some points the same Tosefta passages, and also, from time to time, the same external Tannaite formulations. When, therefore, in Chapters Eight through Eleven, we come to their points of difference, beginning with the fact that the second Talmud scarcely intersects with the first except at the formal points of juncture just now listed, we shall find all the more striking the fact that the second Talmud goes its own way and forms a writing that, while formally like the first Talmud, substantively differs from it, beginning, middle, and end.

Now to the formal likenesses, establishing the fixed traits of theological style and form, making the fundamental points for the future: since both are formed into commentaries to some of the same passages of

---

writing, even the writing to which it compares? The answer comes in two parts. First, the two Talmuds look alike. Second, the two Talmuds also say the same things. Here we see the likeness in form, in Chapter Six, the likeness in substance.

[5]But I hasten to add, my sustained comparison of the two Talmuds reveals remarkably little evidence that the framers of the two documents drew upon a common core of available, already-formulated compositions; and there is no evidence whatsoever that they shared a common core of completed composites. Where there is a corpus of shared materials, it is in the Mishnah and other sayings given Tannaite status and also in some, very few, statements of authorities who flourished in the third century; these sayings, when occurring in both Talmuds, tend to be utilized in the second Talmud in a manner unlike their use in the first. This is spelled out in *The Bavli's Unique Voice*.

the Mishnah, and since both are laid out in the same way, that is, as ad hoc treatments of phrases or even whole paragraphs of the Mishnah, the two Talmuds are identical in form, species of a genus. Not only so, but in their canonical context, they also are different from all other documents of the Judaism of the Dual Torah in the formative age. The two Talmuds therefore comprise a genus, talmud, made up of two species, the Talmud of the Land of Israel and the Talmud of Babylonia. But – as we shall see in due course – what speciates vastly overrides what unites the species into a genus; the form is common, and we shall see, so, too, much of the burden of thought. Where the Talmuds differ, it is in the deepest layers of discourse, but not on the surface of the medium or in the messages they set forth. Since the differences form the basis for my argument concerning the Bavli's theologization of the religious system put forth by the Yerushalmi, we had best dwell on the points in common, which allow us to compare and then contrast the two writings.

How then do the two Talmuds form a common genus? Among Mishnah-centered writings in the canon – the Tosefta, Sifra, the two Sifrés, the Bavli, and the Yerushalmi – only the two Talmuds conduct sustained analytical inquiries over a broad range of problems. The Tosefta is not an analytical document; we have to supply the missing analytical program (as the authors of the two Talmuds, but particularly the Bavli, themselves discovered early on).[6] Sifra (as we shall see in Chapter Six) treats the Mishnah in only a single aspect,[7] while the two Talmuds cover that aspect generously, along with a far more elaborate program. They pursue no encompassing exegetical program. So the two Talmuds are unique in context.

And – also in context – they are unique in a second, somewhat more subtle way: both are made up mainly, though not exclusively, of writing we may call "talmud" – talmud as a moving ("dialectical") argument,[8] from point to point, in which all possibilities are systematically taken up

---

[6]*The Tosefta. An Introduction* (Atlanta, 1992: Scholars Press for South Florida Studies in the History of Judaism) spells out this point.

[7]This is spelled out in *Uniting the Dual Torah: Sifra and the Problem of the Mishnah* (Cambridge and New York, 1989: Cambridge University Press). I did not include discussion of the two Sifrés, but, as a matter of fact, where the Mishnah intrudes in the two Sifrés, it commonly is in this same regard; otherwise the Mishnah passage in the two compilations is cited for purposes of mere illustration. But that is a judgment that awaits refinement.

[8]It is clear to me that the character of the dialectical argument of the Yerushalmi has to be distinguished from that of the Bavli, and this is spelled out in massive detail in *The Bavli's Unique Voice* and summarized below in Chapters Eight and Nine, then translated into theological hermeneutics in Chapters Ten and Eleven. But for the present part of the argument, these characterizations pertain to both Talmuds equally.

and examined.[9] That mode of discourse – sustained, unfolding analysis, formed of proposal and response, proposition and refutation, evidence and argument, counter argument and disqualifying evidence – is unique to the two Talmuds in the entire canon of Judaism, from ancient times to our own day. And the mode of discourse brings to realization in words a generative mode of thought, discourse being merely written-down intellection.

What is talmudic about the two Talmuds is that mode of thought, which is to be defined in two aspects: [1] a critical, systematic application of applied reason and practical logic, [2] moving from a point starting with a proposition through argument and evidence, met head-on by contrary proposition, with its argument and evidence, exchanging balanced responses, each to the position, argument, and evidence of the other, onward. This is carried on for so long as it takes fully to expose every possibility of proposition, argument, and evidence – (ordinarily)

---

[9]I recognize, of course, that the dialectical argument is not unique to the two Talmuds, since philosophy from Socrates onward knows that mode of dynamic analysis as well; but in the context of the Judaic canon, it is indeed unique, and that is what is at issue here. A person better qualified in philosophy than I will want to explain how the one dialectic differs in method from the other. I do not know how to conduct the comparison of systems of dialectical thinking. But for this particular context, treating talmud as a *kind* of writing, namely, a sustained, analytical exercise in which each proposition set forth is challenged and refined, as argument moves from point to point, then a talmud(ic passage) as an example of such a talmud, and the two Talmuds as collections of talmud writing, coheres to the character of the evidence. In the Bavli, we will find a passage of the Tosefta or a set of statements bearing the mark, "Tannaite," subjected to precisely the same analytical inquiry as we find imposed upon the Mishnah; there is in fact no way of distinguishing the reading of the Mishnah from the reading of the Tosefta or of Tannaite statements – all exhibit the same traits of mind and inquiry. Hence we cannot regard as an adequate definition of "talmud" "a commentary to the Mishnah." That definition, necessary but not sufficient, is too specific to the facts. But then "talmud" becomes a type of reading of a received allegation as to facts of principles, that is to say, "talmud" finds its definition in not the literary but the intellectual context. I first realized that fact when my best way of characterizing a long analytical discussion of a Tosefta passage was, "a talmud" to this Tosefta passage, in the analogy of "a talmud" to this Mishnah passage. But then I realized that it is perfectly common for talmuds to be supplied to a variety of received prior statements as to principle or rule or fact, and that these talmuds could be characterized by reason of traits applicable to them all. That is the basis on which I treat "talmud" as a genus for a kind of analytical thinking, and "a Talmud" as a genus for the species, Talmuds (Yerushalmi, Bavli). I do not claim that my definition of "a talmud" is exhaustive; it is provisional, and, as we compare the Yerushalmi and the Bavli, the differentiation of talmud into talmuds will proceed apace.

ending with a firm and (occasionally even an articulated) conclusion.[10]
Now in light of the fact that both Talmuds are made up of dialectical
arguments of just this kind,[11] we stand on firm ground in insisting that,
in the Talmuds, we encounter the theologization of the religion set forth
in the two parts of the Torah, Written and Oral, where we have stories
and rules, but few propositions and generalizations, and no effort
whatsoever (apart from the work of the compilers) to state the whole in
its entirety: balanced, harmonious, and unitary.

Theological thinking about the Torah therefore does not commence
with the Bavli, even though the theology of Judaism reaches its full
statement only in the Bavli. For, so far as our working definition of
theology requires the presence of a rigorous, generalizing mode of
thought, inclusive of rational reflection, concern with argument, and the
attempt to solve conceptual problems (in Dalferth's definition, given
earlier), both Talmuds, not only the Bavli, exhibit ample evidence of a
philosophical reading of religious writings, a philosophical
demonstration of unity of the Torah and its traits of perfection.

Let us now dwell on the character of the genus, talmud, so that later
on, we may appreciate the particular qualities of the principal of the two
species, the Talmud of Babylonia, that provided the principal medium
for the theology of Judaism in its mature formulation. What traits are
shared by both species of the genus, talmud?[12] Both Talmuds not only
are made up of two elements, Mishnah paragraph, then talmudic
amplification, but, in the case of both documents, each element bears its
own literary traits and program of discussion, alike in both documents.
Since the Mishnah passage at the head of each set of Talmudic units of
discourse defines the limits and determines the theme and, generally, the
problematic of the whole, our attention first – if casually – is drawn to the
traits of the Mishnah passages as a group. If, knowing only Hebrew and
Aramaic but nothing about the document, we for the first time saw these
types of pericopes of the Mishnah (embedded as they are in the Talmuds
and separated from one another), we should discern that they adhere to a
separate and quite distinctive set of literary and conceptual canons from
what follows and surrounds them. And on that basis alone, we also
could not differentiate one Talmud from the other, as I shall now explain.

---

[10]One problem in Talmud study, particularly in the Bavli, is that these sustained
arguments may shade over into tedium; further, it is not difficult to lose one's
way, forgetting by the end why an issue is raised to begin with.

[11]Though, as I said, the genus, talmudic dialectic, is to be speciated.

[12]In what follows, "talmud" or "talmudic" refers to both Talmuds without
distinction.

To describe the two Talmuds severally and jointly, we have to begin with their relationship to the Mishnah, which is the two Talmuds' own starting point, the definition of structure and order for them both. Here, too, we cannot differentiate the two commentaries. While the Mishnah admits to no antecedents and neither alludes to nor cites anything prior to its own materials, a passage of either of the two Talmuds is often incomprehensible without knowledge of the passage of the Mishnah around which the Talmuds' discourse centers. Yet in describing and defining the Talmuds, we should err if we were to say that, in common, they only, or mainly, form step-by-step commentaries on the Mishnah, with their respective discussions defined solely by the Mishnah's interests.

We may not even say that the Talmuds are commentaries on the Mishnah and important passages of the Tosefta. Units of discourse that serve these prior compilations stand side by side with many that do not. In fact, both of the Talmuds are in full command of their respective programs of thought and inquiry. Their distinct groups of framers, responsible for the units of discourse, chose what in the Mishnah will be analyzed and what ignored. True, there could be no Talmud without the Mishnah and Tosefta. But knowing only those two works, we could never have predicted the character of the Talmuds' discourse at any point – let alone (even in naked logic) reproducing that discourse.

To develop a taxonomy of the units of discourse contained equally within either of the two Talmuds, we begin by describing gross redactional traits. These are visible to the naked eye. What kinds of units of discourse do the documents exhibit in common and how are they arranged? Both Talmuds invariably do to the Mishnah one of these four things:

(1)   text criticism;
(2)   exegesis of the meaning of the Mishnah, including glosses and amplifications;
(3)   addition of scriptural prooftexts of the Mishnah's central propositions; and
(4)   harmonization of one Mishnah passage with another such passage or with a statement of Tosefta.

The first two of these four procedures remain wholly within the narrow frame of the Mishnah passage subject to discussion. Therefore, in the natural order of things, what the two Talmuds will find interesting in a given Mishnah passage will respond to the same facts and commonly will do so in much the same way. The second pair take an essentially independent stance vis-à-vis the Mishnah pericope at hand. That is where the Talmuds, engaged in a theological enterprise within the

definition offered here, will each take its own path. And that is precisely
the point at which theological, as distinct from literary-critical,
considerations enter in. Where the Talmuds are talmudic, it is in the
theological program of systematic recapitulation of cases, formulation of
propositions of an abstract character, expression of theology through a
prevailing hermeneutics, not merely exposition of a passage through a
constant exegetical plan.

At stake is the re-formation of the (oral part of the) Torah in a way
not envisaged by its writers. The Talmuds do not merely clarify the
Mishnah; both of them in point of fact re-present the Torah – a very
different thing. We understand that fact when we remember what the
Mishnah looks like as it stands on its own.[13] The writers of the Mishnah
created a coherent document, with a topical program formed in accord
with the logical order dictated by the characteristics of a given topic, and
with a set of highly distinctive formulary and formal traits as well. But
these are obscured when the document is taken apart into bits and pieces
and reconstituted in the way in which the Talmuds do. The redefinition
of the Torah accomplished by the Talmuds therefore represented a vast
revision of the initial writing down of the oral component of the Torah –
a point at which the hermeneutics shaded over into a profoundly
theological activity.

For now the Mishnah is read by the Talmuds as a composite of
discrete and essentially autonomous rules, a set of atoms, not an
integrated molecule, so to speak. In so doing, the most striking formal
traits of the Mishnah are obliterated. More important, the Mishnah as a
whole and complete statement of a viewpoint no longer exists. Its
propositions are reduced to details. But what is offered instead? The
answer is, a statement that, on occasion, recasts details in generalizations
encompassing a wide variety of other details across the gaps between
one tractate and another. This immensely creative and imaginative
approach to the Mishnah vastly expands the range of discourse. But the
consequence is to deny to the Mishnah both its own mode of speech and
its distinctive and coherent message. So, as I said at the outset, the two
Talmuds formulate their own hermeneutics, to convey their theological
system: [1] defining the Torah and [2] demonstrating its perfection and
comprehensive character: unity, harmony, lineal origin from Sinai. What
the second Talmud would later on add to that first stage in theological

---

[13]My account of the Mishnah in its own terms is in my *History of the Mishnaic Law*
(Leiden, 1974-1986: E.J. Brill), in forty-three volumes, and in *Judaism. The Evidence
of the Mishnah* (Chicago, 1981: University of Chicago Press). Second printing,
1985. Third printing, 1986. Second edition, augmented (Atlanta, 1987: Scholars
Press for Brown Judaic Studies).

re-presentation of the Torah is instantiation of modes of analysis of the unity, lineal formation, and harmony of the Torah. But, I claim, the framers of the first Talmud assuredly affirmed the same points.

Both authorships take an independent stance when facing the Mishnah, making choices, reaching decisions of their own. Both Talmuds' framers deal with Mishnah tractates of their own choice, and neither provides a Talmud to the entirety of the Mishnah. What the Mishnah therefore contributed to the Talmuds was not received in a spirit of humble acceptance by the sages who produced either of the two Talmuds. Important choices were made about what to treat, hence what to ignore. The exegetical mode of reception did not have to obscure the main lines of the Mishnah's system. But it surely did so. The discrete reading of sentences, or, at most, paragraphs, denying all context, avoiding all larger generalizations except for those transcending the specific lines of tractates – this approach need not have involved the utter reversal of the paramount and definitive elements of the Mishnah's whole and integrated worldview (its "Judaism"). But doing these things did facilitate the revision of the whole into a quite different pattern. That represents a re-presentation of the Torah, one of considerable originality indeed.

A second trait, already familiar to us, in common joins with the foregoing. The Mishnah rarely finds it necessary to adduce prooftexts from the Written Torah in support of its statements. The Talmuds, by contrast, find it appropriate whenever possible to cite scriptural prooftexts for the propositions of the Mishnah.[14] While the various tractates of the Mishnah relate in different ways to Scripture, the view of the framers of the Talmud on the same matter is not differentiated. So far as they are concerned, prooftexts for Mishnaic rules are required. These will be supplied in substantial numbers. And that is the main point. The Mishnah now is systematically represented as not standing free and separate from Scripture, but dependent upon it. The authority of the Mishnah's laws then is reinforced. But the autonomy of the Mishnah as a whole is severely compromised. Just as the Mishnah is represented in the Talmud as a set of rules, rather than as a philosophical essay, so it is presented, rule by rule, as a secondary and derivative development of Scripture. It would be difficult to imagine a more decisive effort to re-formulate the Torah than is accomplished by this work.

The undifferentiated effort to associate diverse Mishnah laws with Scripture is to be viewed together with the systematic breakup of the Mishnah into its diverse laws. The two quite separate activities produce a single effect in both Talmuds. They permit the Talmuds to represent

---

[14] Tosefta, Sifra, and the two Sifrés concur in doing the same.

the state of affairs pretty much as the framers of the Talmuds wish to do. Theology as a creative venture here determines to (re)define the Torah. And how is this done? Everything is shown to be continuous: Scripture, Mishnah, the Tosefta where cited, the authoritative sayings labeled Tannaite where used, ending in – the Talmud itself (whichever Talmud we examine, the effect being the same)! Then all things, as now shaped by the rabbis of the Talmud(s), have the standing of Scripture and represent the authority of Moses (now called "our rabbi"). Accordingly, once the Mishnah enters either of the two Talmuds it nowhere emerges intact. It is wholly preserved, but in bits and pieces, shaped and twisted in whatever ways the Talmuds wish. The Torah now forms a single, continuous statement. And that is the work of the first Talmud, not only of the second.

The question has now to be asked, when do the Talmuds speak for themselves not for the Mishnah? Second, what sorts of units of discourse contain such passages that bear what is "Talmudic" in the two Talmuds? These two questions produce the same answers for both Talmuds, which once more validates comparing and therefore also contrasting them.

1. THEORETICAL QUESTIONS OF LAW NOT ASSOCIATED WITH A PARTICULAR PASSAGE OF THE MISHNAH. In the first of the two Talmuds there is some tendency, and in the second, a very marked tendency, to move beyond the legal boundaries set by the Mishnah's rules themselves. More general inquiries are taken up. These of course remain within the framework of the topic of one tractate or another, although there are some larger modes of thought characteristic of more than a single tractate.

2. EXEGESIS OF SCRIPTURE SEPARATE FROM THE MISHNAH. It is under this rubric that we find the most important instances in which the Talmuds present materials essentially independent of the Mishnah.

3. HISTORICAL STATEMENTS. The Talmuds contain a fair number of statements that something happened, or narratives about how something happened. While many of these are replete with biblical quotations, in general they do not provide exegesis of Scripture, which serves merely as illustration or reference point.

4. STORIES ABOUT, AND RULES FOR, SAGES AND DISCIPLES, SEPARATE FROM DISCUSSION OF A PASSAGE OF THE MISHNAH. The Mishnah contains a tiny number of tales about rabbis. These serve principally as precedents for, or illustrations of, rules.

The Talmuds by contrast contain a sizable number of stories about sages and their relationships to other people. When the Talmuds present us with ideas or expressions of a world related to, but fundamentally separate from, that of the Mishnah, that is, when the Talmuds wish to say something other than what the Mishnah says and means, they will take up one of two modes of discourse. Either we find exegesis of biblical passages, with the value system of the rabbis read into the scriptural tales; or we are told stories about holy men and paradigmatic events, once again through tales told in such a way that a didactic and paranaetic purpose is served.

If, therefore, we want to point to what is Talmudic in either of the two Talmuds it is the exegesis of Scripture, on the one side, and the narration of historical or biographical tales about holy men, on the other. Since much of the biblical exegesis turns upon holy men of biblical times, we may say that the Talmuds speak for themselves alone, as distinct from addressing the problems of the Mishnah, when they tell about holy men now and then. But what is genuinely new in the Talmuds, in comparison and contrast to the Mishnah, is the inclusion of extensive discourse on the meaning imputed to Scripture.

Our Talmuds therefore stand essentially secondary to two prior documents: Mishnah (encompassing for this purpose the whole corpus labeled Tannaite, whenever and wherever produced, much being later than the Mishnah and some being Babylonian), on the one side, and Scripture, on the other. The Mishnah is read in the Talmuds pretty much within the framework of meaning established by the Mishnah itself. Scripture is read as an account of a world remarkably like that of the rabbis of the Talmuds. When the rabbis speak for themselves, as distinct from the Mishnah, it is through exegesis of Scripture. (But any other mode of reading Scripture, to them, would have been unthinkable. They took for granted that they and Scripture's heroes and sages lived in a single timeless plane.)

It follows that the Talmuds are composites of three kinds of materials: [1] exegeses of the Mishnah (and other materials classified as authoritative, that is, Tannaite), [2] exegeses of Scripture, and [3] accounts of the men who provide both.[15] Both Talmuds then constitute elaborate reworkings of the two antecedent documents: the Mishnah, lacking much reference to Scripture, and the Scripture itself. The Talmuds bring the two together into a synthesis of their compilers' own making, both in reading Scripture into Mishnah, and in reading Scripture alongside of, and separate from, Mishnah.

Let me now turn to three more questions, the answers to which characterize both Talmuds:

---

[15]I have dwelt on the stories about sages, where and how they figure and form part of the larger canon and the medium for its systemic statement, in, among other works, *Judaism and Story: The Evidence of The Fathers According to Rabbi Nathan* (Chicago, 1992: University of Chicago Press); and *Why No Gospels in Talmudic Judaism* (Atlanta, 1988: Scholars Press for Brown Judaic Studies).

[1]   What do rabbis in the two Talmuds do in common when they read the Mishnah?

[2]   What are their modes of thought, their characteristic ways of analysis?

[3]   What do we learn about their worldview from the ways in which they receive and interpret the worldview they have inherited in the Mishnah?

These are the very questions, we now realize, that the Talmuds answer on their own account, not only the Mishnah's. The Talmudic exegetes of the Mishnah brought to the document no distinctive program of their own. The exegetes did not know in advance of their approach to a law of the Mishnah facts about the passage not contained within the boundaries of the language of the Mishnah passage itself (except only for facts contained within other units of the same document). Rejecting propositions that were essentially a priori, they proposed to explain and expand precisely the wording and the conceptions supplied by the document under study.

I cannot point to a single instance in which the Talmudic exegetes in either Talmud appear to twist and turn the language and message of a passage, attempting to make the words mean something other than what they appear to say anyhow. While the Talmuds follow a coherent hermeneutics that is very much their own, there is no exegetical program revealed in the Talmuds' reading of the Mishnah other than that defined, to begin with, by the language and conceptions of one Mishnah passage or another.[16] Seen whole, the Talmuds appear to be nothing more than secondary developments of the Mishnah. If there is nothing *in particular* that is Talmudic, nonetheless, there is much *in general* that in both Talmuds is Talmudic. This is in entirely familiar respects.

First, the Mishnah was set forth by Rabbi (that is, Judah the Patriarch, whose name stands for the people who wrote up the Mishnah) whole and complete, a profoundly unified, harmonious document. The Talmud insists upon obliterating the marks of coherence. It treats in bits and pieces what was originally meant to speak whole. That simple fact constitutes what is original, stunningly new and, by definition, Talmudic.

Second, the Mishnah, also by definition, delivered its message in the way chosen by Rabbi. That is to say, by producing the document as he did, Rabbi left no space for the very enterprises of episodic exegesis undertaken so brilliantly by his immediate continuators and heirs.

---

[16]That the second Talmud has its own hermeneutical program, as distinct from an exegetical one, of course is also the fact. But that the second Talmud has its own distinctive hermeneutics does not affect my contention that, in the ways specified here, the two Talmuds are identical.

True, a rather limited process of explanation and gloss of words and phrases, accompanied by a systematic inquiry into the wording of one passage or another, got under way, probably at the very moment, and within the very process, of the Mishnah's closure. But insofar as the larger messages and meanings of the document are conveyed in the ways Rabbi chose through formalization of language, through contrasts, through successive instances of the same normally unspecified, general proposition, for example, the need for exegesis was surely not generated by Rabbi's own program for the Mishnah. Quite to the contrary, Rabbi chose for his Mishnah a mode of expression and defined for the document a large-scale structure and organization, which, by definition, were meant to stand firm and autonomous. Rabbi's Mishnah speaks clearly and for itself.

For the Mishnah did not merely come to closure. At the very moment at which it was completed, the Mishnah also formed a closed system, that is, a whole, complete statement that did not require facts outside of its language and formulation, so made no provision for commentary and amplification of brief allusions, as the Talmuds' style assuredly does. The Mishnah refers to nothing beyond itself except, episodically, Scripture. It promises no information other than what is provided within its limits. It raises no questions for ongoing discussion beyond its decisive, final, descriptive statements of enduring realities and fixed relationships.

The Talmuds' single irrevocable judgment is precisely opposite: this text needs a commentary. The Talmuds' first initiative is to reopen the Mishnah's closed system, almost at the moment of its completion and perfection. That at the foundations is what is Talmudic about the Talmuds: their daring assertion that the concluded and completed demanded clarification and continuation. Once that assertion was made to stick, nothing else mattered very much. The two Talmuds' message was conveyed in the very medium of the Talmud: a new language, focused upon a new grid of discourse to review a received writing.

In the two Talmuds in common we address a program of criticism of the Mishnah framed by independent and original minds. How is this made manifest? Let us quickly bypass the obvious points of independent judgment, the matter of insistence that the very word choices of the Mishnah require clarification, therefore prove faulty. The meanings and amplification of phrases represent the judgment that Rabbi's formulation, while stimulating and provocative, left much to be desired. These indications of independence of judgment among people disposed not merely to memorize but to improve upon the text provided by Rabbi hardly represent judgments of substance. Rather, let us turn to the two most striking: first, the provision of scriptural prooftexts for the propositions of various passages of the Mishnah; second, the rewriting, in the Mishnah's own idiom, if not in its redactional and disciplinary patterns, of much of the law.

As to the former, of course, the message is familiar and clear. The propositions of the Mishnah cannot stand by themselves but must be located within the larger realm of scriptural authority. As to the latter, the Tosefta's and other Tannaite passages, serving as an exegetical complement to the Mishnah's corresponding passages, phrased in the way in which the Mishnah's sentences are written (as distinct from the utterly different way in which the Talmuds' own sentences are framed, for example, in Hebrew rather than in the Talmuds' Aramaic), show equivalent independence of mind. They indicate that, where sages of the time of the Talmuds took up Mishnaic passages, they were not at all limited to the work of gloss and secondary expansion. They recognized and exercised a quite remarkable freedom of initiative. They undertook to restate in their own words, but imitating the Mishnah's style, the propositions of the Mishnah passage at hand.

That is, they both cite what the Mishnah had said and also continue, in imitation of the Mishnah's language, the discourse of the Mishnah passage itself. These Toseftan or other Tannaite complements to the Mishnah – a vast number of them demonstrably written after the closure of the Mishnah – are Talmudic in two senses. First, they come to expression in the period after the Mishnah had reached closure, as is clear from the fact that the exact language of the Mishnah is cited prior to the labor of extension expansion and revision. So they are the work of the Talmuds' age and authority. Second, they derive from precisely the same authorities responsible for the formation of the Talmud as a whole.

Accordingly, both the insistence upon adducing prooftexts for passages Rabbi judged not to need them and the persistent revision and expansion of the Mishnah, even in clumsy imitation of the Mishnah's syntax, rhetoric, and word choices, tell us once more this simple truth: The Talmuds are distinctively Talmudic precisely when the Mishnah itself defines the Talmuds' labor, dictates its ideas, displays its rhetoric, determines its results. The very shift in usable language, from "the Mishnah" (as a whole) to "the Mishnah passage" or "the Mishnaic law at hand" indicates the true state of affairs. On the surface, in all manner of details, the two Talmuds are little more than secondary and derivative documents, explaining the Mishnah itself in trivial ways, or expanding it in a casuistic and logic-chopping manner. But viewing that same surface from a different, more distant perspective and angle, we see things quite differently. In detail the Talmuds changed nothing. Overall, the Talmuds left nothing the same. And, it follows, in general, the two

Talmuds stand close together, not only in form, but in program and much else.

In the two Talmuds we find little to deem Talmudic in particular. But in them both, equally, there is much that is talmudic in general. The particular bits and pieces are Mishnaic. But – as I have stressed in pointing to the theological character of both Talmuds – the Talmuds leave nothing of the Mishnah whole and intact. Their work upon the whole presents an essentially new construction. Through the Mishnah, Rabbi contributed to the Talmud most of the bricks, but little of the mortar, and none of the joists and beams. The design of the whole bore no relationship to Rabbi's plan for the Mishnah. The sages of the Talmud did the rest. They alone imagined, then built, the building. They are the architects, theirs is the vision. The building is a monument to the authority of the sage above all.

What is most definitively indicative of the Talmudic sages' freedom of imagination is the exercise – by each set of authors – of free choice even among the Mishnah's tractates awaiting exegesis. We do not know why some tractates were chosen for Talmudic expansion and others left fallow. We may speculate that the Yerushalmi's omission of all reference to the entire division of Holy Things, on the everyday conduct of the Temple, and to most of the division of Purities, on the sources of uncleanness, objects subject to uncleanness, and modes of removing contamination, constitutes a radical revision of the law of Judaism. What for Rabbi was close to 50 percent of the whole story in volume, forming two of his six divisions in structure, for that Talmud's designers (I assume early as much as late) was of no importance. Here, too, we find the Torah once more subject to (re)definition; nothing of course would be omitted; but choices clearly were made about what is to be brought to the fore.

Both Talmuds in common address the tractates of Appointed Times, Women, and Damages, the second, third, and fourth divisions of the Mishnah. That is then where the comparisons and contrasts have to take place. Interest in the division of Appointed Times involved extensive discussion of the conduct of the cult on extraordinary days. Perhaps at issue here was not what had to be omitted (the cult on appointed times) but what people wanted to discuss, the home and village on those same holy occasions. So the former came in the wake of the latter. Inclusion of the divisions of Women, on the family and the transfer of women from father to husband and back, and Damages, on civil law and institutions, is not hard to explain. The sages fully expected to govern the life of Israel, the Jewish people, in its material and concrete aspects. These divisions, as well as some of the tractates of the division on Appointed Times, demanded and received attention. Ample treatment of the laws in the first division, governing the priests' rations and other sacred segments of the agricultural produce of the Holy Land, is to be expected among authorities living not only in, but also off, the Holy Land.

If we stand back and reflect on the Mishnah's program, we recognize how different is that of the Talmuds. The Mishnah covers a broad variety of topics. The Talmuds contribute none of their own, but trawl across the entire surface of the Mishnah. The Mishnah is organized topically. The Talmuds may be broken down into discrete compositions and neatly joined composites, none of them framed as free-standing, topical formations, all of them in one way or another depending upon the Mishnah for order and coherence. The Mishnah lays out rules and facts about a world beyond itself. The Talmuds negotiate rules and recast facts into propositions that concern the Mishnah – a different focus of discourse and perspective altogether. Continuous with the Mishnah, the two Talmuds in point of fact redirect the Mishnah not only by destroying its integrity and picking and choosing with its topical (and propositional) program, but also by forming of the detritus of the receiving writing a statement of their own. But it was not a statement that, in the end, concerned the Mishnah at all, rather, a statement about the Torah, and a statement of the Torah.

In accepting authority, in centering discourse upon the ideas of other men, in patiently listing even the names behind authoritative laws from olden times to their own day, the sages and framers of the Talmud accomplished exactly the opposite of what they apparently wished to do. They made a commentary. But they obliterated the text.[17] They loyally explained the Mishnah. But they turned the Mishnah into something else than what it had been. They patiently hammered out chains of tradition, binding themselves to the authority of the remote and holy past. But it was, in the end, a tradition of their own design and choosing. That is, it was not tradition but a new creation. And so these Talmuds of ours, so loyal and subservient to the Mishnah of Rabbi, turn out to be less reworkings of received materials than works – each one of them – of remarkably independent judgment. The Talmuds speak humbly and subserviently about received truth, always in the name only of Moses

---

[17]So theirs is a different kind of commentary from, e.g., the true genius Rashi's, whose commentary always highlights the wholeness and integrity of the text on which he comments. It is difficult to find in modern and contemporary commentaries to the received Torah (either part) much profound reflection on the nature of commentary; people more or less "know" what they are supposed to do and do it. The result is intellectual chaos: a ragbag of interesting bits of information, not a hermeneutics at all. So nothing is at stake except (some) information (of some sort or other).

and of sages of times past. But in the end it is truth not discovered and demonstrated, but determined and invented and declared.

The redactional program of the men responsible for laying out the materials of Talmuds may now be described. There is a pronounced tendency in both Talmuds to move from close reading of the Mishnah and then Tosefta outward to more general inquiry into the principles of a Mishnah passage and their interplay with those of some other, superficially unrelated passage, and, finally, to more general reflections on law not self-evidently related to the Mishnah passage at hand or to anthologies intersecting only at a general topic. Unlike the Mishnah, the Talmuds reveal no effort to systematize sayings in larger constructions, or to impose a pattern upon all individual sayings. If the Mishnah is framed to facilitate memorization, then we must say that the Talmuds' materials are not framed with mnemonics in mind. If the Mishnah focuses upon subsurface relationships in syntax, the Talmud in the main looks like notes of a discussion. These notes may serve to recreate the larger patterns of argument and reasoning, a summary of what was thought and perhaps also said. The Talmud preserves and expresses concrete ideas, reducing them to brief but usually accessible and obvious statements. The Mishnah speaks of concrete things in order to hint at abstract relationships, which rarely are brought to the surface and fully exposed.

The Mishnah hides. The Talmuds spell out. The Mishnah hints. The Talmuds repeat ad nauseam. The Mishnah is subtle, the Talmuds obvious; the one restrained and tentative, the others aimed at full and exhaustive expression of what is already clear. The sages of the Mishnah rarely represent themselves as deciding cases. Only on unusual occasions do they declare the decided law, at best reticently spelling out what underlies their positions. The rabbis of the Talmuds harp on who holds which opinion and how a case is actually decided, presenting a rich corpus of precedents. They seek to make explicit what is implicit in the law. The Mishnah is immaterial and spiritual, the Talmud earthy and social. The Mishnah deals in the gossamer threads of philosophical principle, the Talmud in the coarse rope that binds this one and that one into a social construction.

The Mishnah speaks of a world in stasis, an unchanging, eternal present tense where all the tensions of chaos are resolved. The Talmuds address the real Israel in the here and now of ever-changing times, the gross matter of disorder and history. Clearly, the central traits of the Mishnah, revealed in the document at its time of closure in ca. A.D. 200, were revised and transformed into those definitive of the Talmud at its time of closure in ca. A.D. 400 for the earlier Talmud, 600 for the later. We know only that when we compare the Mishnah to the Talmuds we

find in each case two intertwined documents, quite different from one
another both in style and in values. Yet they are so tightly joined that the
Talmud appears in the main to provide mere commentary and
amplification for the Mishnah.   So the two Talmuds are
indistinguishable.

Were we to stop our analysis of the Talmuds here, we should have a
simple definition of the theologizing of Judaism.   The religious
convictions of Judaism reached theological formulation when the (first)
Talmud composed a commentary to the Mishnah to prove first the unity
of the Torah and second its perfection; these points were formulated as a
hermeneutics and demonstrated in a repetitive commentary to the
received writing.   That, sum and substance, would constitute the
theology of Judaism: propositions of vast implications, but, in the end,
only propositions.   But, then, that theology could in no way be described
as a re-presentation of the Torah at all, merely as an apologia and a
recapitulation.   But in fact, in the theology of Judaism we have a free-
standing theological structure and system, exposed only in the second of
the two Talmuds, a theological method that demonstrates over and over
again the character of a statement, an entire re-presentation of the Torah.
The real point of common between the Yerushalmi and the Bavli,
however, has now to be specified: it is that both of them state the same
religious system, as I shall now show.   The second Talmud says little that
the first Talmud had not already stated – and set forth with authority,
clarity, and precision.

6

Alike and Not Alike:
Two Media for the Same Message.

The Examples of the Torah
and the Messiah

The Talmuds are alike in category and conviction. They utilize the same categories and they also set forth the same substance to them. It follows that in the theological program set forth in its pages, we cannot distinguish the second Talmud from the first.

Both Talmuds organize data within the same category formation, meaning, the second Talmud's conforms to that of the first. If we spell out the category formation of the first Talmud, with its interest in anti-politics, anti-economics, and a gnostic Torah,[1] we find ample data that serve for the statement of the second. And, more to the point, when we interrogate the second Talmud about its ethos, ethics, and ethnos, that is, its theory of the social order for its Israel, so far as I can see, it responds in ways wholly congruent to those of the first Talmud. That is what I mean when I say, the category formation of the second Talmud is indistinguishable from that of the first; the differences, so far as there are differences, are in inconsequential matters of detail, not in order, structure, or generative symbol and governing myth. A single theological paradigm defines matters for both.

That explains why I cannot point to a single important category governing in the second but absent in the first, nor do I discern any material change in the definition of any inherited category worked out

---

[1]Terms spelled out in *The Transformation of Judaism. From Philosophy to Religion* (Champaign, 1992: University of Illinois Press).

by the framers of the Talmud of Babylonia.[2]   Accordingly, when we wish
to differentiate the two Talmuds, we cannot point to either new
categories or new doctrines formulated for received categories.   The
differences are rarely doctrinal, ordinarily hermeneutical.   That fact takes
on weight, when we compare the category formations that organize the
Mishnah's chosen data and the Talmud of the Land of Israel's reception
of those same categories, on the one side, but also its invention of its
own, counterpart categories, on the other.   The continuity in category
formation and, consequently, in doctrine, exhibited by the Bavli therefore
requires us to focus attention solely on the second Talmud's modes of
thought and explication of the Mishnah.

To show the identity of viewpoint between the two Talmuds, so
highlighting the distinction in hermeneutics but not in proposition that
sets the Bavli apart, we consider a very brief account of the unfolding,
along documentary lines, of two principal conceptions of the Judaism of
the Dual Torah set forth in the end by the Bavli: [1] the symbol of the
Torah; [2] the Messiah theme.   In both cases the upshot is the same: the
Yerushalmi recast these matters, the Bavli recapitulated the Yerushalmi's
results, perhaps refining or improving here and there, but essentially
saying the same thing in the same way.   The major shift in the unfolding
of the symbol of the Torah and in the theme of the Messiah occurs
between the Mishnah and the Yerushalmi.   That is what I shall now
briefly show.[3]

---

[2]For the comparison of details of the two Talmuds, I refer readers to the items in
Baruch M. Bokser, "The Palestinian Talmud," in J. Neusner, ed., *The Study of
Ancient Judaism* (Atlanta, 1992: Scholars Press for South Florida Studies in the
History of Judaism). II. *The Palestinian and Babylonia Talmuds*. Bokser summarizes
the work that has been done in comparing the two Talmuds' treatment of various
matters; the triviality of the differences in proposition, myth, symbolic structure,
and category formation with reference to the social order underscores the simple
statement here that we cannot differentiate the Talmuds in generative aspects at
all. My differentiation is in hermeneutics, as is already clear and as will be amply
spelled out; and that of course will explain such trivial differences in substance as
have been identified.

[3]For the results briefly summarized here, on the Messiah and on the Torah,
respectively, see my *The Foundations of Judaism. Method, Teleology, Doctrine*
(Philadelphia, 1983-1985: Fortress Press), I-III. II. *Messiah in Context. Israel's
History and Destiny in Formative Judaism*.   Second printing (Lanham, 1988:
University Press of America). Studies in Judaism Series. III. *Torah: From Scroll to
Symbol in Formative Judaism*. Second printing (Atlanta, 1988: Scholars Press for
Brown Judaic Studies).   These are summarized in a larger context in *The
Foundations of Judaism* (Philadelphia, 1988: Fortress); that title has now appeared
in Dutch and Italian.

1. The Torah

Judaism reached its now familiar definition when "the Torah" lost its capital letter and definite article and ultimately became "torah." What for nearly a millennium had been a particular scroll or book thus came to serve as a symbol of an entire system. When a rabbi spoke of torah, he no longer meant only a particular object, a scroll and its contents. Now he used the work to encompass a distinctive and well-defined worldview and way of life. Torah had come to stand for something one does. Knowledge of the Torah promised not merely information about what people were supposed to do, but ultimate redemption or salvation.

THE MISHNAH AND THE TORAH: The Torah of Moses clearly occupied a critical place in all systems of Judaism from the closure of the Torah book, the Pentateuch, in the time of Ezra onward. But in late antiquity, for one group alone the book developed into an abstract and encompassing symbol, so that in the Judaism that took shape in the formative age, the first seven centuries C.E., everything was contained in that one thing. How so? When we speak of torah, in rabbinical literature of late antiquity, we no longer denote a particular book, on the one side, or the contents of such a book, on the other. Instead, we connote a broad range of clearly distinct categories of noun and verb, concrete fact and abstract relationship alike. "Torah" stands for a kind of human being. It connotes a social status and a sort of social group. It refers to a type of social relationship. It further denotes a legal status and differentiates among legal norms. As symbolic abstraction, the word encompasses things and persons, actions and status, points of social differentiation and legal and normative standing, as well as "revealed truth." In all, the main points of insistence of the whole of Israel's life and history come to full symbolic expression in that single word. If people wanted to explain how they would be saved, they would use the word Torah. If they wished to sort out their parlous relationships with gentiles, they would use the world Torah. Torah stood for salvation and accounted for Israel's this-worldly condition and the hope, for both individual and national alike, of life in the world to come. For the kind of Judaism under discussion, therefore, the word Torah stood for everything. The Torah symbolized the whole, at once and entire. When, therefore, we wish to describe the unfolding of the definitive doctrine of Judaism in its formative period, the first exercise consists in paying close attention to the meanings imputed to a single word.

Every detail of the religious system at hand exhibits essentially the same point of insistence, captured in the simple notion of the Torah as the generative symbol, the total, exhaustive expression of the system as a whole. That is why the definitive ritual of the Judaism under study consisted in studying the Torah as the generative symbol, the total, exhaustive expression of the system as a whole. That is why the definitive myth explained that one who studied Torah would become holy, like Moses "our rabbi," and like God, in whose image humanity was made and whose Torah provided the plan and the model for what God wanted of a humanity created in his image. As for Christians it was in Christ God made flesh, so the framers of the system of Judaism at hand found in the Torah that image of God to which Israel should aspire, and to which the sage in fact conformed.

The meaning of the several meanings of the Torah should require only brief explanation. When the Torah refers to a particular thing, it is to a scroll containing divinely revealed words. The Torah may further refer to revelation, not as an object but as a corpus of doctrine. When one "does Torah," the disciple "studies" or "learns," and the master "teaches," Torah. Hence while the word Torah never appears as a verb, it does refer to an act. The word also bears a quite separate sense, torah as category or classification or corpus of rules, for example, "the torah of driving a car" is a usage entirely acceptable to some documents. This generic usage of the word does occur. The word Torah very commonly refers to a status, distinct from and above another status, as "teachings of Torah" as against "teachings of scribes." For the two Talmuds that distinction is absolutely critical to the entire hermeneutic enterprise. But it is important even in the Mishnah. Obviously, no account of the meaning of the word Torah can ignore the distinction between the two Torahs, Written and Oral. It is important only in the secondary stages of the formation of the literature. Finally, the word Torah refers to a source of salvation, often fully worked out in stories about how the individual and the nation will be saved through Torah. In general, the sense of the word "salvation" is not complicated. It is simply salvation in the way in which Deuteronomy and the Deuteronomic historians understand it: kings who do what God wants win battles, those who do not, lose. So, too, here, people who study and do Torah are saved from sickness and death, and the way Israel can save itself from its condition of degradation also is through Torah.

If we examine the documents of the Oral Torah in their chronological sequence, we see that it was with the Yerushalmi that the doctrine of the Dual Torah comes to full expression. The Mishnah places a high value upon studying the Torah and upon the status of the sage. A *"mamzer* disciple of a sage takes priority over a high-priest *am haares*," as at M. Hor. 3:8. But that judgment shows only that the Mishnah pays due honor to the sage. But if the Mishnah does not claim to constitute part of the Torah, then what makes a sage a sage is not mastery of the Mishnah in particular. What we have in hand merely continues the established and familiar position of the wisdom writers of old. Wisdom is important. Knowledge of the Torah is definitive. But to maintain that position, one need hardly profess the fully articulated Torah myth of Rabbinic Judaism. The issue is whether we find in the Mishnah the assertion that whatever the sage has on the authority of his master goes back to Sinai. We seek a definitive view that what the sage says falls into the classification of Torah, just as what Scripture says constitutes Torah from God to Moses. That is what distinguishes wisdom from the Torah as it emerges in the context of Rabbinic Judaism. We do not find the Torah in the Mishnah, and the Mishnah is not part of the Torah.

When the authors of the Mishnah surveyed the landscape of Israelite writings down to their own time, they saw only Sinai, that is, what we now know as Scripture. Based on the documents they cite or mention, we can say with certainty that they knew the pentateuchal law. We may take for granted that they accepted as divine revelation also the Prophets and the Writings, to which they occasionally make reference. That they regarded as a single composition, that is, as revelation, the Torah, Prophets, and Writings appears from their references to the Torah, as a specific "book", and to a Torah scroll. Accordingly, one important meaning associated with the word Torah was concrete in the extreme. The Torah was a particular book or sets of books, regarded as holy, revealed to Moses at Sinai. That fact presents no surprise, since the Torah scroll(s) had existed, it is generally assumed, for many centuries before the closure of the Mishnah in 200. So the concrete and physical meaning attaching to the word Torah, that is, the Torah, the Torah revealed by God to Moses at Mount Sinai (including the books of the Prophets and the Writings), bore a contrary implication. Beyond The Torah there was no torah. Besides the Pentateuch, Prophets, and Writings, not only did no physical scroll deserve veneration, but no corpus of writings demanded obedience.

A generation or so after the closure of the Mishnah, tractate Abot draws into the orbit of Torah talk the names of authorities of the Mishnah. But Abot does not claim that the Mishnah forms part of the Torah. Nor, obviously, does the tractate know the doctrine of the two Torahs. Only in the Talmuds do we begin to find clear and ample evidence of that doctrine. Abot, moreover, does not understand by the word Torah much more than the framers of the Mishnah do. Not only does the established classification scheme remain intact, but the sense essentially replicates already familiar usages, producing no innovation. On the contrary, I find a diminution in the range of meanings. Yet Abot in the aggregate does differ from the Mishnah. The difference has to do with the topic at hand. The other sixty-two tractates of the Mishnah contain Torah sayings here and there. But they do not fall within the framework of Torah discourse. They speak about other matters entirely.

The consideration of the status of Torah rarely pertains to that speech. Abot, by contrast, says a great deal about Torah study. The claim that Torah study produces direct encounter with God forms part of Abot's thesis about the Torah. That claim, by itself, would hardly have surprised Israelite writers of wisdom books over a span of many centuries, whether those assembled in the Essene commune at Qumran, on the one side, or those represented in the pages of Proverbs and in many of the Psalms, or even the Deuteronomistic circle, on the other.

A second glance at tractate Abot, however, produces a surprising fact. In Abot, Torah is instrumental. The figure of the sage, his ideals and conduct, forms the goal, focus, and center. Abot regards study of Torah as what a sage does. The substance of Torah is what a sage says. That is so whether or not the saying relates to scriptural revelation. The content of the sayings attributed to sages endows those sayings with self-validating status. The sages usually do not quote verses of Scripture and explain them, nor do they speak in God's name. Yet, it is clear, sages talk Torah. What follows? It is this: If a sage says something, what he says is Torah. More accurately, what he says falls into the classification of Torah. Accordingly, as I said, Abot treats Torah learning as symptomatic, an indicator of the status of the sage, hence, as I said, as merely instrumental. The simplest proof of that proposition lies in the recurrent formal structure of the document, the one thing the framers of the document never omit and always emphasize: (1) the name of the authority behind a saying, from Simeon the Righteous on downward, and (2) the connective attributive "says." So what is important to the redactors is what they never have to tell us. Because a recognized sage makes a statement, what he says constitutes, in and of itself, a statement in the status of Torah.

At issue in Abot is not the Torah, but the authority of the sage. It is that standing that transforms a saying into a Torah saying, or to state matters more appropriately, that places a saying into the classification of the Torah. Abot then stands as the first document of the doctrine that the sage embodies the Torah and is a holy man, like Moses "our rabbi," in the likeness and image of God. The beginning is to claim that a saying falls into the category of Torah if a sage says it as Torah. The end will be to view the sage himself as Torah incarnate.

THE TALMUDS AND THE TORAH: When we come to the Yerushalmi, we are in a different world. Now the Mishnah is held in the Talmud of the Land of Israel to be equivalent to Scripture (Y. Hor. 3:5). But the Mishnah is not called Torah. Still, once the Mishnah entered the status of Scripture, it would take but a short step to a theory of the Mishnah as part of the revelation at Sinai – hence, Oral Torah. In the first Talmud we find the first glimmerings of an effort to theorize in general, not merely in detail, about how specific teachings of Mishnah relate to specific teachings of Scripture. The citing of scriptural prooftexts for Mishnah propositions, after all, would not have caused much surprise to the framers of the Mishnah; they themselves included such passages, though not often. But what conception of the Torah underlies such initiatives, and how do Yerushalmi sages propose to explain the phenomenon of the Mishnah as a whole? The following passage gives us one statement. It refers to the assertion at M. Hag. 1:8D that the laws on cultic cleanness presented in the Mishnah rest on deep and solid foundations in the Scripture.

[V.A]   The laws of the Sabbath [M. 1:8B]: R. Jonah said R. Hama bar Uqba raised the question [in reference to M. Hag. 1:8D's view that there are many verses of Scripture on cleanness], "And lo, it is written only, 'Nevertheless a spring or a cistern holding water shall be clean; but whatever touches their carcass shall be unclean.' (Lev. 11:36). And from this verse you derive many laws. [So how can M. 8:8D say what it does about many verses for laws of cultic cleanness?]"

[B]   R. Zeira in the name of R. Yohanan: "If a law comes to hand and you do not know its nature, do not discard it for another one, for lo, many laws were stated to Moses at Sinai, and all of them have been embedded in the Mishnah."

Y. Hagigah 1:7

The truly striking assertion appears at B. The Mishnah now is claimed to contain statements made by God to Moses. Just how these statements found their way into the Mishnah, and which passages of the Mishnah contain them, we do not know. That is hardly important, given the fundamental assertion at hand. The passage proceeds to a further, and far more consequential, proposition. It asserts that part of the Torah was written down, and part was preserved in memory and transmitted orally. In context, moreover, that distinction must encompass the Mishnah, thus explaining its origin as part of the Torah. Here is a clear and unmistakable expression of the distinction between two forms in which a single Torah was revealed and handed on at Mount Sinai, part in writing, part orally.

While the passage below does not make use of the language, Torah-in-writing and Torah-by-memory, it does refer to "the Written" and "the Oral." I believe myself fully justified in supplying the word Torah in square brackets. The reader will note, however, that the word Torah likewise does not occur at K, L. Only when the passage reaches its climax, at M, does it break down into a number of categories – Scripture, Mishnah, Talmud, laws, lore. It there makes the additional point that everything comes from Moses at Sinai. So the fully articulated theory of two Torahs (not merely one Torah in two forms) does not reach final expression in this passage. But short of explicit allusion to Torah-in-writing and Torah-by-memory, which (so far as I am able to discern) we find mainly in the Talmud of Babylonia, the ultimate theory of Torah of formative Judaism is at hand in what follows.

[V.D] R. Zeirah in the name of R. Eleazar: "'Were I to write for him my laws by ten thousands, they would be regarded as a strange thing' (Hos. 8:12). Now is the greater part of the Torah written down? [Surely not. The oral part is much greater.] But more abundant are the matters which are derived by exegesis from the Written [Torah] than those derived by exegesis from the Oral [Torah]."

[E] And is that so?

[F] But more cherished are those matters which rest upon the Written [Torah] than those which rest upon the Oral [Torah]....

[J] R. Haggai in the name of R. Samuel bar Nahman, "Some teachings were handed on orally, and some things were handed on in writing, and we do not know which of them is the more precious. But on the basis of that which is written, "And the Lord said to Moses, 'Write these words; in accordance with these words I have made a covenant with you and with Israel' (Ex. 34:27), [we conclude] that the ones which are handed on orally are the more precious."

[K] R. Yohanan and R. Yudan b. R. Simeon – one said, "If you have kept what is preserved orally and also kept what is in writing, I shall make a covenant with you, and if not, I shall not make a covenant with you."

[L] The other said, "If you have kept what is preserved orally and you have kept what is preserved in writing, you shall receive a reward, and if not, you shall not receive a reward."

[M] [With reference to Deut. 9:10: "And on them was written according to all the words which the Lord spoke with you in the mount,"] said R. Joshua b. Levi, "He could have written, 'On them,' but wrote, 'And on them.' He could have written, 'All,' but wrote, 'According to all.' He could have written, 'Words,' but wrote, 'The words.' [These then serve as three encompassing clauses, serving to include] Scripture, Mishnah, Talmud, laws, and lore. Even what an experienced student in the future is going to teach before his master already has been stated to Moses at Sinai."

[N] What is the scriptural basis for this view?

[O] "There is no remembrance of former things, nor will there be any remembrance of later things yet to happen among those who come after" (Qoh. 1:11).

[P] If someone says, "See, this is a new thing," his fellow will answer him, saying to him, "This has been around before us for a long time."

Y. Hagigah 1:7

Here we have absolutely explicit evidence that people believed part of the Torah had been preserved not in writing but orally. Linking that part to the Mishnah remains a matter of implication. But it surely comes fairly close to the surface, when we are told that the Mishnah contains Torah traditions revealed at Sinai. From that view it requires only a small step to the allegation that the Mishnah is part of the Torah, the oral part.

To define the category of the Torah as a source of salvation, as the Yerushalmi states matters, I point to a story that explicitly states the proposition that the Torah constitutes a source of salvation. In this story we shall see that because people observed the rules of the Torah, they expected to be saved. And if they did not observe, they accepted their punishment. So the Torah now stands for something more than revelation and life of study, and (it goes without saying) the sage now appears as a holy, not merely a learned, man. This is because his knowledge of the Torah has transformed him. Accordingly, we deal with a category of stories and sayings about the Torah entirely different from what has gone before.

> [II.A] As to Levi ben Sisi: Troops came to his town. He took a scroll of the Torah and went up to the roof and said, "Lord of the ages! If a single word of this scroll of the Torah has been nullified [in our town], let them come up against us, and if not, let them go their way."
>
> [B] Forthwith people went looking for the troops but did not find them [because they had gone their way].
>
> [C] A disciple of his did the same thing, and his hand withered, but the troops went their way.
>
> [D] A disciple of his disciple did the same thing. His hand did not wither, but they also did not go their way.
>
> [E] This illustrates the following apophthegm: You can't insult an idiot, and dead skin does not feel the scalpel.
>
> Y. Taanit 3:8

What is interesting here is how taxa into which the word Torah previously fell have been absorbed and superseded in a new taxon. The Torah is an object: "He took a scroll...." It also constitutes God's revelation to Israel: "If a single word...." The outcome of the revelation is to form an ongoing way of life, embodied in the sage himself: "A disciple of his did the same thing...." The sage plays an intimate part in the supernatural event: "His hand withered...." Now can we categorize this story as a statement that the Torah constitutes a particular object, or a source of divine revelation, or a way of life? Yes and no. The Torah here stands not only for the things we already have catalogued. It represents one more thing which takes in all the others. Torah is a source of salvation. How so? The Torah stands for, or constitutes, the way in which the people Israel saves itself from marauders. This straightforward sense of salvation would not have surprised the author of Deuteronomy.

In the canonical documents up to the Yerushalmi, we look in vain for sayings or stories that fall into such a category. In the Yerushalmi and the Bavli, such sayings are commonplace. True, we may take for granted that everyone always believed that, in general, Israel would be saved by obedience to the Torah. That claim – a commonplace, systemically inert in any system that appealed to the Pentateuch – would not have surprised any Israelite writer from the first prophets down through the final redactors of the Pentateuch in the time of Ezra and onward through the next seven hundred years. But, in the rabbinical corpus from the Mishnah forward, the specific and concrete assertion that by taking up the scroll of the Torah and standing on the roof of one's house, confronting God in Heaven, a sage in particular could take action against the expected invasion – that kind of claim is not located, so far as I know, in any composition surveyed so far. No stories containing such a viewpoint appear in any rabbinical document associated with the Mishnah. So what is critical here is not the generalized category – the genus – of conviction that the Torah serves as the source of Israel's salvation. It is the concrete assertion – the speciation of the genus – that in the hands of the sage and under conditions specified, the Torah may be utilized in pressing circumstances as Levi, his disciple, and the disciple of his disciple used it. That is what is new.

This stunningly new usage of Torah found in the Talmud of the Land of Israel and recapitulated in the Bavli emerges from a group of stories not readily classified in our established categories. All of these stories treat the word Torah (whether scroll, contents, or act of study) as source and guarantor of salvation. Accordingly, evoking the word Torah forms the centerpiece of a theory of Israel's history, on the one side, and an account of the teleology of the entire system, on the other. Torah indeed has ceased to constitute a specific thing or even a category or classification when stories about studying the Torah yield not a judgment as to status (i.e., praise for the learned man) but promise for supernatural blessing now and salvation in time to come.

To the rabbis the principal salvific deed was to "study Torah," by which they meant memorizing Torah sayings by constant repetition, and, as the Talmud itself amply testifies (for some sages) profound analytic inquiry into the meaning of those sayings. That that is the case for the Bavli is shown by the story of how Heaven required Rabbah's Torah, which we examined in Chapter Four. The innovation now is that this act of "study of Torah" imparts supernatural power of a material character. For example, by repeating words of Torah, the sage could ward off the angel of death and accomplish other kinds of miracles as well. So Torah formulas served as incantations. Mastery of Torah transformed the man engaged in Torah learning into a supernatural figure, who could do things ordinary folk could not do. The category of "Torah" had already vastly expanded so that through transformation of the Torah from a concrete thing to a symbol, a Torah scroll could be compared to a man of Torah, namely, a rabbi. Now, once the principle had been established, that salvation would come from keeping God's will in general, as Israelite holy men had insisted for so many centuries, it was a small step for rabbis to identify their particular corpus of learning, namely, the Mishnah and associated sayings, with God's will expressed in Scripture, the universally acknowledged medium of revelation.

The key to the first Talmud's theory of the Torah lies in its conception of the sage, to which that theory is subordinate. Once the sage reaches his full apotheosis as Torah incarnate, then, but only then, the Torah becomes (also) a source of salvation in the present concrete formulation of the matter. That is why we traced the doctrine of the Torah in the salvific process by elaborate citation of stories about sages, living Torahs, exercising the supernatural power of the Torah, and serving, like the Torah itself, to reveal God's will. Since the sage embodied the Torah and gave the Torah, the Torah naturally came to stand for the principal source of Israel's salvation, not merely a scroll, on the one side, or a source of revelation, on the other.

The history of the symbolization of the Torah proceeds from its removal from the framework of material objects, even from the limitations of its own contents, to its transformation into something quite different and abstract, quite distinct from the document and its teachings. The Torah stands for this something more, specifically, when it comes to be identified with a living person, the sage, and endowed with those particular traits that the sage claimed for himself. While we cannot say that the process of symbolization leading to the pure abstraction at hand moved in easy stages, we may still point to the stations that had to be passed in sequence. The word Torah reached the apologists for the Mishnah in its long-established meanings: Torah scroll, contents of the Torah scroll. But even in the Mishnah itself, these meanings provoked a secondary development, status of Torah as distinct from other (lower) status, hence, Torah teaching in contradistinction to scribal teaching. With that small and simple step, the Torah ceased to denote only a concrete and material thing – a scroll and its contents. It now connoted an abstract matter of status. And once made abstract, the symbol entered a secondary history beyond all limits imposed by the concrete object, including its specific teachings, the Torah scroll.

I believe that Abot stands at the beginning of this process. In the history of the word Torah as abstract symbol, a metaphor serving to sort out one abstract status from another regained concrete and material reality of a new order entirely. For the message of Abot, as we saw, was that the Torah served the sage. How so? The Torah indicated who was a sage and who was not. Accordingly, the apology of Abot for the Mishnah was that the Mishnah contained things sages had said. What sages said formed a chain of tradition extending back to Sinai. Hence it was equivalent to the Torah. The upshot is that words of sages enjoyed the status of the Torah. The small step beyond, I think, was to claim that what sages said was Torah, as much as what Scripture said was Torah. And, a further small step (and the steps need not have been taken separately or in the order here suggested) moved matters to the position that there were two forms in which the Torah reached Israel: one [Torah] in writing, the other [Torah] handed on orally, that is, in memory. The final step, fully revealed in the Talmud at hand, brought the conception of Torah to its logical conclusion: what the sage said was in the status of the Torah, was Torah, because the sage was Torah incarnate. So the abstract symbol now became concrete and material once more. We recognize the many, diverse ways in which the Talmud stated that conviction. Every passage in which knowledge of the Torah yields power over this world and the next, capacity to coerce to the sage's will the natural and supernatural worlds alike, rests upon the same viewpoint.

The first Talmud's theory of the Torah carries us through several stages in the processes of the symbolization of the word Torah. First transformed from something material and concrete into something abstract and beyond all metaphor, the word Torah finally emerged once more in a concrete aspect, now as the encompassing and universal mode of stating the whole doctrine, all at once, of Judaism in its formative age. It suffices to allege as fact: The second Talmud concurred in all that the first Talmud set forth and in no way recast the category, Torah, as the Yerushalmi had defined it.

2. The Messiah

THE MISHNAH AND THE MESSIAH; THE QUESTION OF HISTORY: The Mishnah set forth a Judaic system in which history did not define the main framework by which the issue of teleology took a form other than the familiar eschatological one and in which historical events were absorbed, through their trivialization in taxonomic structures, into an ahistorical system. In the kind of Judaism in this document, messiahs played a solely taxonomic hierarchical part. But these "anointed men" had no historical role. They were merely a species of priest, falling into one classification rather than another. That fact becomes transparent when we ask the Mishnah to answer the questions at hand. What of the

Messiah? When will he come? To whom, in Israel, will he come? And what must, or can, we do while we wait to hasten his coming? If we now reframe these questions and divest them of their mythic cloak, we ask about the Mishnah's theory of the history and destiny of Israel and the purpose of the Mishnah's own system in relationship to Israel's present and end: the implicit teleology of the philosophical law at hand. Answering these questions out of the resources of the Mishnah is not possible.

The Mishnah presents no large view of history. It contains no reflection whatever on the nature and meaning of the destruction of the Temple in A.D. 70, an event which surfaces only in connection with some changes in the law explained as resulting from the end of the cult. The Mishnah pays no attention to the matter of the end time. The word "salvation" is rare, "sanctification" commonplace. More strikingly, the framers of the Mishnah are virtually silent on the teleology of the system; they never tell us why we should do what the Mishnah tells us, let alone explain what will happen if we do. Incidents in the Mishnah are preserved either as narrative settings for the statement of the law, or, occasionally, as precedents. Historical events are classified and turned into entries on lists. But incidents in any case come few and far between. True, events do make an impact. But it always is for the Mishnah's own purpose and within its own taxonomic system and rule-seeking mode of thought. To be sure, the framers of the Mishnah may also have had a theory of the Messiah and of the meaning of Israel's history and destiny. But they kept it hidden, and their document manages to provide an immense account of Israel's life without explicitly telling us about such matters.

The Messiah in the Mishnah does not stand at the forefront of the framers' consciousness. The issues encapsulated in the myth and person of the Messiah are scarcely addressed. The framers of the Mishnah do not resort to speculation about the Messiah as a historical-supernatural figure. So far as that kind of speculation provides the vehicle for reflection on salvific issues, or in mythic terms, narratives on the meaning of history and the destiny of Israel, we cannot say that the Mishnah's philosophers take up those encompassing categories of being: Where are we heading? What can we do about it? That does not mean questions found urgent in the aftermath of the destruction of the Temple and the disaster of Bar Kokhba failed to attract the attention of the Mishnah's sages. But they treated history in a different way, offering their own answers to its questions. To these we now turn.

By "history" I mean not merely events, but how events serve to teach lessons, reveal patterns, tell us what we must do and what will happen to us tomorrow. In that context, some events contain richer lessons than others; the destruction of the Temple of Jerusalem teaches more than a crop failure, being kidnapped into slavery more than stubbing one's toe. Furthermore, lessons taught by events – "history" in the didactic sense – follow a progression from trivial and private to consequential and public. The framers of the Mishnah explicitly refer to very few events, treating those they do mention with a focus quite separate from the unfolding events themselves. They rarely create narratives; historical events do not supply organizing categories or taxonomic classifications. We find no tractate devoted to the destruction of the Temple, no complete chapter detailing the events of Bar Kokhba nor even a sustained celebration of the events of the sages' own historical lives. When things that have happened are mentioned, it is neither to narrate nor to interpret and draw lessons from the events. It is either to illustrate a point of law or to pose a problem of the law – always *en passant*, never in a pointed way.

The Mishnah absorbs into its encompassing system all events, small and large. With them the sages accomplish what they accomplish in everything else: a vast labor of taxonomy, an immense construction of the order and rules governing the classification of everything on earth and in Heaven. The disruptive character of history – one-time events of ineluctable significance – scarcely impresses the philosophers. They find no difficulty in showing that what appears unique and beyond classification has in fact happened before and so falls within the range of trustworthy rules and known procedures. Once history's components, one-time events, lose their distinctiveness, then history as a didactic intellectual construct, as a source of lessons and rules, also loses all pertinence.

So lessons and rules come from sorting things out and classifying them from the procedures and modes of thought of the philosopher seeking regularity. To this labor of taxonomy, the historian's way of selecting data and arranging them into patterns of meaning to teach lessons proves inconsequential. One-time events are not important. The world is composed of nature and supernature. The laws that count are those to be discovered in Heaven and, in Heaven's creation and counterpart, on earth. Keep those laws and things will work out. Break them, and the result is predictable: calamity of whatever sort will supervene in accordance with the rules. But just because it is predictable, a catastrophic happening testifies to what has always been and must always be, in accordance with reliable rules and within categories already discovered and well explained. That is why the lawyer-philosophers of the mid second century produced the Mishnah – to explain how things are. Within the framework of well-classified rules, there could be messiahs, but no single Messiah.

If the end of time and the coming of the Messiah do not serve to explain, for the Mishnah's system, why people should do what the Mishnah says, then what alternative teleology does the Mishnah's first apologetic, Abot, provide? Only when we appreciate the clear answers given in that document, brought to closure at ca. 250, shall we grasp how remarkable is the shift, which took place in later documents of the rabbinic canon, to a messianic framing of the issues of the Torah's ultimate purpose and value. Let us see how the framers of Abot, in the aftermath of the creation of the Mishnah, explain the purpose and goal of the Mishnah: an ahistorical, nonmessianic teleology.

Abot agreed with the other sixty-two tractates: history proved no more important here than it had been before. With scarcely a word about history and no account of events at all, Abot manages to provide an ample account of how the Torah – Written and Oral, thus in later eyes, Scripture and Mishnah – came down to its own day. Accordingly, the passage of time as such plays no role in the explanation of the origins of the document, nor is the Mishnah presented as eschatological. Occurrences of great weight ("history") are never invoked. How then does the tractate tell the story of Torah, narrate the history of God's revelation to Israel, encompassing both Scripture and Mishnah? The answer is that Abot's framers manage to do their work of explanation without telling a story or invoking history at all. They pursue a different way of answering the same question, by exploiting a nonhistorical mode of thought and method of legitimation. And that is the main point: teleology serves the purpose of legitimation, and hence is accomplished in ways other than explaining how things originated or assuming that historical fact explains anything.

Disorderly historical events entered the system of the Mishnah and found their place within the larger framework of the Mishnah's orderly world. But to claim that the Mishnah's framers merely ignored what was happening would be incorrect. They worked out their own way of dealing with historical events, the disruptive power of which they not only conceded but freely recognized. Further, the Mishnah's authors did not intend to compose a history book or a work of prophecy or apocalypse. Even if they had wanted to narrate the course of events, they could hardly have done so through the medium of the Mishnah. Yet the Mishnah presents its philosophy in full awareness of the issues of historical calamity confronting the Jewish nation. So far as the philosophy of the document confronts the totality of Israel's existence, the Mishnah by definition also presents a philosophy of history.

The Mishnah's subordination of historical events contradicts the emphasis of a thousand years of Israelite thought. The biblical histories, the ancient prophets, the apocalyptic visionaries all had testified that events themselves were important. Events carried the message of the living God. Events constituted history, pointed toward, and so explained, Israel's destiny. An essentially ahistorical system of timeless sanctification, worked out through construction of an eternal rhythm which centered on the movement of the moon and stars and seasons, represented a life chosen by few outside of the priesthood. Israel had suffered enormous loss of life. The Talmud of the Land of Israel takes these events seriously and treats them as unique and remarkable. The memories proved real. The hopes evoked by the Mishnah's promise of sanctification of a world in static perfection did not. For they had to compete with the grief of an entire century of mourning.

THE TALMUDS AND THE MESSIAH; THE CENTRALITY OF HISTORY: The most important change is the shift in historical thinking adumbrated in the pages of the Talmud of the Land of Israel, a shift from focus upon the Temple and its supernatural history to close attention to the people Israel and its natural, this-worldly history. Once Israel, holy Israel, had come to form the counterpart to the Temple and its supernatural life, that other history – Israel's – would stand at the center of things. Accordingly, a new sort of memorable event came to the fore in the Talmud of the Land of Israel. Let me give this new history appropriate emphasis: it was the story of Israel's suffering, remembrance of that suffering, on the one side, and an effort to explain events of such tragedy, on the other. So a composite "history" constructed out of the Yerushalmi's units of discourse which were pertinent to consequential events would contain long chapters on what happened to Israel, the Jewish people, and not only, or mainly, what had earlier occurred in the Temple.

The components of the historical theory of Israel's sufferings were manifold. First and foremost, history taught moral lessons. Historical events entered into the construction of a teleology for the Yerushalmi's system of Judaism as a whole. What the law demanded reflected the consequences of wrongful action on the part of Israel. So, again, Israel's own deeds defined the events of history. Rome's role, like Assyria's and Babylonia's, depended upon Israel's provoking divine wrath as it was executed by the great empire. The framers of the Talmud of the Land of Israel were not telling the Jews to please God by doing commandments in order that they should thereby gain control of their own destiny. To the contrary, the paradox of the Yerushalmi's system lies in the fact that Israel can free itself of control by other nations only by humbly agreeing to accept God's rule. The nations – Rome, in the present instance – rest on one side of the balance, while God rests on the other. Israel must then choose between them. There is no such thing for Israel as freedom from both God and the nations, total autonomy and independence. There is only a choice of masters, a ruler on earth or a ruler in Heaven.

With propositions such as these, the framers of the Mishnah will certainly have concurred. And why not? For the fundamental affirmations of the Mishnah about the centrality of Israel's perfection in stasis – sanctification – readily prove congruent to the attitudes at hand. Once the Messiah's coming had become dependent upon Israel's condition and not upon Israel's actions in historical time, then the Mishnah's system would have imposed its fundamental and definitive character upon the Messiah myth. An eschatological teleology framed through that myth then would prove wholly appropriate to the method of the larger system of the Mishnah. When this fact has been fully and completely spelled out in the final chapter, we shall then have grasped the distinctive history of the myth of the Messiah in the formative history of Judaism.

What, after all, makes a messiah a false messiah? In this Talmud, it is not his claim to save Israel, but his claim to save Israel without the help of God. The meaning of the true Messiah is Israel's total submission, through the Messiah's gentle rule, to God's yoke and service. So God is not to be manipulated through Israel's humoring of Heaven in rite and cult. The notion of keeping the commandments so as to please Heaven and get God to do what Israel wants is totally incongruent to the text at hand. Keeping the commandments as a mark of submission, loyalty, humility before God is the rabbinic system of salvation. So Israel does not "save itself." Israel never controls its own destiny, either on earth or in Heaven. The only choice is whether to place one's fate into the hands of cruel, deceitful men, or to trust in the living God of mercy and love. We shall now see how this critical position is spelled out in the setting of discourse about the Messiah in the Talmud of the Land of Israel. Bar Kokhba, above all, exemplifies arrogance against God. He lost the war because of that arrogance. In particular, he ignored the authority of sages:

> [K] Said R. Yohanan, "There were eighty thousand pairs of trumpeteers surrounding Betar. Each one was in charge of a number of troops. Ben Kozeba was there and he had two hundred thousand troops who, as a sign of loyalty, had cut off their little fingers.
>
> [L] "Sages sent word to him, 'How long are you going to turn Israel into a maimed people?'
>
> [M] "He said to them, 'How otherwise is it possible to test them?'
>
> [N] "They replied to him, 'Whoever cannot uproot a cedar of Lebanon while riding on his horse will not be inscribed on your military rolls.'
>
> [O] "So there were two hundred thousand who qualified in one way, and another two hundred thousand who qualified in another way."

[P] When he would go forth to battle, he would say, "Lord of the world! Do not help and do not hinder us! 'Hast thou not rejected us, O God? Thou dost not go forth, O God, with our armies'(Ps. 60:10)."

[Q] Three and a half years did Hadrian besiege Betar.

[R] R. Eleazar of Modiin would sit on sackcloth and ashes and pray every day, saying "Lord of the ages! Do not judge in accord with strict judgment this day! Do not judge in accord with strict judgment this day!"

[S] He got into the city through a drain pipe. He went and found R. Eleazar of Modiin standing and praying. He pretended to whisper something in his ear.

[T] The townspeople saw [the Samaritan] do this and brought him to Ben Kozeba. They told him, "We saw this man having dealings with your friend."

[U] [Bar Kokhba] said to him, "What did you say to him, and what did he say to you?"

[V] He said to [the Samaritan], "If I tell you, then the king will kill me, and if I do not tell you, then you will kill me. It is better that the king kill me, and not you.

[W] "[Eleazar] said to me, 'I should hand over my city.' ['I shall make peace....']"

[X] He turned to R. Eleazar of Modiin. He said to him, "What did this Samaritan say to you?"

[Y] He replied, "Nothing."

[Z] He said to him, "What did you say to him?"

[AA] He said to him, "Nothing."

[BB] [Ben Kozeba] gave [Eleazar] one good kick and killed him.

[CC] Forthwith an echo came forth and proclaimed the following verse:

[DD] "'Woe to my worthless shepherd, who deserts the flock! May the sword smite his arm and his right eye! Let his arm be wholly withered, his right eye utterly blinded!' (Zech. 11:17).

[EE] "You have murdered R. Eleazar of Modiin, the right arm of all Israel, and their right eye. Therefore may the right arm of that man wither, may his right eye be utterly blinded!"

[FF] Forthwith Betar was taken, and Ben Kozeba was killed.

Y. Taanit 4:5

We notice two complementary themes. First, Bar Kokhba treats Heaven with arrogance, asking God merely to keep out of the way. Second, he treats an especially revered sage with a parallel arrogance. The sage had the power to preserve Israel. Bar Kokhba destroyed Israel's one protection. The result was inevitable. The Messiah, the centerpiece of salvation history and hero of the tale, emerged as a critical figure. The historical theory of this Yerushalmi passage is stated very simply. In sages' view Israel had to choose between wars, either the war fought by Bar Kokhba or the "war for Torah." "Why had they been punished? It was because of the weight of the war, for they had not wanted to engage in the struggles over the meaning of the Torah" (Y. Ta. 3:9 XVI I). Those struggles, which were ritual arguments about ritual matters, promised the only victory worth winning. Then Israel's history would be written in terms of wars over the meaning of the Torah and the decision of the law.

True, the skins are new, but the wine is very old. For while we speak of sages and learning, the message is the familiar one. It is Israel's history that works out and expresses Israel's relationship with God. The critical dimension of Israel's life, therefore, is salvation, the definitive trait, a movement in time from now to then. It follows that the paramount and organizing category is history and its lessons. In the Yerushalmi we witness, among the Mishnah's heirs, a striking reversion to biblical convictions about the centrality of history in the definition of Israel's reality. The heavy weight of prophecy and apocalyptic and biblical historiography, with their emphasis upon salvation and on history as the indicator of Israel's salvation, stood against the Mishnah's quite separate thesis of what truly mattered. What, from their viewpoint, demanded description and analysis and required interpretation? It was the category of sanctification, for eternity. The true issue framed by history and apocalypse was how to move toward the foreordained end of salvation, how to act in time to reach salvation at the end of time. The Mishnah's teleology beyond time and its capacity to posit an eschatology without a place for a historical Mishnah take a position beyond that of the entire antecedent sacred literature of Israel. Only one strand, the priestly one, had ever taken so extreme a position on the centrality of sanctification and the peripheral nature of salvation. Wisdom had stood in between, with its own concerns, drawing attention both to what happened and to what endured. But to Wisdom what finally mattered was not nature or supernature, but rather abiding relationships in historical time.

The Talmud of Babylonia, at the end, carried forward the innovations we have seen in the Talmud of the Land of Israel. In the view expressed here, the principal result of Israel's loyal adherence to the Torah and its religious duties will be Israel's humble acceptance of God's rule. The humility, under all conditions, makes God love Israel.

> "It was not because you were greater than any people that the Lord set his love upon you and chose you" (Deut. 7:7). The Holy One, blessed be He, said to Israel, "I love you because even when I bestow greatness upon you, you humble yourselves before me. I bestowed greatness upon Abraham, yet he said to me, 'I am but dust and ashes' (Gen. 18:27); upon Moses and Aaron, yet they said, 'But I am a worm and no man' (Ps. 22:7). But with the heathens it is not so. I bestowed greatness upon Nimrod, and he said, 'Come, let us build us a city' (Gen. 11:4); upon Pharaoh, and he said, 'Who are they among all the gods of the counties?' (2 Kgs. 18:35); upon Nebuchadnezzar, and he said, 'I will ascend above

the heights of the clouds' (Isa. 14:14); upon Hiram, king of Tyre, and he
said, 'I sit in the seat of God, in the heart of the seas' (Ezek. 28:2)."

B. Hullin 89a

So the system emerges complete, each of its parts stating precisely the
same message as is revealed in the whole. The issue of the Messiah and
the meaning of Israel's history framed through the Messiah myth convey
in their terms precisely the same position that we find everywhere else in
all other symbolic components of the rabbinic system and canon. The
heart of the matter then is Israel's subservience to God's will, as
expressed in the Torah and embodied in the teachings and lives of the
great sages. When Israel fully accepts God's rule, then the Messiah will
come. Until Israel subjects itself to God's rule, the Jews will be
subjugated to pagan domination. Since the condition of Israel governs,
Israel itself holds the key to its own redemption. But this it can achieve
only by throwing away the key!

The paradox must be crystal clear: Israel acts to redeem itself
through the opposite of self-determination, namely, by subjugating itself
to God. Israel's power lies in its negation of power. Its destiny lies in
giving up all pretense at deciding its own destiny. So weakness is the
ultimate strength, forbearance the final act of self-assertion, passive
resignation the sure step toward liberation. (The parallel is the crucified
Christ.) Israel's freedom is engraved on the tablets of the
commandments of God: To be free is freely to obey. That is not the
meaning associated with these words in the minds of others who, like the
sages of the rabbinical canon, declared their view of what Israel must do
to secure the coming of the Messiah. The passage, praising Israel for its
humility, completes the circle begun with the description of Bar Kokhba
as arrogant and boastful. Gentile kings are boastful; Israelite kings are
humble. There is no distinguishing the Bavli's from the Yerushalmi's
Messiah doctrine or use of the Messiah theme; differences emerge in
nuance alone, not in the characterization and definition of the category
nor in the functioning of the category.

When constructing a systematic account of Judaism – that is, the
worldview and way of life for Israel presented in the Mishnah – the
philosophers of the Mishnah did not make use of the Messiah myth in
the construction of a teleology for their system. They found it possible to
present a statement of goals for their projected life of Israel which was
entirely separate from appeals to history and eschatology. Since they
certainly knew, and even alluded to, long-standing and widely held
convictions on eschatological subjects, beginning with those in Scripture,
the framers thereby testified that, knowing the larger repertoire, they
made choices different from others before and after them. Their

document accurately and ubiquitously expresses these choices, both affirmative and negative.

Second, the appearance of a messianic eschatology fully consonant with the larger characteristic of the rabbinic system – with its stress on the viewpoints and prooftexts of Scripture, its interest in what was happening to Israel, its focus upon the national-historical dimension of the life of the group – indicates that the encompassing rabbinic system set forth by the first, then the second, Talmud stands essentially autonomous of the prior, Mishnaic system. True, what had gone before was absorbed and fully assimilated, but the rabbinic system first appearing in the Talmud of the Land of Israel is different in the aggregate from the Mishnaic system, and there is no differentiating the second from the first Talmud in the matter of the Messiah.

Having alleged that the second Talmud's hermeneutics forms the theological medium for the first Talmud's religious message, my task is now to demonstrate how hermeneutics in a rabbinic document in fact conveys a theological proposition. For that purpose we take up a document that defines for itself a major position in the sequence of writings through which Judaism stated its theology.

7

Out of Hermeneutics:
How a Scriptural Text Yields
Its Theological Program

Having alleged that the Bavli's theology reaches us through the medium of its hermeneutics, and, further, that its hermeneutics marked a fundamental step beyond that of the Yerushalmi, I now pause to make certain my premise is clear. It is that hermeneutics can bear a theological message, and that how a text is explicated constitutes, in itself, a profoundly theological statement. Without having been shown how these premises yield concrete results, results that are, as a matter of fact, blatant and incontrovertible, readers will find difficult what are, in fact, the rather obvious propositions of Chapters Eight through Eleven. So we turn aside to examine a fine case in which a text yields its theological program, not by specifying the propositions of that program in so many words, but by repeatedly reading a received text in such a way as to make clear the propositions that are subject to demonstration.

Sifra, a commentary to Leviticus, provides a definitive example of what I mean by finding theology set forth in and as hermeneutics.[1] It

---

[1] It is an appropriate choice for a subjective reason as well. It was when I was translating and analyzing Sifra that I realized for the first time how the hermeneutics of the text – and no other element or component of that text – was utilized to convey, instantiate, and demonstrate a single, sustained, and unfolding theological argument. This is spelled out in *Uniting the Dual Torah: Sifra and the Problem of the Mishnah* (Cambridge and New York, 1989: Cambridge University Press); and *Sifra in Perspective: The Documentary Comparison of the Midrashim of Ancient Judaism* (Atlanta, 1988: Scholars Press for Brown Judaic Studies). At that time I even considered a further exercise, showing that there is a sequential hermeneutics in Sifra, with a shift from point one to point two and onward through the document; but it struck me as demonstrable but not worth the effort, at this time. I did bury some hints on that matter in *Uniting the Dual*

places on display the union of the message, method, and medium of the theology of Judaism. That is to say, when a document repeatedly raises a single question, the character of that question – more than the answers that it elicits – bears the weight of the structure, the main beam of the document's construction. The premise of the question then defines the document's principal point. Governing thought by focusing attention on one problem, rather than some other, the paramount question imposes a reading on the document and makes of the entire writing an exercise in demonstrating the premise of the perennial inquiry. For example, writers of a commentary to a text may formulate the same question time and again. That question may produce diverse answers, but it governs how we shall read the received text and dictates what we shall find out about it. Then the program for reading the document – the principles of hermeneutics that govern throughout – not only guides understanding the text at hand; it also contains a deeper point, a subtext that the text throughout is made to bear.

Now, if that principle of reading the received text has a bearing on the character of the Torah – its definition, its composition, the relationship of its parts – then the document's authors have given us not merely a set of statements about the meaning of a book of the Torah (whether a pentateuchal book or a Mishnah tractate). They have also made out of their exegesis of the received text a theological statement, itself nowhere articulated but everywhere present. And that becomes the definition of their document and – so I maintain – their purpose in writing their commentary. These then form the program that requires clarification and demonstration:

[1] Judaism states its theology through a distinctive hermeneutics, and [2] the document the hermeneutics of which re-presents that theology is the Talmud, so that, [3] when we know the unique hermeneutics of the Talmud, we also can define the theology of Judaism, which is to say, the intellectual quest for clarity about the Torah and its view of reality in the eternal perspective of the Torah.

That entire burden depends upon that interpretation of the meaning of the Talmud's hermeneutics. For (so I allege) here we describe a system whose theology is given form in hermeneutics. That theology is brought to expression through repetition of the same hermeneutical program. This is done in such a way as to demonstrate not solely the right meaning of one or another passage of the Torah (Written or Oral)

Torah. But it seems to me that if someone wants to show the unfolding of a program in the substrate of the exegetical results of the treatment of a given document of the Written or Oral Torah, the work should be done on a broader basis than a single document.

but the deep layers of truth that the Torah, all together and everywhere, exposes through a particular and universal rationality. That is what I mean when I maintained in Chapter Two that the hermeneutics of a text may form the medium for its theological system and itself not only convey but constitute the theological message of that system. That is to say, the message will be never stated in so many words but always repeated in a single result, everywhere achieved; none able to grasp the result (which is, in the nature of things, abstruse) could ever have missed the message.

My concrete example of what I mean by a theological re-presentation of a religious (revealed) truth is provided by Sifra, a compilation of exegesis of the book of Leviticus in Sifra, in fact, a sustained and disciplined theological disquisition in the form of a commentary and in the medium of the hermeneutics of that commentary. Focused upon the relationship between the Mishnah and Scripture, Sifra cites the Mishnah verbatim and therefore derives from the period ca. 200-300. What we shall see is, first, how Dalferth's definition of theology as philosophical method applied to religious data comes to expression in a writing, and, more to the point, second, my insistence that hermeneutics bears the theological re-presentation. First, to meet the simplest of Dalferth's requirements of a theological writing:

1. A. "And the Lord said to Moses, Say to all the congregation of the people of Israel, You shall be holy, [for I the Lord your God am holy. Every one of you shall revere his mother and his father, and you shall keep my sabbaths; I am the Lord your God. Do not turn to idols or make for yourselves molten gods; I am the Lord your God]" (Lev. 19:1-4):

2. A. "You shall be holy":
    B. "You shall be separate."

3. A. "You shall be holy, for I the Lord your God am holy":
    B. That is to say, "If you sanctify yourselves, I shall credit it to you as though you had sanctified me, and if you do not sanctify yourselves, I shall hold that it is as if you have not sanctified me."
    C. Or perhaps the sense is this: "If you sanctify me, then lo, I shall be sanctified, and if not, I shall not be sanctified"?
    D. Scripture says, "For I...am holy," meaning, I remain in my state of sanctification, whether or not you sanctify me.
    E. Abba Saul says, "The king has a retinue, and what is the task thereof? It is to imitate the king."

Sifra CXCV:I.1-3

The important point comes at No. 3, where the framer of the passage not only interprets the received declaration "you shall be holy" as "you shall be separate," but also conducts an argument on his interpretation, thus 3.C raises that issue in so many words. Where the argument is joined,

3.C, theological reconsideration of religious truth gets underway; then the argument comes to resolution in the citation of yet another established fact, D, which is invoked to set the first proposition, A-B, into its proper position. Here is where exegesis shades over into argument, religion into theology. That is a small matter, but an important consideration.

Sifra in fact employs a well-defined and restricted program of formal and rhetorical conventions to set forth within a single system of logical cogency an encompassing argument and determinate proposition. And the proposition at hand, as a matter of fact, is argued as a philosophical one, concerning the sources of (hierarchical) classification. But it concerns the character of the Torah, hence is to be classified as theological. The issue of philosophy concerns the principles of hierarchical classification: how we classify things and order them. The Mishnah's framers maintain that on the basis of the inherent traits of things it is entirely possible to conduct the labor of classification, therefore also of the hierarchization of things. That philosophical position, fully in accord with the norms of natural history, is subjected to severe criticism by Sifra. The framers of Sifra cogently argue, to the contrary, on the basis of the evidence of reason alone – that is, the premises of the Mishnah itself – that hierarchical classification can be conducted solely on the foundations of the revealed categories of the Torah.

Their premise is the religious one that the Torah encompasses all truth. Their mode of argument is a philosophical one, rigorous argument, appealing to monothetic and polythetic taxonomy and its rules, concerning the correct media of classification. Their achievement is to present a theological statement. That statement, rigorously argued, carefully spelled out in numerous examples, is about the proper means of classification deriving solely from the Torah: from philosophy, through religion, to theology. It is a statement made not in so many words but in a great many examples of a single, singular reading of the Written Torah and the Oral Torah together, wholly in communication with one another. The means of that re-presentation of the character of the Torah is the hermeneutics that governs in the reading of Leviticus. So, as I said, here I present my first significant example of the message, method, and medium of the theology of Judaism.

We start with the literary-critical problem: the formal conventions characteristic of Sifra in particular. All compositions and composites of the document conform to one of three forms. The first, the dialectical, is the demonstration that if we wish to classify things, we must follow the taxa – the classification system – dictated by Scripture rather than relying solely upon the traits of the things we wish to classify. The second, the citation form, invokes the citation of passages of the Mishnah or the Tosefta in the setting of Scripture. The third is what I call commentary form, in which a phrase of Scripture is followed by an amplificatory clause of some sort. The forms of the document admirably expressed the polemical purpose of the authorship at hand. What they wished to prove was that a taxonomy resting on the traits of things without reference to Scripture's classifications cannot serve. They further wished to restate the Oral Torah in the setting of the Written Torah. And, finally, they wished to accomplish the whole by rewriting the Written Torah – writing with Scripture is what I call it. The dialectical form accomplishes the first purpose, the citation form the second, and the commentary form the third.

The simple commentary form requires a verse, or an element of a verse, that is cited, and then a very few words explain the meaning of that verse. Second come the complex forms, in which a simple exegesis is augmented in some important way, commonly by questions and answers, so that we have more than simply a verse and a brief exposition of its elements or of its meaning as a whole. The authorship of the Sifra time and again wishes to show that prior documents, Mishnah or Tosefta, cited verbatim, require the support of exegesis of Scripture for important propositions, presented in the Mishnah and the Tosefta not on the foundation of exegetical proof at all. In the main, moreover, the authorship of Sifra tends not to attribute its materials to specific authorities, and most of the pericopae containing attributions are shared with Mishnah and Tosefta. When Sifra uses forms other than those in which its exegeses are routinely phrased, it commonly, though not always, draws upon materials also found in Mishnah and Tosefta. It is uncommon for Sifra to make use of nonexegetical forms for materials peculiar to its compilation. As a working hypothesis, to be corrected presently, the forms of rhetorical patterning of language in Sifra are two, simple and complex.

Every example of a complex form, that is, a passage in which we have more than a cited verse and a brief exposition of its meaning, may be called "dialectical," that is, moving or developing an idea through questions and answers, sometimes implicit, but commonly explicit. What "moves" is the argument, the flow of thought, from problem to problem. The movement is generated by the raising of contrary questions and theses. There are several subdivisions of the dialectical exegesis, so distinctive as to be treated by themselves. But all exhibit a flow of logical argument, unfolding in questions and answers, characteristic, in the later literature, of the Talmud. One important subdivision of the stated form consists of those items, somewhat few in number but all rather large in size and articulation, intended to prove that logic alone is insufficient, and that only through revealed law will a reliable view of what is required be attained. The polemic in these items is pointed and obvious; logic (DYN) never wins the argument, though at a few points flaws in the text seem to suggest disjunctures in the flow of logic. There are some few instances of this form in Mekhilta Attributed to R. Ishmael.

The rhetorical plan of Sifra leads us to recognize that the exegetes, while working verse by verse, in fact have brought a considerable well-defined program to their reading of the book of Leviticus. They did not look at the book of Leviticus first, but knew what they wished to find there before they opened the book. What they wanted to say concerns the interplay of the Oral Torah, represented by the Mishnah, with the Written Torah, represented by the book of Leviticus. That question demanded, in their view, not an answer comprising mere generalities. They wished to show their results through details, masses of details, and, like the rigorous philosophers that they were, they furthermore argued essentially through an inductive procedure, amassing evidence that in its accumulation made the point at hand. The syllogism I have identified about the priority of the revelation of the Written Torah in the search for truth is nowhere expressed in so many words, because the philosopher exegetes of the rabbinic world preferred to address an implicit syllogism and to pursue or to test that syllogism solely in a sequence of experiments of a small scale. Sifra's authorship therefore finds in the Mishnah and Tosefta a sizable laboratory for the testing of propositions.

To clarify these general remarks, let us now address a particular chapter of Sifra and out of its details form a theory of the repertoire of forms on which our authorship has drawn.

14.
Parashat Vayyiqra Dibura Denedabah Parashah 7

I.1   A.   ["If his offering to the Lord is a burnt-offering of birds, he shall choose [bring near] his offering from turtledoves or pigeons. The priest shall bring it to the altar, pinch off its head, and turn it into smoke on the altar; and its blood shall be drained out against the side of the altar. He shall remove its crop with its contents and cast it into the place of the ashes, at the east side of the altar. The priest shall tear it open by its wings, without severing it, and turn it into smoke on the altar, upon the wood that is on the fire. It is a burnt-offering, an offering by fire, of pleasing odor to the Lord" (Lev. 1:14-17)]:

        B.   "[The priest] shall bring it [to the altar]":

        C.   What is the sense of this statement?

        D.   Since it is said, "He shall choose [bring near] his offering from turtledoves or pigeons," one might have supposed that there can be no fewer than two sets of birds.

E.   Accordingly, Scripture states, "[The priest] shall bring it [to the altar]," to indicate, [by reference to the "it,"] that even a single pair suffices.

Reduced to its simplest syntactic traits, the form consists of the citation of a clause of a verse, followed by secondary amplification of that clause. We may call this commentary form, in that the rhetorical requirement is citation plus amplification. Clearly, the form sustains a variety of expressions, for example, the one at hand: "What is the sense of this statement...since it is said...accordingly Scripture states...." But for our purposes there is no need to differentiate within the commentary form.

2.   A.   "The priest shall bring it to the altar, pinch off its head":
     B.   Why does Scripture say, "The priest...pinch off..."?
     C.   This teaches that the act of pinching off the head should be done only by a priest.
     D.   But is the contrary to that proposition not a matter of logic:
     E.   If in the case of a beast of the flock, to which the act of slaughter at the north side of the altar is assigned, the participation of a priest in particular is not assigned, to the act of pinching the neck, to which the act of slaughter at the north side of the altar is not assigned, surely should not involve the participation of the priest in particular!
     F.   That is why it is necessary for Scripture to say, "The priest...pinch off...,"
     G.   so as to teach that the act of pinching off the head should be done only by a priest.
3.   A.   Might one compose an argument to prove that one should pinch the neck by using a knife?
     B.   For lo, it is a matter of logic.
     C.   If to the act of slaughter [of a beast as a sacrifice], for which the participation of a priest is not required, the use of a correct utensil is required, for the act of pinching the neck, for which the participation of a priest indeed is required, surely should involve the requirement of using a correct implement!
     D.   That is why it is necessary for Scripture to say, "The priest...pinch off...."
4.   A.   Said R. Aqiba, "Now would it really enter anyone's mind that a nonpriest should present an offering on the altar?
     B.   "Then why is it said, 'The priest...pinch off...'?
     C.   "This teaches that the act of pinching the neck must be done by the priest using his own finger [and not a utensil]."
5.   A.   Might one suppose that the act of pinching may be done either at the head [up by the altar] or at the foot [on the pavement down below the altar]?
     B.   It is a matter of logic:
     C.   If in the case of an offering of a beast, which, when presented as a sin-offering is slaughtered above [at the altar itself] but when slaughtered as a burnt-offering is killed below [at the pavement, below the altar], in the case of an offering of fowl, since when

presented as a sin-offering it is slaughtered down below, surely in the case of a burnt-offering it should be done down below as well!

D.   That is why it was necessary for Scripture to make explicit [that it is killed up by the altar itself]: "The priest shall bring it to the altar, pinch off its head, and turn it into smoke on the altar."

E.   The altar is explicitly noted with respect to turning the offering into smoke and also to pinching off the head.

F.   Just as the offering is turned into smoke up above, at the altar itself, so the pinching off of the head is to be done up above, at the altar itself.

The form at hand is to be characterized as a dialectical exegetical argument, in which we move from point to point in a protracted, yet very tight, exposition of a proposition. The proposition is both implicit and explicit. The implicit proposition is that "logic" does not suffice, a matter vastly spelled out in *Uniting the Dual Torah*. The explicit proposition concerns the subject matter at hand. We may identify the traits of this form very simply: citation of a verse or clause + a proposition that interprets that phrase, then "it is a matter of logic" followed by the demonstration that logic is insufficient for the determination of taxa.

III.1   A.   "...and its blood shall be drained out [against the side of the altar]":

         B.   all of its blood: he takes hold of the head and the body and drains the blood out of both pieces.

This is commentary form.

III.2   A.   "...against the side of the altar":

         B.   not on the wall of the ramp up to the altar, and not on the wall of the foundation, nor on the wall of the courtyard.

III.3   A.   It is to be on the upper half of the wall.

         B.   Might one suppose it may be on the lower half of the wall?

         C.   It is a matter of logic: In the case of the sacrifice of a beast, which, if done as a sin-offering, has its blood tossed on the upper part of the wall, and if done as a burnt-offering, has its blood tossed on the lower part of the wall,

         D.   in the case of the sacrifice of a bird, since, if it is offered as a sin-offering, the blood is tossed at the lower half of the wall, should logic not dictate that if it is offered as a burnt-offering, its blood should be tossed on the lower part of the wall as well?

         E.   That is why it is necessary for Scripture to frame matters in this way:

         F.   "The priest shall bring it to the altar, pinch off its head, and turn it into smoke on the altar; and its blood shall be drained out against the side of the altar,"

         G.   the altar is noted with respect to turning the carcass into smoke and also with reference to the draining of the blood.

> H.   Just as the act of turning the carcass into smoke is done at the
> topside of the altar, so the draining of the blood is done at the
> topside of the altar.

This is the dialectical exegetical form. Now we come to a third usage.

> III.4   A.   How does the priest do it?
>   B.   **The priest went up on the ramp and went around the circuit. He**
>   **came to the southeastern corner. He would wring off its head**
>   **from its neck and divide the head from the body. And he drained**
>   **off its blood onto the wall of the altar [M. Zeb. 6:5B-E].**
>   C.   **If one did it from the place at which he was standing and**
>   **downward by a cubit, it is valid. R. Simeon and R. Yohanan ben**
>   **Beroqah say, "The entire deed was done only at the top of the**
>   **altar" [T. Zeb. 7:9C-D].**

What we have now is the verbatim citation of a passage of the
Mishnah or of the Tosefta, joined to its setting in the exegetical
framework of Sifra by some sort of joining formula. We shall call this
formal convention Mishnah citation form. Its formal requirement is
simply appropriate joining language.

The operative logics of Sifra are mainly propositional. What the
authorship of Sifra wished to prove was that a taxonomy resting on the
traits of things without reference to Scripture's classifications cannot
serve. They further wished to restate the Oral Torah in the setting of the
Written Torah. And, finally, they wished to accomplish the whole by
rewriting the Written Torah. The dialectical form accomplished the first
purpose, the citation form the second, and the commentary form the
third.

For its topical program the authorship of Sifra takes the book of
Leviticus. For propositions Sifra's authorship presents episodic and ad
hoc sentences. If we ask how these sentences form propositions other
than amplifications of points made in the book of Leviticus itself, and
how we may restate those propositions in a coherent way, so far as I can
see, nothing sustained and coherent emerges. Without leading the
reader through all two hundred seventy-seven chapters of Sifra, I state
simply that Sifra does not constitute a propositional document in any
dimension ever transcending its precipitating text. I fail to see a topical
program distinct from that of Scripture, nor do I find it possible to set
forth important propositions that transcend the cases at hand. Sifra
remains wholly within Scripture's orbit and range of discourse,
proposing only to expand and clarify what it found within Scripture.

Where the authorship moves beyond Scripture, it is not toward fresh
theological or philosophical thought, but rather to a quite different set of
issues altogether. These concern the Mishnah and Tosefta, which frame
the program of Sifra. Even at the very surface we observe a simple fact.

Without the Mishnah or the Tosefta, our authorship would have had virtually nothing to say about one passage after another of the Written Torah in Leviticus. It follows that the three basic and definitive traits of Sifra, are, first, its total adherence to the topical program of the Written Torah for order and plan; second, its very common reliance upon the phrases or verses of the Written Torah for the joining into coherent discourse of discrete thoughts, for example, comments on, or amplifications of, words or phrases; and third, its equally profound dependence upon the Oral Torah for its program of thought: the problematic that defines the issues the authorship wishes to explore and resolve.

While Sifra in detail presents no paramount propositions, Sifra seen whole demonstrates a highly distinctive and vigorously demonstrated proposition. While in detail we cannot reconstruct a topical program other than that of Scripture, viewed in its indicative and definitive traits of rhetoric, logic, and implicit proposition, Sifra does take up a well-composed position on a fundamental issue, namely, the relationship between the Written Torah, represented by the book of Leviticus, and the Oral Torah, represented by the passages of the Mishnah deemed by the authorship of Sifra to be pertinent to the book of Leviticus. In a simple and fundamental sense, Sifra joins the two Torahs into a single statement, accomplishing a re-presentation of the Written Torah in topic and in program and in the logic of cogent discourse, and within that rewriting of the Written Torah, a re-presentation of the Oral Torah in its paramount problematic and in many of its substantive propositions.

Stated simply, the Written Torah provides the form, the Oral Torah, the content. What emerges is not merely a united, Dual Torah, but *The* Torah, stated whole and complete, in the context defined by the book of Leviticus. Here the authorship of Sifra presents, through its re-presentation, The Torah as a proper noun, all together, all at once, and, above all, complete and utterly coherent. In order to do so our authorship has constructed through its document, first, the sustained critique of the Mishnah's mode of thought, worked out through making lists to prove the hierarchical structure of all being, properly classified and ordered, then, the defense of the Mishnah's propositions on the foundation of scriptural principles of taxonomy, hierarchical classification in particular.

The compilers of Sifra and the other documents of its class do not merely assemble this and that, forming a hodgepodge of things people happen to have said: scrapbooks. In the case of each document we can answer the question of topic as much as of rhetoric and logic: Why this, not that? That is to say, why discuss this topic in this pattern of language and resort to this logic of cogent discourse, rather than treating some other topic in a different set of language patterns and relying on other modes of making connections and drawing conclusions? These are questions that we have now answered for Sifra. Sifra presents a proposition distinctive to its authorship, solving a problem identified by that authorship as urgent. Now to see how in a concrete text these things are accomplished.

The authorship of Sifra thus undertook a vast polemic against the logic of classification that forms the foundation of the system of the Mishnah. This they did two ways. The first, and less important, was to demonstrate that the Mishnah's rules required exegetical foundations. The second, and paramount, way was to attack the very logic by which the Mishnah's authorship developed its points. To understand the theological polemic of Sifra, therefore, we have to grasp the fundamental logical basis for the workings of the Mishnah. Then we shall see in its polemical context the recurrent statement of the authorship of Sifra: *Classification does not work, because there is no genus, but only species.*

Therefore the Mishnah's insistence on listing things that have the same traits and identifying the rule that governs those things, then setting things into relationship (higher, lower) with one another – its insistence that things are either like one another, therefore follow the same rule, or opposite to one another, therefore follow the opposite rule – these fundamental building blocks of Mishnaic thought prove deeply flawed. For if nothing is ever really like something else, then we cannot classify different things together, as the same thing. And, it follows, we also can make no lists of things that, whether in a polythetic or a monothetic framework, follow the same rule and therefore generate a generalization. Since, as we shall now see, the logic of the Mishnah begins with the premise that diverse species form a single genus, so can be subjected to comparison and contrast, that dogged insistence, time and again, upon the incomparability of species, forms a fundamental critique of the practical reason of the Mishnah. A full appreciation of matters now requires that we dwell at some length upon the system of the Mishnah.

First, we shall observe a sequence of cases in which Sifra's authorship demonstrates that *Listenwissenschaft* is a self-evidently valid mode of demonstrating the truth of propositions. Second, we shall note, in the same cases, that *the* source of the correct classification of things is Scripture and only Scripture. Without Scripture's intervention into the taxonomy of the world, we should have no knowledge at all of which things fall into which classifications and therefore are governed by which rules. Let us begin with a sustained example of the right way of doing things. Appropriately, the opening composition of Sifra shows the contrast between relying on Scripture's classification, and the traits imputed by Scripture to the taxa it identifies, and appealing to categories not defined and endowed with indicative traits by Scripture.

Parashat Vayyiqra Dibura Denedabah Parashah 1

I.1 A. "The Lord called [to Moses] and spoke [to him from the tent of meeting, saying, 'Speak to the Israelite people and say to them']" (Lev. 1:1):

B. He gave priority to the calling over the speaking.

C. That is in line with the usage of Scripture.

D. Here there is an act of speaking, and in connection with the encounter at the bush [Ex. 3:4: "God called to him out of the bush, 'Moses, Moses'"], there is an act of speaking.

E. Just as in the latter occasion, the act of calling is given priority over the act of speaking [even though the actual word, "speaking" does not occur, it is implicit in the framing of the verse], so here, with respect to the act of speaking, the act of calling is given priority over the act of speaking.

I.2 A. No, [you cannot generalize on the basis of that case,] for if you invoke the case of the act of speaking at the bush, which is the first in the sequence of acts of speech [on which account, there had to be a call prior to entry into discourse],

B. will you say the same of the act of speech in the tent of meeting, which assuredly is not the first in a sequence of acts of speech [so there was no need for a preliminary entry into discourse through a call]?

C. The act of speech at Mount Sinai [Ex. 19:3] will prove to the contrary, for it is assuredly not the first in a sequence of acts of speech, yet, in that case, there was an act of calling prior to the act of speech.

I.3 A. No, [the exception proves nothing,] for if you invoke in evidence the act of speech at Mount Sinai, which pertained to all the Israelites, will you represent it as parallel to the act of speech in the tent of meeting, which is not pertinent to all Israel?

B. Lo, you may sort matters out by appeal to comparison and contrast, specifically:

C. The act of speech at the bush, which is the first of the acts of speech, is not of the same classification as the act of speech at Sinai, which is not the first act of speech.

D. And the act of speech at Sinai, which is addressed to all Israel, is not in the same classification as the act of speech at the bush, which is not addressed to all Israel.

I.4 A. What they have in common, however, is that both of them are acts of speech, deriving from the mouth of the Holy One, addressed to Moses, in which case, the act of calling comes prior to the act of speech,

B. so that, by way of generalization, we may maintain that every act of speech which comes from the mouth of the Holy One to Moses will be preceded by an act of calling.

I.5 A. Now if what the several occasions have in common is that all involve an act of speech, accompanied by fire, from the mouth of the Holy One, addressed to Moses, so that the act of calling was given priority over the act of speaking, then every case in which there is an act of speech, involving fire, from the mouth of the Holy One, addressed to Moses, should involve an act of calling prior to the act of speech.

B.   But then an exception is presented by the act of speech at the tent of meeting, in which there was no fire.

C.   [That is why it was necessary for Scripture on this occasion to state explicitly,] "The Lord called [to Moses and spoke to him from the tent of meeting, saying, 'Speak to the Israelite people and say to them']" (Lev. 1:1).

D.   That explicit statement shows that, on the occasion at hand, priority was given to the act of calling over the act of speaking.

II.1   A.   ["The Lord called to Moses and spoke to him from the tent of meeting, saying, 'Speak to the Israelite people and say to them'" (Lev. 1:1)]: Might one suppose that the act of calling applied only to this act of speaking alone?

B.   And how on the basis of Scripture do we know that on the occasion of all acts of speaking that are mentioned in the Torah, [there was a prior act of calling]?

C.   Scripture specifies, "From the tent of meeting,"

D.   which bears the sense that on every occasion on which it was an act of speaking from the tent of meeting, there was an act of calling prior to the act of speaking.

II.2   A.   Might one suppose that there was an act of calling only prior to the acts of speech alone?

B.   How on the basis of Scripture do I know that the same practice accompanied acts of saying and also acts of commanding?

C.   Said R. Simeon, "Scripture says not only, '...spoke,...,' but '...and he spoke,' [with the inclusion of the *and*] meant to encompass also acts of telling and also acts of commanding."

The exercise of generalization addresses the character of God's meeting with Moses. The point of special interest is the comparison of the meeting at the bush and the meeting at the tent of meeting. And at stake is asking whether all acts of God's calling and talking with, or speaking to, the prophet are the same, or whether some of these acts are of a different classification from others. In point of fact, we are able to come to a generalization, worked out at I:I.5.A. And that permits us to explain why there is a different usage at Lev. 1:1 from what characterizes parallel cases. I:II.1-2 proceeds to generalize from the case at hand to other usages entirely, a very satisfying conclusion to the whole. I separate I:II from I:I because had I:I ended at 5, it could have stood complete and on its own, and therefore I see I:II as a brief appendix. The interest for my argument should not be missed. We seek generalizations, governing rules, that are supposed to emerge by the comparison and contrast of categories or of classifications. The way to do this is to follow the usage of Scripture, that alone. And the right way of doing things is then illustrated.   Now we seek rules that emerge from Scripture's classification.

LIV.1 A.   How on the basis of Scripture do we know that every act of speech involved the call to Moses, Moses [two times]?

B.   Scripture says, "God called to him out of the bush, 'Moses, Moses'" (Ex. 3:4).

C.   Now when Scripture says, "And he said," it teaches that every act of calling involved the call to Moses, Moses [two times].

LIV.2 A.   And how on the basis of Scripture do we know, furthermore, that at each act of calling, he responded, "Here I am"?

B.   Scripture says, "God called to him out of the bush, 'Moses, Moses,' and he said, 'Here I am'" (Ex. 3:4).

C.   Now when Scripture says, "And he said," it teaches that in response to each act of calling, he said, "Here I am."

LIV.3 A.   "Moses, Moses" ((Ex. 3:4), "Abraham, Abraham" (Gen. 22:11), "Jacob, Jacob" (Gen. 46:2), "Samuel, Samuel" (1 Sam. 3:10).

B.   This language expresses affection and also means to move to prompt response.

LIV.3 A.   Another interpretation of "Moses, Moses":

B.   This was the very same Moses both before he had been spoken with [by God] and also afterward.

The final unit completes the work of generalization which began with the opening passage. The point throughout is that there are acts of calling and speech, and a general rule pertains to them all. No. 3 and No. 4 conclude with observations outside of the besought generalization. The first of the two interprets the repetition of a name, the second, a conclusion particular to Moses personally. These seem to me tacked on. The first lesson in the rehabilitation of taxonomic logic is then clear. Let me state the proposition, which is demonstrated over and over again in rhetoric and logic: *Scripture provides reliable taxa and dictates the indicative characteristics of those taxa.*

The next step in the argument is to maintain that Scripture *alone* can set forth the proper names of things: classifications and their hierarchical order. How do we appeal to Scripture to designate the operative classifications? Here is a simple example of the alternative mode of classification, one that does not appeal to the traits of things but to the utilization of names by Scripture. What we see is how by naming things in one way, rather than in another, Scripture orders all things, classifying and, in the nature of things, also hierarchizing them.

Parashat Vayyiqra Dibura Denedabah Parashah 4

V.1   A.   "...and Aaron's sons the priests shall present the blood and throw the blood [round about against the altar that is at the door of the tent of meeting]":

    B.   Why does Scripture make use of the word "blood" twice [instead of using a pronoun]?

    C.   [It is for the following purpose:] How on the basis of Scripture do you know that if blood deriving from one burnt-offering was confused with blood deriving from another burnt-offering, blood deriving from one burnt-offering with blood deriving from a beast that has been substituted therefor, blood deriving from a burnt-offering with blood deriving from an unconsecrated beast, the mixture should nonetheless be presented?

    D.   It is because Scripture makes use of the word "blood" twice [instead of using a pronoun].

V.2   A.   It is possible to suppose that while if blood deriving from beasts in the specified classifications was confused, it is to be presented, for the simple reason that if the several beasts while alive had been confused with one another, they might be offered up,

    B.   but how do we know that even if the blood of a burnt-offering were confused with that of a beast killed as a guilt-offering, [it is to be offered up]?

    C.   I shall concede the case of the mixture of the blood of a burnt-offering confused with that of a beast killed as a guilt-offering, it is to be presented, for both this one and that one fall into the classification of Most Holy Things.

    D.   But how do I know that if the blood of a burnt-offering were confused with the blood of a beast slaughtered in the classification of peace-offerings or of a thanksgiving-offering, [it is to be presented]?

    E.   I shall concede the case of the mixture of the blood of a burnt-offering confused with that of a beast slaughtered in the classification of peace-offerings or of a thanksgiving-offering, [it is to be presented], because the beasts in both classifications produce blood that has to be sprinkled four times.

    F.   But how do I know that if the blood of a burnt-offering were confused with the blood of a beast slaughtered in the classification of a firstling or a beast that was counted as tenth or of a beast designated as a passover, [it is to be presented]?

    G.   I shall concede the case of the mixture of the blood of a burnt-offering confused with that of a beast slaughtered in the classification of firstling or a beast that was counted as tenth or of a beast designated as a passover, [it is to be presented], because Scripture uses the word "blood" two times.

    H.   Then while I may make that concession, might I also suppose that if the blood of a burnt-offering was confused with the blood of beasts that had suffered an invalidation, it also may be offered up?

    I.   Scripture says, "...its blood," [thus excluding such a case].

    J.   Then I shall concede the case of a mixture of the blood of a valid burnt-offering with the blood of beasts that had suffered an invalidation, which blood is not valid to be presented at all.

    K.   But how do I know that if such blood were mixed with the blood deriving from beasts set aside as sin-offerings to be offered on the inner altar, [it is not to be offered up]?

L.   I can concede that the blood of a burnt-offering that has been mixed with the blood deriving from beasts set aside as sin-offerings to be offered on the inner altar is not to be offered up, for the one is offered on the inner altar, and the other on the outer altar [the burnt-offering brought as a freewill-offering, under discussion here, is slaughtered at the altar "...that is at the door of the tent of meeting," not at the inner altar].

M.   But how do I know that even if the blood of a burnt-offering was confused with the blood of sin-offerings that are to be slaughtered at the outer altar, it is not to be offered up?

N.   Scripture says, "...its blood," [thus excluding such a case].

In place of the rejecting of arguments resting on classifying species into a common genus, we now demonstrate how classification really is to be carried on. It is through the imposition upon data of the categories dictated by Scripture: Scripture's use of language. That is the force of this powerful exercise. No. 1 sets the stage, simply pointing out that the use of the word "blood" twice encompasses a case in which blood in two distinct classifications is somehow confused in the process of the conduct of the cult. In such a case it is quite proper to pour out the mixture of blood deriving from distinct sources, for example, beasts that have served different, but comparable purposes. We then systemically work out the limits of that rule, showing how comparability works, then pointing to cases in which comparability is set aside. Throughout the exposition, at the crucial point we invoke the formulation of Scripture, subordinating logic or in our instance the process of classification of like species to the dictation of Scripture. I cannot imagine a more successful demonstration of what the framers wish to say.

From this simple account of the paramount position of Scripture in the labor of classification, let us turn to the specific way in which, because of Scripture's provision of taxa, we are able to undertake the science of *Listenwissenschaft*, including hierarchical classification, in the right way. What can we do because we appeal to Scripture, which we cannot do if we do not rely on Scripture? It is to establish the possibility of polythetic classification. We can appeal to shared traits of otherwise distinct taxa and so transform species into a common genus for a given purpose. Only Scripture makes that initiative feasible, so our authorship maintains. What is at stake? It is the possibility of doing precisely what the framers of the Mishnah wish to do. That is to join together masses of diverse data into a single, encompassing statement, to show the rule that inheres in diverse cases.

In what follows, we shall see an enormous, coherent, and beautifully articulated exercise in the comparison and contrast of many things of a single genus. The whole holds together, because Scripture makes possible the statement of all things within a single rule. That is, as we have noted, precisely what the framers of the Mishnah proposed to accomplish. Our authorship maintains that only by appeal to The Torah is this fete of learning possible. If, then, we wish to understand all things all together and all at once under a single encompassing rule, we had best revert to The Torah, with its account of the rightful names, positions, and order, imputed to all things.

Parashat Vayyiqra Dibura Denedabah Parashah 11

I.1   A.   [With reference to M. Men. 5:5:] There are those [offerings which require bringing near but do not require waving, waving but not bringing near, waving and bringing near, neither waving nor bringing near: These are offerings which require bringing near but do not require waving: the meal-offering of fine flour and the meal-offering prepared in the baking pan and the meal-offering prepared in the frying pan, and the meal-offering of cakes and the meal-offering of wafers, and the meal-offering of priests, and the meal-offering of an anointed priest, and the meal-offering of gentiles, and the meal-offering of women, and the meal-offering of a sinner. R. Simeon says, "The meal-offering of priests and of the anointed priest – bringing near does not apply to them, because the taking of a handful does not apply to them. And whatever is not subject to the taking of a handful is not subject to bringing near."] [Scripture] says, "When you present to the Lord a meal-offering that is made in any of these ways, it shall be brought [to the priest who shall take it up to the altar]":

        B.   What requires bringing near is only the handful alone. How do I know that I should encompass under the rule of bringing near the meal-offering?

        C.   Scripture says explicitly, "Meal-offering."

        D.   How do I know that I should encompass all meal-offerings?

        E.   Scripture says, using the accusative particle, "The meal-offering."

I.2   A.   I might propose that what requires bringing near is solely the meal-offering brought as a freewill-offering.

        B.   How do I know that the rule encompasses an obligatory meal-offering?

        C.   It is a matter of logic.

        D.   Bringing a meal-offering as a freewill-offering and bringing a meal-offering as a matter of obligation form a single classification. Just as a meal-offering presented as a freewill-offering requires bringing near, so the same rule applies to a meal-offering of a sinner [brought as a matter of obligation], which should likewise require bringing near.

        E.   No, if you have stated that rule governing bringing near in the case of a freewill-offering, on which oil and frankincense have to be added. will you say the same of the meal-offering of a sinner [Lev. 5:11], which does not require oil and frankincense?

        F.   The meal-offering brought by a wife accused of adultery will prove to the contrary, for it does not require oil and frankincense, but it does require bringing near [as is stated explicitly at Num. 5:15].

G. No, if you have applied the requirement of bringing near to the meal-offering brought by a wife accused of adultery, which also requires waving, will you say the same of the meal-offering of a sinner, which does not have to be waved?

H. Lo, you must therefore reason by appeal to a polythetic analogy [in which not all traits pertain to all components of the category, but some traits apply to them all in common]:

I. The meal-offering brought as a freewill-offering, which requires oil and frankincense, does not in all respects conform to the traits of the meal-offering of a wife accused of adultery, which does not require oil and frankincense, and the meal-offering of the wife accused of adultery, which requires waving, does not in all respects conform to the traits of a meal-offering brought as a freewill-offering, which does not require waving.

J. But what they have in common is that they are alike in requiring the taking up of a handful and they are also alike in that they require bringing near.

K. I shall then introduce into the same classification the meal-offering of a sinner, which is equivalent to them as to the matter of the taking up of a handful, and also should be equivalent to them as to the requirement of being drawn near.

L. But might one not argue that the trait that all have in common is that all of them may be brought equally by a rich and a poor person and require drawing near, which then excludes from the common classification the meal-offering of a sinner, which does not conform to the rule that it may be brought equally by a rich and a poor person, [but may be brought only by a poor person,] and such an offering also should not require being brought near!

M. [The fact that the polythetic classification yields indeterminate results means failure once more, and, accordingly,] Scripture states, "Meal-offering,"

N. with this meaning: All the same are the meal-offering brought as a freewill-offering and the meal-offering of a sinner, both this and that require being brought near.

The elegant exercise draws together the various types of meal-offerings and shows that they cannot form a classification of either a monothetic or a polythetic character. Consequently, Scripture must be invoked to supply the proof for the classification of the discrete items. The important language is at H-J: these differ from those, and those from these, but what they have in common is.... Then we demonstrate, with our appeal to Scripture, the sole valid source of polythetic classification, M. And this is constant throughout Sifra.

The strength of argument of our authorship is manifest in its capacity to demonstrate how diverse things relate through points in common, so long as the commonalities derive from a valid source. And that leads us to the central and fundamental premise of all: Scripture, its picture of the classifications of nature and supernature, its account of the rightful names and order of all things, is the sole source for that encompassing and generalizing principle that permits scientific inquiry into the governing laws to take place.   This tripartite subject of [1] the transformation of case to rule in Leviticus through the exercise of exclusion and inclusion; [2] the movement from rule to system and structure, hence the interest in taxonomy based on Scripture's classification system; and [3] the reunification of the two Torahs into a single statement, effected in part through commentary, in part through extensive citation of passages of the Mishnah and of the Tosefta – this is what I take to be the topic addressed by Sifra, together with its simple problematic: the relationship of the two Torahs not only in form but at the deepest structures of thought.

Now how, out of the hermeneutics illustrated in these passages, do I claim to identify a theological issue and our authorship's position on it? One critical polemic, fundamental to Sifra's purpose, is to demonstrate the inadequacy of reason unaided by revelation.   Time and again Sifra asks, Does this proposition, offered with a prooftext, really require the stated proof of revelation?   Will it not stand firmly upon the basis of autonomous reason, unaided by Scripture?   Sometimes Scripture will show that the opposite of the conclusion of reason is the result of exegesis.   Therefore the truth is to be discovered solely through exegesis. At other times Sifra will show that reason by itself is flawed and fallible, not definitive.   At important points it will seek to prove not only a given proposition, but also that that proposition is to be demonstrated solely through revelation, through exegesis of Scripture.   In all it is difficult to avoid the impression that the primary purpose of the compilers of Sifra is to criticize the Mishnah and the Tosefta, documents notoriously uninterested in the exegetical foundations of their laws.

The authorship of Sifra composed the one (and the only truly successful) document to accomplish the union of the two Torahs, Scripture, or the Written Torah, and the Mishnah, or the Oral Torah.   This was achieved not merely formally but through the interior structure of thought.   It was by means of the critique of practical logic and the rehabilitation of the probative logic of hierarchical classification (*Listenwissenschaft*) in particular that the authorship of Sifra accomplished this remarkable feat of intellect.   That authorship achieved the (re)union of the two Torahs into a single cogent statement within the framework of the Written Torah by penetrating into the deep composition of logic that underlay the creation of the world in its correct components, rightly classified, and in its right order, as portrayed by the Torah.

Specifically, by systematically demolishing the logic that sustains an autonomous Mishnah and by equally thoroughly demonstrating the dependency, for the identification of the correct classification of things, not upon the traits of things viewed in the abstract, but upon the classification of things by Scripture in particular, the framers of Sifra recast the two parts of the Torah into a single coherent statement through unitary and cogent discourse. At stake, therefore, for our authorship is the dependency of the Mishnah upon Scripture, at least for the encompassing case of the book of Leviticus. So in choosing, as to form, the base text of Scripture, the authorship of Sifra made its entire statement *in nuce.* Then by composing a document that for very long stretches could not have been put together without the Mishnah and at the same time subjecting the generative logical principles of the Mishnah to devastating critique, that same authorship took up its mediating position. The destruction of the Mishnah as an autonomous and free-standing statement, based upon its own logic, is followed by the reconstruction of (large tracts of the Mishnah) as a statement wholly within, and in accord with, the logic and program of the Written Torah in Leviticus.

One response was represented by the claim that the authorities of the Mishnah stood in a chain of tradition that extended back to Sinai; stated explicitly in the Mishnah's first apologetic, tractate Avot, that circulated from approximately a generation beyond the promulgation of the Mishnah itself, that view required amplification and concrete demonstration. This approach treated the word *torah* as a common noun, as the word that spoke of a status or classification of sayings. A saying was *torah*, that is, enjoyed the status of *torah*, or fell into the classification of *torah*, if it stood in the line of tradition from Sinai.

A second and distinct response took the same view of *torah* as a common noun. This response was to treat the Mishnah as subordinate to, and dependent upon, Scripture. Then *torah* was what fell into the classification of the revelation of *Torah* by God to Moses at Sinai. The way of providing what was needed within that theory was to link statements of the Mishnah to statements ("prooftexts") of Scripture. The Tosefta, ca. 300, a compilation of citations of, and comments upon, the Mishnah, together with some autonomous materials that may have reached closure in the period in which the work of redaction of the Mishnah was going on, as well as the Talmud of the Land of Israel, ca. 400, fairly systematically did just that.

The former solution treated Torah with a small t, that is to say, as a generic classification, and identified the Mishnah with the Torah revealed to Moses at Sinai by claiming a place for the Mishnah's authorities in the process of tradition and transmission that brought torah – no longer, the Torah, the specific writing comprising the Five Books of Moses – to contemporary Israel, the Jewish people. It was a theological solution, expressed through ideas, attitudes, implicit claims, but not through sustained rewriting of either Scripture or the Mishnah.

The latter solution, by contrast, concerned the specific and concrete statements of the Mishnah and required a literary, not merely a theological, statement, one precise and specific to passages of the Mishnah, one after the other. What was demanded by the claim that the Mishnah depended upon, but therefore enjoyed the standing of, Scripture, was a line-by-line commentary upon the Mishnah in light of Scripture. But this too, I stress, treated *torah* as a common noun.

The third way, which is Sifra's, would set aside the two solutions, the theological and the literary, and explore the much more profound issues of the fundamental and generative structure of right thought, yielding, as a matter of fact, both Scripture and the Mishnah. This approach insisted that *torah* always was a proper noun. There was, and is, only The Torah. But this – The Torah – demanded expansion and vast amplification. When we know the principles of logical structure and especially those of hierarchical classification that animate The Torah, we can undertake part of the task of expansion and amplification, that is, join in the processes of thought that, in the mind of God, yielded The Torah. For when we know how God thought in giving The Torah to Moses at Sinai and so accounting for the classifications and their ordering in the very creation of the world, we can ourselves enter into The Torah and participate in its processes.

The solution of Sifra was a hermeneutical one, and its clear and present intent was to make a theological point. Sifra's authorship attempted to set forth the Dual Torah as a single, cogent statement, doing so by reading the Mishnah into Scripture not merely for proposition but for expression of proposition. On the surface that decision represented a literary, not merely a theological, judgment. But within the deep structure of thought, it was far more than a mere matter of how to select and organize propositions. Presenting the two Torahs in a single statement constituted an experiment in logic, that logic, in particular, that made cogent thought possible, and that transformed facts into propositions, and propositions into judgments of the more, or the less, consequential.

While the Mishnah's other apologists wrote the Written Torah into the Mishnah, Sifra's authorship wrote the Oral Torah into Scripture. That is to say, the other of the two approaches to the problem of the Mishnah, the one of Sifra, to begin with claimed to demonstrate that the Mishnah found its correct place within the Written Torah itself. Instead of citing verses of Scripture in the context of the Mishnah, the authorship of Sifra cited passages of the Mishnah in the context of Scripture, Leviticus in particular.

The authorship of Sifra concurs in the fundamental principle that sanctification consists in calling things by their rightful name, or, in philosophical language, discovering the classification of things and determining the rule that governs diverse things. Where that authorship differs from the view of the Mishnah's concerns is – I emphasize – *the origins of taxa*: how do we know what diverse things form a single classification of things. Taxa originate in Scripture. Accordingly, at stake in the critique of the Mishnah is not the principles of logic necessary for understanding the construction and inner structure of creation. All parties among sages concurred that the inner structure set forth by a logic of classification alone could sustain the system of ordering all things in proper place and under the proper rule. The like belongs with the like and conforms to the rule governing the like, the unlike goes over to the opposite and conforms to the opposite rule. When we make lists of the like, we also know the rule governing all the items on those lists, respectively. We know that and one other thing, namely, the opposite rule, governing all items sufficiently like to belong together on lists, but sufficiently unlike to be placed on other lists. That rigorously philosophical logic of analysis, comparison and contrast, served because it was the only logic that could serve a system that proposed to make the statement concerning order and right array.

The thrust of Sifra's authorship's attack on the Mishnah's taxonomic logic is readily discerned. Time and again, we can easily demonstrate, things have so many and such diverse and contradictory indicative traits that, comparing one thing to something else, we can always distinguish one species from another. Even though we find something in common, we also can discern some other trait characteristic of one thing but not the other. Consequently, we also can show that the hierarchical logic on which we rely, the argument a fortiori or *qol vehomer*, will not serve. For if on the basis of one set of traits which yield a given classification, we place into hierarchical order two or more items, on the basis of a different set of traits, we have either a different classification altogether, or, much more commonly, simply a different hierarchy. So the attack on the way in which the Mishnah's authorship has done its work appeals to not merely the limitations of classification solely on the basis of traits of things. The more telling argument addresses what is, to *Listenwissenschaft*, the source of power and compelling proof: hierarchization. That is why, throughout, we must designate the Mishnah's mode of *Listenwissenschaft* a logic of hierarchical classification. Things are not merely like or unlike, therefore following one rule or its opposite. Things also are weightier or less weighty, and that particular point of likeness or difference generates the logical force of *Listenwissenschaft*.

Sifra's authorship repeatedly demonstrates that the formation of classifications based on monothetic taxonomy, that is to say, traits that are not only common to both items but that are shared throughout both items subject to comparison and contrast, simply will not serve. For at every point at which someone alleges uniform, that is to say, monothetic likeness, Sifra's authorship will demonstrate difference. Then how to proceed? Appeal to some shared traits as a basis for classification: this is not like that, and that is not like this, but the indicative trait that both exhibit is such and so, that is to say, polythetic taxonomy. The self-evident problem in accepting differences among things and insisting, nonetheless, on their monomorphic character for purposes of comparison and contrast, cannot be set aside: who says? That is, if I can adduce in evidence for a shared classification of things only a few traits among many characteristic of each thing, then what stops me from treating all things alike?

Polythetic taxonomy opens the way to an unlimited exercise in finding what diverse things have in common and imposing, for that reason, one rule on everything. Then the very working of *Listenwissenschaft* as a tool of analysis, differentiation, comparison, contrast, and the descriptive determination of rules yields the opposite of what is desired. Chaos, not order, a mass of exceptions, not rules, a world of examples, each subject to its own regulation, instead of a world of order and proportion, composition and stability, will result.

Sifra's authorship demonstrates that *Listenwissenschaft* is a self-evidently valid mode of demonstrating the truth of propositions. But *the* source of the correct classification of things is Scripture and only Scripture. Without Scripture's intervention into the taxonomy of the world, we should have no knowledge at all of which things fall into which classifications and therefore are governed by which rules. How then do we appeal to Scripture to designate the operative classifications? Here is a simple example of the alternative mode of classification, one that does not appeal to the traits of things but to the utilization of names by Scripture. What we see is how by naming things in one way, rather than in another, Scripture orders all things, classifying and, in the nature of things, also hierarchizing them.

The reason for Scripture's unique power of classification is the possibility of polythetic classification that only Scripture makes possible. Because of Scripture's provision of taxa, we are able to undertake the science of *Listenwissenschaft*, including hierarchical classification, in the right way. What can we do because we appeal to Scripture, which we cannot do if we do not rely on Scripture? It is to establish the possibility of polythetic classification. We can appeal to shared traits of otherwise distinct taxa and so transform species into a common genus for a given purpose. Only Scripture makes that initiative feasible, so our authorship maintains. What is at stake? It is the possibility of doing precisely what the framers of the Mishnah wish to do. That is to join together masses of diverse data into a single, encompassing statement, to show the rule that inheres in diverse cases. In what follows, we shall see an enormous, coherent, and beautifully articulated exercise in the comparison and contrast of many things of a single genus. The whole holds together, because Scripture makes possible the statement of all things within a single rule. That is, as we have noted, precisely what the framers of the Mishnah proposed to accomplish. Our authorship maintains that only by appeal to The Torah is this fete of learning possible. If, then, we wish to understand all things all together and all at once under a single encompassing rule, we had best revert to The Torah, with its account of the rightful names, positions, and order, imputed to all things.

When the logic operative throughout the Mishnah is subjected to criticism, the language of the Mishnah will rarely, if ever, be cited in context. The operative language in dealing with the critique of the applied logic of *Listenwissenschaft* as represented by the framers of the Mishnah ordinarily is, "is it not a matter of logic?" Then the sorts of arguments against taxonomy pursued outside of the framework of Scripture's classifications will follow. When, by contrast, the authorship of Sifra wishes to introduce into the context it has already established a verbatim passage of the Mishnah, it will ordinarily, though not always, use, *mikan amru*, which, in context, means, "in this connection [sages} have said." It is a simple fact that when the intent is to demolish improper reasoning, the Mishnah's rules in the Mishnah's language rarely, if ever, occur. When the authorship of Sifra wishes to incorporate paragraphs of the Mishnah into their re-presentation of The Torah, they will do so either without fanfare, as in the passage at hand, or by the neutral joining language "in this connection [sages] have said."

The authorship of Sifra never called into question the self-evident validity of taxonomic logic, for its critique is addressed only to how the Mishnah's framers identify the origins of, and delineate, taxa. But that critique proves fundamental to the case that that authorship proposed to make. For, intending to demonstrate that *The Torah* was a proper noun, and that everything that was valid came to expression in the single, cogent statement of The Torah, the authorship at hand identified the fundamental issue. It is the debate over the way we know things. In insisting, in agreement with the framers of the Mishnah, that there are not only cases but also rules, not only species but also genera, the authorship of Sifra also made its case in behalf of the case for The Torah as a proper noun. This carries us to the theological foundation for Sifra's authorship's sustained critique of applied reason.

Here is where hermeneutics shades over into theology. For at stake in the hermeneutics is to demonstrate a proposition concerning the character of the Torah and what it is, in The Torah, that we wish to discern. And the answer to that question requires theological, not merely literary and philosophical, reflection on our part. For I maintain that in their delineation of correct hierarchical logic, our authorship uncovered, within the Torah (hence by definition, written and oral components of the Torah alike) an adumbration of the working of the mind of God. That is because the premise of all discourse is that The Torah was written by God and dictated by God to Moses at Sinai. And that will in the end explain why our authorship for its part has entered into The Torah long passages of not merely clarification but active intrusion, making itself a component of the interlocutorial process. To what end we know: it was to unite the Dual Torah. But on what basis?

If Sifra had taken first place in the curriculum of Judaism, its representation of the Written Torah and the Oral Torah all together and all at once would have opened a different path altogether. For it is one thing to absorb the Torah, Oral and Written, and it is quite another to join in the processes of thought, the right way of thinking, that sustain the Torah. The authorship of Sifra proposed to regain access to the modes of thought that guided the formation of the Torah, Oral and Written alike: comparison and contrast in this way, not in that, identification of categories in one manner, not in another. Since those were the modes of thought that, in our authorship's conception, dictated the structure of intellect upon which the Torah, the united Torah, rested, a simple conclusion is the sole possible one.

Now to answer the question of the basis on which our authorship represented itself as participants in, and interlocutors of, The Torah, such that they were prepared to re-present, that is to say, simply rewrite (and therefore, themselves write) The Torah. And that is what I meant when I said at the outset: Theology dictates hermeneutics, and hermeneutics, the principles by which the particular verses are to be read. And, it therefore must follow, an examination of the hermeneutics, beginning with the literary structures that bear the detailed formulation of the document time and again, yields the theology. When we turn in due course to the Talmud's hermeneutics, identifying what is unique to that writing, we shall pursue the same set of questions I have addressed here for Sifra.

Let me conclude with a clear statement of the theology that the hermeneutics of the exemplary document yields – a theology to which the second Talmud will lead us back at the end. In their analysis of the deepest structures of intellect of the Torah, the authorship of Sifra supposed to enter into the mind of God, showing how God's mind worked when God formed the Torah, Written and Oral alike. And there, in the intellect of God, humanity gained access to the only means of uniting the two components of the Torah, because that is where the

Torah originated. But in discerning how God's mind worked – the principles of taxonomy and the hierarchization of the classes of things that governed the making of the world – the intellectuals who created Sifra claimed for themselves a place in that very process of thought that had given birth to The Torah. Our authorship could rewrite the Torah because, knowing how The Torah originally was written, they, too, could write (though not reveal) the Torah.

Part Three

THE SECOND TALMUD:
FROM CASES TO PRINCIPLES

Prologue

The Second Stage in the Formation of the Theology of Judaism

The Integrity of Truth

The initial theological statement yielded a Judaism that was illuminating and informative, rich in belief and norms of behavior. The Torah (to shift categories slightly) of that Judaism consisted of nearly every dogma and dictate of behavior that it would contain at the end of the formative age. And the hermeneutics would have yielded two generative propositions. But concluded at that point, the systemic statement would have come to not only fruition but closure. And, as we shall now see, the theological adventure inaugurated by the Judaic statement of its theology meant never to come to a conclusion; the very power of the second Talmud's re-presentation derived from its transformation of theology from a statement of a system alone – in Judaic terms, the contents of the Torah, how they cohere, what they maintain – to a recapitulation of God's intellect, revealed as it is in God's giving of the Torah and demonstration therein of the intellectual principles that secured Torah's unity and coherence. That is what is truly at stake in the theological phase of the formation of Judaism, represented by the Bavli and associated Midrash compilations.

The Yerushalmi prepared the way, laying down the generative hermeneutics of proposition; its associated Midrash compilations, for which Sifra stands, showed how through sound hermeneutics propositions are attained out of Scripture, whether those of abstraction as we saw in Sifra or those of a concrete order, as we should identify in Genesis Rabbah, Leviticus Rabbah, and other Midrash compilations in the Yerushalmi's neighborhood. Still, had the formation of Judaism concluded with the Talmud of the Land of Israel and its associated Midrash compilations, Judaism would have reached a statement to be classified as theological, but not the theological statement that it ultimately gained for itself.

For the statement of the earlier Talmud consisted of declarations of facts, rules, propositions nicely spelled out. The Judaic theological method would have been the philosophical ordering of religious truths; the medium, the sustained exegesis of the Mishnah in conformity with an ample hermeneutics; the message, the unity of the Torah, the perfection of its parts. In point of fact, everything was in place for a complete re-presentation of the Torah. The Yerushalmi and associated Midrash compilations fully realized the work; the Torah attained its re-presentation in accord with philosophy's rules of rigorous thought and clear articulation. But, while necessary to the final outcome, that is not a sufficient description of the Torah as it actually emerged in the Talmud of Babylonia and its companion Midrash compilations. The final statement of the theology of Judaism opened up for exploration depths of intellect not conceived in earlier writings, reframed the issue of theology altogether, recast tradition from received propositions to an active act of knowing. And, accordingly, for Judaism, the re-presentation by the Bavli made all the difference: the Torah underwent an entire redefinition, that of which the tradition consisted being reframed in terms beyond all prior imagining.

Because of the character of the evidence for the religion and also the theology of Judaism, which is wholly literary, these statements depend upon a characterization of the difference between one writing and the next. They bear full meaning only in the context of the description of how the Bavli formed a fresh hermeneutics, congruent with the received one but vastly denser and more complex. Alike in program and proposition, in fact the two Talmuds have nothing in common except for form and function. For the initial statement contained no intellectual medium of extension and expansion; had it made the final statement, the door would have been closed to anyone's ongoing participation in those processes of the Torah – processes of thought that because of the character of the Torah as now defined recapitulated those of God's mind – that in the divine intellect had produced the propositions of the Torah. The repertoire of facts – practices and propositions alike – would have come to closure; the conversation would have come to its conclusion.

But the second Talmud's representation of the Torah opened that door, and it never closed. That is because the second Talmud's Torah taught (in ordinary language) not only what to think but how to think, set forth the rules of analysis by which the Torah was attained in its propositional form. And this was accomplished (as Sifra has already adumbrated) by deriving from the results of the Torah an account of the modes of rationality that produced those results: God's mind revealed in the Torah, as much as God's will. What the Bavli contributed to the Torah was not only the re-presentation but the redefinition of what the Torah teaches: not only God's words, but working from words to word – logos is what I mean – God's own logic. The Talmud's representation represented theology in the most precise and concrete sense of the word.[1]

As a matter of fact, the second Talmud stands independent of the first in everything but form and fundamental convention and protocol. When the authors of its compositions and the framers of its composites looked at the same Mishnah paragraph as those of the other Talmud, they saw a different thing before them from what the others had earlier perceived. The reason is, of course, they gazed through different spectacles and expected to see something other than what their predecessors had examined.

The formal and doctrinal identity of the two Talmuds makes all the more stunning the simple fact that, for the bulk of their thirty-seven tractates, the Bavli's writers simply go their own way, utilizing what they received from the Land of Israel (not from its Talmud but from the authorities who occur, also, in its Talmud) for their own purposes, in their own idiom, and on their own terms. That fact begins with the Babylonian sages' choice of tractates and divisions, since they ignore an entire division covered in the other Talmud, the first, and they treat an entire division ignored in the other Talmud, the fifth. It is really not an interesting question to find out whether the later Talmud's framers knew the earlier document – the answer being slightly embarrassing, if they

---

[1]Comparativists may find interesting the implications of these observations for the reception of the Quran, on the one side, understood as the perfect and literal record of God's words, in God's own writing, just as the Torah is so understood in the theology of Judaism; and also for the formation, among Christianities, of a principal medium of religious discourse in theological issues, debate, and creed making, on the other side. My schematization would suggest that the three heirs of ancient Israel define "the word" in three ways: Christ, Quran, and Torah; God incarnate, book, and Torah in the sense in which Torah is realized in the Bavli: an entire statement, written and oral. That would situate Judaism between Islam and Christianity, that is, between book in a broad sense, as for Islam; but a statement made in the chain of tradition formed by humanity in God's image, after God's likeness, extending from Heaven, thus from Sinai, that is established by the discipleship of Moses to God, and the discipleship of Joshua to Moses, hence the relationship of master and disciple, expressed through the communication of learning – proposition and process alike. Then all things depend on the nature of tradition – process, proposition, above all, pattern of intellection. So the stakes here are very high; they do not get any higher.

did: they knew it and thought it third rate. We know that is so, because what they themselves set forth is so much more elegant. But I prefer to think they had ample access to episodic sayings and even brief compositions, but went their own way, using the sayings and revising the compositions as they liked.[2]

Since the Bavli's framers produced their document, it is generally agreed, hundreds of years after the Yerushalmi's finished their work, we may conclude that, if they had access to the Yerushalmi's compositions and composites, they chose not to use them but preferred to make their own statement in their own way and for their own purpose. Where sayings are shared by the two Talmuds, they are episodic, ad hoc, singular; rarely do entire compositions make their way from the former to the latter document, and whole composites, never. Referring in common with the authors of the Yerushalmi's composites and even compositions to the same Scripture, Mishnah, Tosefta, Sifra, and the two Sifrés, the Bavli's authorship drew upon composites and compositions that differed, beginning to end and top to bottom, from the Yerushalmi's counterparts. The materials shared in common are episodic and seldom.

Now that we realize the differences in literary character, these writings that exhibit formal congruence await differentiation as to the substantive side of matters. With the two Talmuds, that work is exceptionally simple. In fact, they intersect at only a few points, each set of writers doing pretty much whatever it likes with exactly those sayings, stories, and even compositions that it shares with the other. For even as commentaries to the Mishnah, they intersect at only a few points, and then along lines that, so far as I can see, begin within the program of Mishnah exegesis and are governed by the dictates of the substrate of that program (whether logical, whether topical). The two Talmuds use Scripture in the same way, but each for its own purpose.

The Talmud of Babylonia speaks in a unique voice to make a statement wholly its own. While the Bavli cannot be represented as the document that theologized the Torah, some fundamental and formative

---

[2]How they made such revisions of compositions is spelled out in rich detail in my comparative studies of versions of the same saying or story in these works:

> *Development of a Legend. Studies on the Traditions Concerning Yohanan ben Zakkai* (Leiden, 1970: E.J. Brill.)
>
> *The Rabbinic Traditions about the Pharisees before 70* (Leiden, 1971: E.J. Brill), I-III. I. *The Rabbinic Traditions about the Pharisees before 70. The Masters;* II. *The Rabbinic Traditions about the Pharisees before 70. The Houses;* III. *The Rabbinic Traditions about the Pharisees before 70. Conclusions.*
>
> *Eliezer ben Hyrcanus. The Tradition and the Man* (Leiden, 1973: E.J. Brill), I-II. I. *Eliezer ben Hyrcanus. The Tradition and the Man. The Tradition; and* II. *Eliezer ben Hyrcanus. The Tradition and the Man. The Man.*

work having been done by the Yerushalmi, the Bavli fully accomplished a sustained and systematic theological statement, delivered through its ubiquitous and distinctive hermeneutics; the Yerushalmi did no such thing and exercised no influence whatsoever. The Bavli's voice is unique because, at its foundations, the Bavli is different from the Yerushalmi not in detail, but in definitive, intellectual character. In fact the Talmuds have too little in common to permit our isolating differences for episodic and ad hoc explanation. The Bavli's statement belongs to its compositions' authors and to its composites' compilers and to its penultimate and ultimate authorship – to them, to them alone, to them uniquely. Everything in this account of the Talmud's re-presentation of the Torah depends upon the difference between the two Talmuds; the first set forth a religious structure and presented it as a cogent system, one we have no difficulty in classifying as theology. The second restated the whole in the theological re-presentation that would define the Torah and prevail as Judaism.

What makes the Bavli's voice unique, unrelated to the Yerushalmi's, therefore, is that it forms a statement distinctive of those who framed the whole, and, also, in very great measure, particular to those who wrote up nearly the entirety of the principal parts of the document: nearly all of the composites, and the vast majority of the compositions. It stands for different people, talking to different people about different things, from the Yerushalmi's authors, their address, their audience, their intent. All the Bavli has in common with the Yerushalmi are the prior documents and compilations, Scripture, the Mishnah, the Tosefta, and some sort of collections of sayings assigned Tannaite status. But these form corpera of inert materials, used in whatever way the framers of the Bavli chose to use them, dictating nothing of the consequent analytical inquiry, and never permitting us to predict the shape and structure of the treatment of a given saying or even of a given problem by the two Talmuds in common. So between the two Talmuds there is virtually nothing in common beyond inert facts.

How about the corresponding Midrash compilations of the final phase in the formation of Judaism? The Bavli made a theological statement through its hermeneutics, concerning the unity of truth and its integrity. For their part, the Midrash compilations would turn to Scripture to form, out of the mass of details presented by the exegesis of a book of the Written Torah, an explicit statement of the specific propositions that are expressed only in the context of detailed narrative. They, too, went in search of the main point, that is, truth that exhibits integrity amidst the diversity of the details of story line and detailed message. And of course, having looked, they saw what they expected to find: a clear statement of a proposition, not various propositions that illustrated a single principle, as in the case of Sifra, nor even various propositions produced through various facts of Scripture shaped into syllogisms, as shown by Genesis Rabbah and (more effectively still) by Leviticus Rabbah, but a single encompassing point or proposition. Sifré to Deuteronomy and Sifra say the same thing about many things, but that is not equivalent to what we find here. Indeed, the formation of an encompassing, singular proposition is something that I do not find in any prior compilation of Midrash exegeses, but do find in the compilations produced alongside the Bavli.

So the Bavli re-presented the Torah through a hermeneutic designed to show the law behind the laws and demonstrate the integrity of truth, and the associated Midrash compilations re-presented the Torah by stating out of complex and vast detail some singular principle among its principal parts. Since both Talmuds say the same thing in pretty much the same way, what evidence validates my claim that the second Talmud radically differs from the first? It is the demonstration of two facts. First comes decisive, detailed evidence of the utter independence of the Bavli from the prior Talmud. Second in line is the demonstration that the foundation of the autonomy of the Bavli – and the best possible explanation for its difference for the Yerushalmi – derives from the latter's distinctive hermeneutics. Accordingly, first we address the indications that the second Talmud makes its own statement, then, in Chapter Nine pay attention to the character of that statement. Chapters Ten and Eleven, finally, require us to identify specific examples of the hermeneutic difference and to interpret them in the context of theological premise and discourse. So it is in the differences between the two Talmuds that we identify the hermeneutics of the second, hence, also, its theological statement.[3]

---

[3]Only when we fully appreciate that fact will the theological message of the Bavli's unique hermeneutics demand attention, spelled out in detail in Chapters Nine and Ten.

8

The Independence of the Talmud of Babylonia

The Bavli differs from the Yerushalmi because the framers of the Bavli drew upon their distinctive, local sources for compositions and composites, and the framers of the Yerushalmi made use of their equivalently distinctive, local sources for compositions and composites. The two Talmuds routinely treat the same Mishnah but only very rarely intersect other than at a given Mishnah paragraph. The reason is that the penultimate and ultimate framers of the two Talmuds utilized what they had in hand, and each document's framers drew upon a corpus of materials utterly different from the one used by (therefore also: available to) the other. If, for instance, there were compilations of sayings of principal sages circulating independent of fully formulated discourses and drawn upon in the framing of those discourses – something akin to Q's collection of sayings attributed to Jesus upon which (it is commonly thought) Mark, Matthew, and Luke drew in writing their Gospels – then that source, or those sources, made remarkably slight impact upon the framing of the compositions and, all the more so, the composites, of which the two Talmuds are made up, respectively.[1]

That means that the second Talmud stands autonomous of the first. The two meet at the received, completed documents, in Scripture, the Mishnah, the Tosefta, some Tannaite sayings, Sifra, and the two Sifrés.

---

[1] And that fact calls into question the approach to the analysis of the forming of the Talmuds that begins with the individual sayings and moves upward and outward from there. The correct approach is from the document back to its composites, and thence to the compositions, and then to the joined sayings (e.g., two or more sages' views of a given rule) given a place in the compositions by the author(s) of the compositions. Last in line, then, is what an individual sage is supposed to have said on a given subject.

Both appeal to episodic passages that we now find, also, in the Tosefta, and a few sayings. But they never meet in the workshops of sages writing up compositions or compiling composites of composites; in the enormous sample of my probe, I did not find a single composition in which the Bavli lifted whole a piece of writing of the Yerushalmi, let alone a composite of any size shared by the two Talmuds.[2]

The framers of the Bavli's compositions, all the more so, of its composites, do precisely what they wish with such shared sayings or stories. So far as I can discern in the sample I have examined, they rarely, if ever, respond to, carry forward, or build on, a composition, all the more so, a composite, shared with the earlier Talmud. The Talmud of Babylonia speaks with a single voice to deliver a message unique to itself, by which I mean, to the authors of its compositions and the compilers of its composites and the authorships of its massive and whole statements: chapters, tractates – the lot. When they had completed their statement, Judaism received its theology, a theology distinguished by the invitation it extended to generations to come to participate, and by the lessons it afforded on how to do so.

Both Talmuds are made up of materials – compositions and also composites[3] – that reached closure before the final forming of the Talmudic composites in the documents as we know them; each draws upon its own corpus of locally written compositions, made up of completed units of thought that also were locally written, whether free-standing sayings or disputes or little stories or extensive and sustained analyses. So the comparison of the two Talmuds really requires the contrast of the character of the available compositions and even

---

[2]That people did lift up compositions and even composites and move them about in the compilation of Talmuds is a fact of the writing of the Yerushalmi, approximatley 40% of which is simply filler, that is, materials that occur in one place and then recur somewhere else; we always can identify the primary position of such peregrinating writings and invariably know where secondary use has been made of them. In the Bavli, too, sayings and stories recur here and about, but it is exceedingly rare to find a composition in more than a single passage, and I can say confidently that not a single composite is used more than once. The point, then, is that, within the literary repertoire of the writers of the two Talmuds lay the power to move writings hither and yon, and that happened commonly in the Yerushalmi, occasionally in the Bavli, but – so far as it now appears, in my probe of the question in *The Bavli's Unique Voice* – never, I repeat, never in the relationships between the two Talmuds. The Bavli borrowed nothing, though it shared much.

[3]This distinction is critical to all analysis of all rabbinic writings of late antiquity; it is set forth in *The Rules of Composition of the Talmud of Babylonia. The Cogency of the Bavli's Composite* (Atlanta, 1991: Scholars Press for South Florida Studies in the History of Judaism).

composites. And that is precisely where, entirely and consistently and nearly ubiquitously, the Bavli differs from the Yerushalmi.

Whether or not the framers of the Bavli "knew" the Yerushalmi is not at issue here; the received scholarship,[4] with which I concur, is certain that they did not. To be sure, I cannot understand why the later sages should not have known the earlier document as a whole, since, we all assume, it was composed and completed two centuries before the closure of the Bavli. What matters is, what difference did the document make to them? And the answer is, demonstrably, no difference at all. If they knew the document, they certainly were not so impressed by it as to turn themselves into its continuators and commentators; theirs is no super-commentary to the Yerushalmi's commentary to the Mishnah; it is not only not incremental, it is not even connected with the first commentary. Nonetheless, I do think that the work of Mishnah commentary is common to the sages of both countries. It is clear that that work involved an interest, among the authors of compositions and even framers of composites, in details of Mishnah rules, and other Tannaite rules, as these were read in the other country: the Babylonian writers very frequently address opinion formulated in the Land of Israel on this, that, and the other thing. That makes the utter autonomy of the second Talmud from the first all the more striking.

What does it mean to allege that the second Talmud makes an utterly independent statement in its own behalf? In literary terms, I refer to the fact that while the Bavli is made up of cogent composition and large-scale composites, as well as massive miscellanies of compositions, in the samples that I have examined, covering all divisions and numerous chapters, not a single massive miscellany of the Bavli occurs also in the Yerushalmi. I cannot identify a single composite in the Talmud of Babylonia that finds a place also in the Talmud of the Land of Israel. As to compositions, it is rare for the same composition to occur in the earlier and then in the later document. But, when that is the case, it is difficult to show, for more than a saying or a brief story, that the earlier document's version of the composition has been taken over and revised line by line in the later document's version of the same matter. Where the Talmuds share materials other than passages of Scripture, the Mishnah, the Tosefta, or compilations of formulations of rules accorded Tannaite status, the points of intersection are few and far between.

---

[4]A review of prior research, including attention to this question, will be found in Baruch M. Bokser, "The Palestinian Talmud," in J. Neusner, ed., *The Study of Ancient Judaism* (New York, 1981: Ktav). Second printing (Atlanta, 1992: Scholars Press for South Florida Studies in the History of Judaism). II. *The Palestinian and Babylonian Talmuds.*

Both Talmuds do appeal to some sources in common, Scripture, Mishnah, episodic passages that we now find, also, in the Tosefta, and a few sayings attributed to authorities who flourished after the closure of the Mishnah, for example, earlier masters in the Talmudic process that yielded the Talmuds of each country, Yohanan and Simeon b. Laqish, for the Land of Israel, Rab and Samuel, for Babylonia, for example. But the common use of received sayings rarely permits us to predict the direction and purpose of the compositions of the two Talmuds; each will go its own way, guided by its own concerns, pursuing its own interests.

The Bavli speaks about its region's reading of the Mishnah; its particularity is the localization of the Torah to the mind of its place. The compositions and composites that comprise the Talmud of Babylonia occasionally use imported parts, that is, sayings from the other locale, but in any event are manufactured at home – and the document all the more so. The one whole Torah of Moses, our rabbi – written, in Scripture, oral, in the Mishnah and related sayings classified as Tannaite – divides by place, and traditions are bound by place, and the Torah governs here in particular, if everywhere else, also and equally in all due particularity.

What would represent contraindications to the theory of a wholly independent second Talmud? One important contrary fact would be appeal to a common prior source or collection of earlier authorities' sayings, in the context of Gospels' research, a "source" or Quelle (Q).[5] So let me ask, first of all, do the Bavli and Yerushalmi draw on (a) "Q"? That is to say, is there a corpus of sayings available to the authors of compositions and framers of composites used in both Talmuds and prior to and independent of each? If such a source of sayings circulated, then the Bavli cannot be said to stand independent of the Yerushalmi, since it would then be joined to the Yerushalmi not only by common sources upon which both draw or comment, but something far more definitive of the character of the Bavli in the tradition of the Yerushalmi.

Now, it is a demonstrable fact that, here and there, the Bavli cites the same saying in the same wording that the Yerushalmi presents in its composition on a given Mishnah pericope. That is in three aspects. First, it is the simple fact that, occasionally, sayings not found in any prior

---

[5]Stories in the Talmuds about communications sent from one community of sages to another, citations of one locale's principal authorities in the Talmud of the other, allegations that the Babylonian sages humbly accepted the priority of those of the Land of Israel, the appearance of sages of the one country in the Talmud of the other – these form ample grounds for the hypothesis of a "Q" to substitute for the absence of fully articulated compositions and composites. "Q" would then stand in the way of the theory of an utterly free-standing Talmud, such as I set forth here and proceed to explain and interpret in the following chapters. Hence my null hypothesis.

document are shared in the same or nearly the same wording by the Yerushalmi and the Bavli. That is not surprising. Stories in both Talmuds speak of constant communications among the authorities of each country's Jewish polity. That the Bavli had access to sayings assigned to the Yerushalmi's authorities is shown on virtually every other page of the document, where Simeon b. Laqish or Yohanan or their colleagues are cited. What I take that to mean is, the stories about circulating sayings are matched by the data themselves, which show the Babylonians' utilizing sayings in the names of the other country's sages. But whether or not collections of such sayings existed, as a counterpart to Q, and, if they did, what such collections looked like, is a separate question.

For a saying to occur in the rabbinic "Q," I should want it to be cited in both Talmuds, in the same context or for the same purpose. If a saying imputed to a Yerushalmi figure occurs only in the Bavli, for example, in a dispute involving Rab and Samuel, Simeon b. Laqish and Yohanan, that may show that the Babylonians had access to sayings from the Land of Israel (if we take the names at face value), but it does not show that a common corpus of sayings circulated in both countries and influenced the formation of both Talmuds along the same lines (yielding a Bavli dependent on "Q" dependent on the Yerushalmi or closely tied to it); it shows the exact opposite. If a saying assigned to a Yerushalmi sage occurs in both the Yerushalmi and the Bavli but not in the same context, for example, "R. Simeon b. Laqish says, 'It is unfit,'" that is inconsequential, because it is simply indeterminate.

But if, in the same setting, for example, of Mishnah exegesis or analysis of legal principle or premise, the same saying occurs in the same way in both documents (but in no other, prior or contemporary document, for example, the Mishnah, Tosefta, or Sifra), and if that saying is so worded as to be particular to the issue (not just "R. Yohanan declares unclean"), or distinctive to the context, then we may propose that that saying derives from a circulating collection of sayings of Yerushalmi sages (or Babylonian ones, for that matter); and then there was a "Q." And if there was a "Q," then, while not directly connected, the Bavli stands in an established relationship to the Yerushalmi – as against my interpretation of the facts I have established, which is, the Bavli is independent of the earlier Talmud (within the amply specified qualifications about prior common sources of the Torah, Scripture and the Mishnah, for example).

I state very simply that, in the sample I examined, there are too few such sayings to suggest that the framers of the Bavli drew to any extent on a corpus of set sayings in the formation of their compositions. But the issue is not quantity but effect. If there was such a "Q," the part of it the existence of which we can demonstrate through hard evidence was both trivial and lacking in all influence. I have simply never found a case in which that shared saying, from a hypothetical "Q," influenced the authors of the two Talmuds' compositions to say the same thing in the same way. To the contrary, shared sayings were used in different ways, with the consequence that, if there was a "Q," it made no difference to the authors of the Bavli's compositions as they contemplated their exegetical or hermeneutical program.

A specific case is now called for. If there was a "Q," what would it have looked like? Here is a candidate for consideration: At M. Niddah 1:1 neither set of authors does more than give a reprise of received materials. But if I had to specify the character of the received materials, I should have to say that, as to wording, they do not appear the same in both Talmuds; it is the gist that can be shown to play a role in both Talmuds' compositions, not the wording – so surely no "Q" by any definition that pertains. I underline what I take to be the candidate for "Q."

[I.A] Samuel said, "This teaching [of A] applies only to a virgin and an old lady. But as to a pregnant woman and a nursing mother, they assign to her the entire period of her pregnancy or the entire period of her nursing [respectively, for the blood ceases, and what does flow is inconsequential, so there is no retroactive contamination at all]."

[B] Rab and R. Yohanan – both of them say, "<u>All the same are the virgin, the old lady, the pregnant woman, and the nursing mother [= B].</u>"

VIII.1 A. **And of what case did they speak when they said, "Sufficient for her is her time"? In the case of the first appearance of a drop of blood. But in the case of the second appearance of such a drop of blood, she conveys uncleanness to whatever she touched during the preceding twenty-four hours.**

B. Said Rab, "<u>**The statement [But in the case of the second appearance of such a drop of blood, she conveys uncleanness to whatever she touched during the preceding twenty-four hours]**</u> applies to all the listed cases."

[C] Said R. Zeira, "The opinion of Rab and R. Yohanan accords with the position of R. Haninah, and all of them differ from the position of Samuel."

C. And Samuel said, "It refers only to the virgin and the old lady, but as to the pregnant woman and the nursing mother, throughout all the days of pregnancy or through all the days of nursing, it is sufficient for them to reckon uncleanness not retroactively but only from the time of observing a flow."

D. And so said R. Simeon b. Laqish, "The statement [**But in the case of the second appearance of such a drop of blood, she conveys uncleanness to whatever she touched during the preceding twenty-four hours**] applies to all the listed cases."

E. And R. Yohanan said, "It refers only to the virgin and the old lady, but as to the pregnant woman and the nursing mother, throughout all the days of pregnancy or through all the days of nursing, it is sufficient for them to reckon uncleanness not retroactively but only from the time of observing a flow."

F. *The dispute follows the lines of a dispute among Tannaite versions:*

[D] For R. Eleazar said in the name of R. Haninah, "On one occasion Rabbi gave instruction in accord

with the lenient rul-
ings of R. Meir and in
accord with the le-
nient rulings of R.
Yosé."

[E] What was the nature
of the case?

[F] [If] the fetus was no-
ticeable, and then [the
woman] produced a
drop of blood –

[G] R. Meir says, "She is
subject to the rule of
the sufficiency of her
time [of actually dis-
covering the blood]."

G. "A pregnant woman
or a nursing mother
who were [11A]
bleeding profusely –
throughout all the
days of pregnancy or
through all the days of
nursing, it is sufficient
for them to reckon
uncleanness   not
retroactively but only
from the time of
observing a flow," the
words of R. Meir.

[H] R. Yosé says, "She
imparts uncleanness
retroactively   for
twenty-four hours."

[I] [If] she produced
many drops of blood,
then missed three pe-
riods, and afterward
produced a drop of
blood,

[J] R. Meir says, "She
imparts uncleanness
retroactively   for
twenty-four hours."

[K] R. Yosé says, "She is
subject to the rule of
the sufficiency of her
time [of actually
discovering blood]."

[L] Now if you say that
they assign to her the
entire period of her
pregnancy or the en-
tire period of her
nursing, what need do
I have for the lenient
ruling of R. Yosé? The
teaching of R. Meir [in
such a case] produces
a still more lenient

H. R. Yosé and R. Judah
and R. Simeon say,
"The ruling that
sufficient for them is
the time of their
actually seeing a drop
of blood applies only
to the first appearance
of a drop of blood, but
the second imparts
uncleanness for the
preceding twenty-four
hours or from one
examination to the
prior examination."

ruling than does that of R. Yosé. [For so far as Meir is concerned, if we read his view in the light of Samuel's opinion (A), the nursing mother and the pregnant woman enjoy the stated leniency throughout the period of nursing or pregnancy. The issue, then, is that Meir deems this drop of blood (I) as a second one. Yosé regards the cessation of the period as consequential.]

[M] Said R. Mana before R. Yosé, "Or perhaps we should assign [Rabbi's ruling] to the case of the milk [dealt with above, in which Meir and Yosé dispute about whether the woman who hands over her son to a wet nurse retains the stated leniency. At issue then is whether the matter depends upon the status of the woman's milk or on the status of the child]."

[N] He said to him, "The matter was explicitly stated in regard to the present issue."

I see no material differences as to the gist of the law, between the two Talmuds' representation of the matter. But this kind of intersection has proven very, very rare in our sample. So all we can conclude is that we have a fine example of what the two Talmuds would have looked like, had the Bavli's authors satisfied themselves with a reprise of the Yerushalmi, a reprise constructed by reference not to the Yerushalmi itself but to some sort of handbook of sayings. "Q" here would then have consisted of something that yielded the underlined wording in the respective documents, that is to say, that would have permitted the

Bavli's composition's author to word matters as he did. If this were our sole evidence, then we should have to posit a "Q" consisting of paraphrases and allusions, the gist of what was said, not the wording; but then the analogy collapses, that is not what Q consists of or how it contributes to the received Gospels.

Second, some items that appear to attest to a "Q" of sayings, not the gist, show the opposite, for what appears to be a shared saying may turn out, on closer examination, to be two distinct sayings, one for each Talmud. Hence, even where a saying appears to originate in the rabbinic counterpart to Q, in fact it shows the opposite: not a well-crafted sourcebook of sayings, but a rather slovenly process of tradition, operating so that handing on whatever was shared was botched. Let me give a single example of such a phenomenon, one in which (as a matter of fact) the Yerushalmi's version is superior to the Bavli's.

M. M.Q. 3:4: We have a somewhat odd situation at Y. 3:4 III and B. 3:4 I.2. As it stands, the latter is incomprehensible, and it clearly presupposes the former. Then there is no discussion, at B.'s version, of Rab's views:

[III.A] Someone lost his tefillin on the intermediate days of a festival. He came to R. Hananel [who was a scribe and who would prepare a new set for him]. He sent him to R. Abba bar Nathan. He said to him, "Give him your *tefillin* [phylacteries] and go, write a new set for yourself."

[B] Said to him Rab, "[It is permitted to] go and write them for him [without practicing deception]."

[C] The Mishnah stands at variance with the view of Rab: A *man may write out tefillin and mezuzahs for his own use* [M. 3:4G].

[D] Lo, for someone else he may not do so.

I.2 A. *Rab instructed R. Hananel, and some say, Rabbah bar bar Hanna instructed R. Hananel,* "The decided law is this: He may write them out and sell them in the ordinary way if it is to make his living."

[E] Interpret the passage
to speak of not doing
so merely by writing
them out and leaving
them [for future sale].

As we have it, B.'s version is strange and out of context; read as a continuation of B. 3:4 I.1, the statement does not intersect with Y.'s case at all; but then how explain the reference to Hananel?! So, in all, here is a case in which a fragment of a formulation has been inserted, and without the Yerushalmi, the fragment is not to be interpreted.

Yet a second look calls that judgment into question. In fact, Rab's instructions to Hananel in B. have to do with writing tefillin and selling them on the intermediate days of the festival if it is to make a living; Y.'s formulation does not introduce that consideration at all. And the reason that the consideration of making a living is introduced at B. 3:4 I.2 is Yosé's reference to it at I.1D! So, in fact, while somewhere in the dim past of both Talmuds' compositions may lie a statement of Rab to Hananel (or: Rabbah bar bar Hanna!), the use of the same by each depends entirely on considerations particular to each Talmud respectively. Here is no instance in which making sense of the Bavli requires that we resort to the Yerushalmi or to "Q"; to the contrary, all we have to do is back up one line to make sense of the Bavli's formulation entirely in the Bavli's own terms.

Do the Bavli and Yerushalmi draw on (a) "Q"? At some points, they do draw on finished, and available, materials, ordinarily, sayings floating hither and yon. It is very common that these finished materials occur also in the Tosefta, which is hardly surprising, but, occasionally, the finished materials are not located in any other document. So there could have been a "Q," but not a "Q" of the size and importance of the one that is attested by Matthew and Mark and used by Luke. But if there was a shared corpus of sayings besides those in available documents, what difference does that fact make for the description of the Bavli? None. The Bavli emerges, all the more so, as a free-standing document, written by its compositions' writers and its composites' compilers, for whatever purpose suited them. They used traditions, whether deriving from Scripture or the Mishnah or the Tosefta or other compilations bearing the sign of Tannaite status; this they did for their own purposes, in their own way, for the presentation of their own statement. They used traditions, they were not traditional.

We proceed to a second null hypothesis. An established, conventional protocol, governing the problematic identified in a given Mishnah paragraph by both Talmuds, can link the Talmuds and compromise the independence of the second one. So we now ask: If there is no shared corpus of sayings, then does a topical protocol define both Talmuds' Mishnah exegesis, that is, a protocol of topics or problems associated with a given Mishnah pericope but not articulated therein? Such a protocol would have told the exegetes of that pericope, or the compilers of compositions deemed pertinent to that pericope, what subject they should treat (over and above the subject of the pericope); or what problem they should investigate (over and above the problem explicit in the pericope). Obviously, every Mishnah pericope treated differently in the two Talmuds gives evidence that there was no such protocol of topics or problems.   But more specific evidence can be adduced, where the Mishnah pericope does not demand attention to a topic, but both Talmuds address said topic. It is at Mishnah Moed Qatan 3:5-6, where the absence of a protocol of problems, over and above those of Scripture, emerges:

[XXXIX.A] **For they have said, "The Sabbath counts in the days of mourning, but does not interrupt the period of mourning, while the festivals interrupt the period of mourning, and do not count in the days of mourning" [M. 3:5C].**	II.1 A. **For they have said, "The Sabbath counts [in the days of mourning] but does not interrupt [the period of mourning], [while] the festivals interrupt [the period of mourning] and do not count [in the days of mourning]":**
[B] ["The festivals do not count,"] R. Simon in the name of R. Yohanan [explained], "because one is permitted on them to have sexual relations."	B. *Judeans and Galilaeans –*
	C. *These say,* [2 3 B] "Mourning pertains to the Sabbath."
[C] R. Jeremiah dealt with R. Judah b. R. Simon, saying to him, "Do all the disciples of R. Yohanan report this tradition? Not one person has ever heard this tradition from him, except for your father!"	D. *And those say,* "Mourning does not pertain to the Sabbath."
	E. *The one who says,* "Mourning pertains to the Sabbath," *cites the Mishnah's statement,* **The Sabbath counts [in the days of mourning].**
[D] Said to him R. Jacob, "If it was said, it was said only by those who say, 'Thus and so is the matter' [without	F. *The one who says,* "Mourning does not pertain to the Sabbath," *cites the Mishnah's statement,* **but does not interrupt**

knowing what they are talking about]!

[E] "For R. Joshua b. Levi said, 'Lo, [on the festival] it is forbidden [for a mourner] to have sexual relations.'"

[F] For R. Simon said in the name of R. Joshua b. Levi, "Have they not said, 'A mourning does not apply on a festival, but people observe mourning discretely'?"

[G] What is the context for this discretion? It has to do with sexual relations [which are not to be performed on the festival by a mourner].

[H] [Reverting to the discussion broken off at B:] They objected, "Lo, in the case of the festival, lo, the mourner is prohibited from having sexual relations, and yet it does not count [toward the days of mourning]. Also in regard to the Sabbath, since a mourner is forbidden to have sexual relations, the Sabbath should not count [among the days of mourning, and yet it does, so the reason proposed at B is not likely]."

[I] Said R. Ba, "It is possible that seven days can pass without a festival, but it is not possible that seven days can pass without a Sabbath[, and if the

[the period of mourning]. *Now if you take the view that mourning applies to the Sabbath, if mourning were observed, would there be any question of its interrupting the counting of the days of mourning?*

G. *Well, as a matter of fact, the same passage does say,* **The Sabbath counts [in the days of mourning]**!

H. *The inclusion of that phrase is on account of what is coming, namely,* **[while] the festivals interrupt [the period of mourning] and do not count [in the days of mourning],** *so the Tannaite formulation to balance matters also stated,* **The Sabbath counts [in the days of mourning].**

I. *And as to the position of him who says,* "Mourning pertains to the Sabbath," *does the passage not say,* **but does not interrupt [the period of mourning]**?

J. *That is because the framer of the passage wishes to include,* **the festivals interrupt [the period of mourning],** *so for the sake of balance he stated as well,* **The Sabbath...does not interrupt [the period of mourning].**

II.2 A. *May we say that at issue is what is under debate among the Tannaite*

Sabbath does not suspend the rites of mourning, there will be eight days of mourning, and not seven]."

authorities in the following:

B.   As to one whose deceased [actually] lies before him, he eats in a different room. If he does not have another room, he eats in the room of his fellow. If he has no access to the room of his fellow, he makes a partition and eats [separate from the corpse]. If he has nothing with which to make a partition, he turns his face away and eats.

C.   He does not recline and eat, he does not eat meat, he does not drink wine, he does not say a blessing before the meal, he does not serve to form a quorum, and people do not say a blessing for him or include him in a quorum.

D.   He is exempt from the requirement to recite the Shema and from the Prayer and from the requirement of wearing phylacteries and from all of the religious duties that are listed in the Torah.

E.   But on the Sabbath he does recline and eat, he does eat meat, he does drink wine, he does say a blessing before the meal, he does serve to form a quorum and people do say a blessing for him and include him in a quorum. And he is liable to carry out all of the religious duties that are listed in the Torah.

F. Rabban Simeon b. Gamaliel says, "Since he is liable for these [religious duties], he is liable to carry out all of them."

G. And [in connection with the dispute just now recorded], R. Yohanan said, "*What is at issue between [Simeon and the anonymous authority]? At issue is the matter of having sexual relations.* [Simeon maintains that the mourner on the Sabbath has the religious obligation to have sexual relations with his wife, and the anonymous authority does not include that requirement, since during the mourning period it does not apply.]"

H. Is now this what is at stake between them, namely, one authority [Simeon b. Gamaliel] maintains, "Mourning pertains to the Sabbath," and the other takes the view, "Mourning does not pertain to the Sabbath"?

I. *What compels that conclusion? Perhaps the initial Tannaite authority takes the view that he does there only because of the simple consideration that the deceased is lying there awaiting burial, but in the present*

		case, in which the deceased is not lying there awaiting burial, he would not take the position that he does. And, further, perhaps Rabban Simeon b. Gamaliel takes the position that he does in that case because, at that point [prior to burial] the restrictions of mourning do not pertain, but, here, where the restrictions of mourning do pertain, he would concur [that the mourning does pertain to the Sabbath].
II.3	A.	[24A] R. Yohanan asked Samuel, "Does mourning pertain to the Sabbath or does mourning not pertain to the Sabbath?"
	B.	He said to him, "Mourning does not pertain to the Sabbath."

Now what is interesting here is not that the passages do not intersect. It is that the Bavli introduces the case of one's deceased's actually lying there in the room, and links that case with the present dispute. But the Yerushalmi treats that situation in a completely different context, namely, at Y. 3:5 VI. What makes that evidence probative is simple. The passage where the Yerushalmi treats the cited question serves *not* our Mishnah pericope at all, but rather M. Ber. 3:1. Since it has nothing to do with the Mishnah passage to which, in the Bavli, the topic is tied, here is no argument from silence. It is, rather, decisive evidence that no topical protocol told sages in both the Land of Israel and Babylonia where and how to address a given theme that was not in the Mishnah but somehow deemed connected to it. Where the framers of the Yerushalmi thought a given subject, not introduced by the Mishnah but held relevant to it, should be addressed, the authors of the compositions and composites of the Bavli had no such notion, and, it goes without saying, vice versa.

Here again, an analogy may clarify for New Testament scholars what is at stake here. It is clear that for the authors of the four canonical Gospels as well as all of the extracanonical ones, a shared protocol, not spelled out, dictated the subjects that should be treated and the order in which they should occur. That is to say, if we propose to talk about Jesus Christ, his life and teachings, we follow an established program. We are going to discuss, for example, the Passion, and, moreover, the Passion is going to appear at the end of the narrative. A biographical narrative will intrude throughout. That protocol governs in all four Gospels, without regard to the character of the Passion narrative, on the one side, or the program of sayings and stories to be utilized in the articulation of the various Gospels, respectively, on the other: a fine example of a blatant topical (narrative) protocol.

If such a protocol were in play, then when discussing a given Mishnah paragraph, compilers of both Talmuds would have introduced the same themes, not mentioned in the Mishnah (whether in the paragraph at hand or in some other paragraph) but held in common to belong to the clarification of that Mishnah paragraph. But where a topic not introduced in a given Mishnah paragraph is treated by both Talmuds, the framers of one Talmud will deal with that topic in one place, those of the other, in a different place; nothing tells them both to treat the same topic in the same context. That is so when it comes to matters of lore; where we have the same story, it will not always serve the same purpose; and it is true when it comes to matters of law.

I dwell on the matter of the null hypothesis because the stakes in a "Q" or a protocol shared by the two Talmuds are high. If the Talmuds are linked not at the surface but at least underneath, then any allegation that the second Talmud considerably recasts the statement of the first, therefore that the second Talmud forms a fresh and original stage in the formation of the hermeneutics that bears the theology of Judaism, would contradict the literary facts of the documents that serve as bearers of the theological re-presentation of the Torah.

But that is not the case. We have seen in the sample of evidence just now reviewed that there is no substantial, shared tradition, either in fully spelled-out statements in so many words, or in the gist of ideas, or in topical conventions, or in intellectual characteristics. The Bavli presents an utterly autonomous statement, speaking in its own behalf and in its own way about its own interests. The shared traits are imposed and extrinsic and formal: documents cited by one set of writers and by another. The differentiating characteristics are intrinsic and substantive: what is to be done with the shared formed statements taken from prior writings. The framers of the Bavli in no way found guidance in the processes by which the Yerushalmi's compositions and composites took shape, either in the dim past of the document, or, it goes without saying, in the results of those processes as well. The Talmuds differ not in general only, but in detail; not in how they make their statements or in what they say but, at a more profound level, in their very generative layers, in the intellectual morphology characteristic of each.

Now that we know how utterly different the Bavli is from the Yerushalmi, it is time to account for the difference. Let me begin with generalizations, presently illustrated. The difference between the Talmuds is that same difference that distinguishes jurisprudence from philosophy. The distinction between the documents lies partly in the quality of mind that characterizes each. The Yerushalmi talks in details, the Bavli in large truths; the Yerushalmi tells us what the Mishnah says, the Bavli, what it means. That is to say, the Bavli demonstrates how the Mishnah's laws form law, the way in which its rules attest to the ontological unity of truth. But the true difference between them derives from not intellection but outcome (to be sure, the product of intellection). The Bavli thinks more deeply about deep things, and, in the end, its authors also think about different things from those that occupy the writers of the Yerushalmi. Their modes of thought, conveyed by their principles of interpretation of the Mishnah and the formation of sustained analytical inquiries show their independence from their predecessors.

How do the Talmuds compare? The example we shall now examine in some detail yields these generalizations: [1] the first Talmud analyzes evidence, the second investigates premises; [2] the first remains wholly within the limits of its case, the second vastly transcends the bounds of the case altogether; and [3] the first wants to know the rule, the second asks about the principle and its implications for other cases. The one Talmud provides an exegesis and amplification of the Mishnah, the other, a theoretical study of the law in all its magnificent abstraction – transforming the Mishnah into testimony to a deeper reality altogether: to the law behind the laws. And it is that to which the Bavli itself attests – a hermeneutics that insists upon inquiry into premises, implications, and principles behind cases and how they coalesce – that forms the theological re-presentation of the Torah accomplished by the Bavli itself. So the contrast between the two Talmuds affords access to more than merely literary data on how two commentaries to the same text differ – much more.

To make these points stick,[6] we turn to Mishnah-tractate Gittin 1:1 as read by both Talmuds. Let us first look at the passage and the way that the Yerushalmi reads it. As usual, passages of the Mishnah or Tosefta are given in boldface type.

---

[6]*The Bavli's Unique Voice* contains a very substantial selection of further examples. This is the positive side of the negative that I could not find points of intersection, let alone duplication in the later Talmud of the earlier Talmud's writings.

Yerushalmi to Gittin 1:1

[A] [43a] He who delivers a writ of divorce from overseas must state, "In my presence it was written, and in my presence it was signed."

[B] Rabban Gamaliel says, "Also: He who delivers [a writ of divorce] from Reqem or from Heger [must make a similar declaration]."

[C] R. Eliezer says, "Even from Kefar Ludim to Lud."

[D] And sages say, "He must state, 'In my presence it was written, and in my presence it was signed,' only in the case of him who delivers a writ of divorce from overseas,

[E] "and him who takes [one abroad]."

[F] And he who delivers [a writ of divorce] from one overseas province to another must state, "In my presence it was written, and in my presence it was signed."

[G] Rabban Simeon b. Gamaliel says, "Even [if he brings one] from one jurisdiction to another [in the same town.]"

[I.A] Now here is a problem. In the case of one who brings a deed of gift from overseas, does he have to state, "Before me it was written and before me it was signed"? [Why is the rule stricter for writs of divorce?]

[B] R. Joshua b. Levi said, "The case [of writs of divorce] is different, for [overseas] they are not expert in the details of preparing writs of divorce [properly]."

[C] Said R. Yohanan, "It is a lenient ruling which [sages] have provided for her, that she should not sit an abandoned wife [unable to remarry]."

[D] And is this a lenient ruling? It is only a stringent one, for if the messenger did not testify, "In my presence it was written, and in my presence it was signed," you are not indeed going to permit the woman to remarry [at all], [so what sort of a lenient ruling do we have here]?

[E] Said R. Yosé, "The strict requirement which you have imposed on the matter at the outset, requiring the messenger to testify, 'Before me it was written and before me it was signed,' turns out to be a lenient ruling which you have set for the case at the end. For if the husband later on should come and call into question the validity of the document, his cavil will be null."

[F] [As to the denial of credibility to the husband's challenge to the validity of the writ of divorce,] R. Mana contemplated ruling, "That applies to a complaint dealing with matters external to the body of the document itself."

[G] But as to a complaint as to the body of the document itself [do we believe him]? [Surely we take seriously his claim that the document is a forgery.]

[H] And as to a complaint [against the writ] which has no substance [one may not take the husband's cavil seriously].

[I] And even in the case of a cavil which has substance [should he not be believed]? [Surely he should be believed.]

[J] Said R. Yosé b. R. Bun, "[No, the original statement stands in all these cases]. [That is to say,] since you have said that the reason you have applied in the case a more stringent requirement at the outset, that the messenger must declare, 'Before me it was [written, and before me it was] signed,' is that you have imposed a lenient ruling at the end, for if the husband later on should come and call into question the validity of the document, his cavil will be null, and we must conclude that there is no difference at all whether the complaint against the validity of the document pertains to matters external to the body of the document or to matters internal to the body of the document, nor is there any difference whether the complaint deals with matters of no substance or matters of substance. [Once the necessary formula is recited by the messenger, the document has been validated against all future doubts.]"

[K]   And yet should one not take account that invalid witnesses may have signed the document?

[L]   Said R. Abun, "The husband is not suspect of disrupting [the wife's future marriage] in a matter which is in the hands of Heaven, [but is suspect of doing so only in a matter which lies before a court]. [Hence we do not take account of the husband's issuing such a complaint as is entered at G.]

[M]   "In a court proceeding he is suspect of disrupting the wife's [future marriage]. For since he knows full well that if he should come and register a complaint against the validity of the document, his complaint will be deemed null, even he sees to it [when he prepares the writ] that it is signed by valid witnesses."

Unit I clarifies the force of the required declaration. Once the messenger so states, the husband cannot later on invalidate the document. Since, in the meantime, it is assumed that the wife will remarry, the importance of limiting the original husband's power is self-evident. That, sum and substance, is what interests the Yerushalmi.

Now let us see how the Bavli reads the same paragraph. I give only part of the discussion, the first nine units of a score that comprise one of the Talmud's great, sustained composites – enough so that the point is abundantly clear. Use of italics here indicates an Aramaic original.

Bavli to Gittin 1:1

A.   He who delivers a writ of divorce from overseas must state, "In my presence it was written, and in my presence it was signed."

B.   Rabban Gamaliel says, "Also: He who delivers [a writ of divorce] from Reqem or from Heger [must make a similar declaration]."

C.   R. Eliezer says, "Even from Kefar Ludim to Lud."

D.   And sages say, "He must state, 'In my presence it was written, and in my presence it was signed,' only in the case of him who delivers a writ of divorce from overseas.

I.1   A.   What is the operative consideration here?

B.   Said Rabbah, **[2B]** "Because [Israelites overseas] are inexpert in the requirement that the writ be prepared for the particular person for whom it is intended."

C. Raba said, "Because valid witnesses are not readily found to confirm the signatures [and the declaration of the agent serves to authenticate the signatures of the witnesses]."

D. *So what is at issue between these two explanations?*

E. *At issue between them is a case in which two persons brought the writ of divorce [in which case Raba's consideration is null], or a case in which a writ of divorce was brought from one province to another in the Land of Israel [in which case the consideration of Rabbah is null], or from one place to another in the same overseas province.*

I.2 A. *And from the perspective of Rabbah, who has said, "Because [Israelites overseas] are inexpert in the requirement that the writ be prepared for the particular person for whom it is intended," there should still be a requirement that the writ of divorce is brought by two persons, such as is the requirement in respect to all acts of testimony that are spelled out in the Torah [in line with Deut. 19:15]!*

B. An individual witness is believed where the question has to do with a prohibition [for example, as to personal status, but not monetary matters].

C. *Well, I might well concede that we do hold,* an individual witness is believed where the question has to do with a prohibition, *for example, in the case of a piece of fat, which may be forbidden fat or may be permitted fat, in which instance the status of a prohibition has not yet been assumed. But here, with regard to the case at hand, where the presence of a prohibition is assumed, namely, that the woman is married, it amounts to a matter involving prohibited sexual relations,* and a matter involving sexual relations is settled by no fewer than two witnesses.

D. Most overseas Israelites are expert in the rule that the document has to be written for the expressed purpose of divorcing this particular woman.

E. *And even R. Meir, who takes account of not only the condition of the majority but even that of the minority [in this case, people not expert in that rule], concedes the ordinary scribe of a court knows the law full well, and it was rabbis who imposed the requirement. But here* **[3A]** *so as to prevent the woman from entering the status of a deserted wife [unable to remarry], they made the rule lenient.*

F. *Is this really a lenient ruling? It is in fact a strict ruling, since, if you require that the writ of divorce be brought by two messengers, there is no possibility of the husband's coming and challenging its validity and having it invalidated, but if only one person brings the document, he can still do so!*

G. Since the master has said, "As to how many persons must be present when the messenger hands over the writ of divorce to the wife, there is a dispute between R. Yohanan and R. Hanina. One party maintains it must be at least two, the other three." *Now, since that is the fact, the messenger will clarify the husband's intentions to begin with, and the husband under such circumstances is not going to come and try to invalidate the writ and so get himself into trouble later on.*

I.3 A. *Now from the perspective of Raba, who said that the operative consideration is, "Because valid witnesses are not readily found to confirm the signatures [and the declaration of the agent serves to authenticate the signatures of the witnesses]," there should still be a* requirement that the writ of divorce is brought by two persons, such as is the requirement in respect to all acts of confirming the validity of documents in general!

B. An individual witness is believed where the question has to do with a prohibition [for example, as to personal status, but not monetary matters].

C. *Well, I might well concede that we do hold,* an individual witness is believed where the question has to do with a prohibition, *for example, in the case of a piece of fat, which may be forbidden fat or may be permitted fat, in which instance the status of a prohibition has not yet been assumed. But here, with regard to the case at hand, where the presence of a prohibition is assumed, namely, that the woman is married, it amounts to a matter involving prohibited sexual relations,* and a matter involving sexual relations is settled by no fewer than two witnesses.

D. *Well, in strict law, there should be no requirement that witnesses confirm the signature on other documents either, in line with what R. Simeon b. Laqish said, for said R. Simeon b. Laqish, "Witnesses who have signed a document are treated as equivalent to those who have been cross-examined in court." It was rabbis who imposed the requirement. But here so as to prevent the woman from entering the status of a deserted wife [unable to remarry], they made the rule lenient.*

E. *Is this really a lenient ruling? It is in fact a strict ruling, since, if you require that the writ of divorce be brought by two messengers, there is no possibility of the husband's coming and challenging its validity and having it invalidated, but if only one person brings the document, he can still do so!*

F. Since the master has said, "As to how many persons must be present when the messenger hands over the writ of divorce to the wife, there is a dispute between R. Yohanan and R. Hanina. One party maintains it must be at least two, the other three." *Now, since that is the fact, the messenger will clarify the husband's intentions to begin with, and the husband under such circumstances is not going to come and try to invalidate the writ and so get himself into trouble later on.*

I.4 A. *So how come Raba didn't give the operative consideration that Rabbah did?*

B. *He will say to you,* "Does the Tannaite rule state, **In my presence it was written** for the purpose of divorcing this woman in particular, **and in my presence it was signed** for the purpose of divorcing this woman in particular?"

C. *And Rabbah?*

D. *Strictly speaking, it should have been formulated for Tannaite purposes in that way. But if you get verbose, the bearer may omit something that is required.*

E. *Yeah, well, even as it is, the bearer may omit something that is required!*

F. *One out of three phrases he may leave out, but one out of two phrases he's not going to leave out.*

G. *So how come Rabbah didn't give the operative consideration that Raba did?*

H. *He will say to you,* "If so, the Tannaite formulate should be, **In my presence it was signed** – *and nothing more! What need do I have for the language,* **In my presence it was written**? *That is to indicate that* *we require that the writ be prepared for the sole purpose of divorcing this particular woman.*

I. And Raba?

J. *Strictly speaking, it should have been formulated for Tannaite purposes in that way.* But if it were done that way, people might come to confuse the matter of the confirmation of documents in general and hold that only a single witness is required for that purpose.

K. And Rabbah?

L. *But is the parallel all that close? There the required language is, "We know that this is Mr. So-and-so's signature," while here it is, "In my presence...." In that case, a woman is not believed to testify, in this case, a woman is believed to testify. In that case, an interested party cannot testify, here an interested party can testify.*

M. And Raba?

N. *He will say to you, "Here, too, if the agent says, 'I know...,' he is believed, and since that is the fact, there really is the consideration [if he says only,* 'In my presence it was signed' (Simon)], *people might come to confuse the matter of the confirmation of documents in general and hold that only a single witness is required for that purpose."*

I.5 A. *From the perspective of Rabbah, who has said,* "Because [Israelites overseas] are inexpert in the requirement that the writ be prepared for the particular person for whom it is intended," *who is the authority that requires that* the writ of divorce be both written for the particular person for whom it is intended *and also requires* [3B] that it be signed for the particular person for whom it is intended? *It obviously isn't R. Meir, for he requires the correct declaration as to the signing of the document, but not as to the writing of the document, for we have learned in the Mishnah:* **They do not write [a writ of divorce] on something which is attached to the ground. [If] one wrote it on something attached to the ground, then plucked it up, signed it, and gave it to her, it is valid [M. 2:4A-B].** [The anonymous rule, assumed to stand for Meir, holds that what matters is the signing, not the writing, of the document.] *It also cannot be R. Eleazar, who maintains that the writing be done properly* [with correct intentionality as to the preparation of the document for the particular woman to whom it is to be given as a writ of divorce], *but as to the signing, he imposes no such requirement. And, further, should you say that, in point of fact, it really is R. Eleazar, and as to his not requiring correct procedure as to the signing of the document with proper specificity* [with correct intentionality as to the preparation of the document for the particular woman to whom it is to be given as a writ of divorce], *that is on the strength of the authority of the Torah, but as to the position of rabbis, he would concur that that requirement must be met — if that is your claim, lo, there are three kinds of writs of divorce that rabbis have declared invalid [but the Torah has not invalidated], and among them, R. Eleazar does not include one that has not been signed with appropriate intentionality for that particular woman, as we see in the following Mishnah:* **There are three writs of divorce which are invalid, but if the wife [subsequently] remarried [on the strength of those documents], the offspring [nonetheless] is valid: [If] he wrote it in his own handwriting, but there are no witnesses on it; there are** witnesses on it, but it is not dated; it is dated, but there is only a single witness – lo, these are three kinds of invalid writs of divorce, but if the wife [subsequently] remarried, the offspring is valid. R. Eleazar says, "Even though there are no witnesses on it [the document itself], but he handed it over to her in the presence of witnesses, it is valid. And she collects [her marriage contract] from mortgaged property. For witnesses sign the writ of divorce only for the good order of the world" [M. Git. 9:4].

B.   *Well, then, it must be R. Meir, and so far as he is concerned, as to his not requiring correct procedure as to the signing of the document with proper specificity* [with correct intentionality as to the preparation of the document for the particular woman to whom it is to be given as a writ of divorce], *that is on the strength of the authority of the Torah, but as to the position of rabbis, he would concur that that requirement must be met.*

C.   Yes, but said R. Nahman, "R. Meir would rule, 'Even if one found it in the garbage [4A] and had it properly signed and handed it over to her, it is a valid writ of divorce'"! *And, as a matter of fact, this ruling is to say, "valid so far as the Torah is concerned," then the language that R. Nahman should have used is not, "R. Meir would rule," but rather, "The rule of the Torah is...."*

D.   *Rather, the position before us represents the view of R. Eleazar, and the case in which R. Eleazar does not require a signature incised for the sake of the particular woman for whom the document is prepared, that is a case in which there are no witnesses at all. But in a case in which there are witnesses, he does impose that requirement. For said R. Abba, "R. Eleazar concurs in the case of a writ disqualified on the basis of its own character that it is invalid* [and here we have invalid witnesses]."

E.   *R. Ashi said, "Lo, who is the authority at hand? It is R. Judah, for we have learned in the Mishnah:* R. Judah declares it invalid, so long as writing it and signing it are [not] on something which is plucked up from the ground."

F.   *So to begin with why didn't we assign the passage to R. Judah?*

G.   *We first of all reverted to R. Meir, for an otherwise unattributed statement in the Mishnah belongs to R. Meir. We reverted to R. Eleazar, because it is an established fact for us that in matters of writs of divorce, the decided law is in accord with his position.*

I.6   A.   *We have learned in the Mishnah:* Rabban Gamaliel says, "Also: He who delivers [a writ of divorce] from Reqem or from Heger [must make a similar declaration]." R. Eliezer says, "Even from Kefar Ludim to Lud":

B.   *And said Abbayye, "We deal with towns that are near the Land of Israel and those that are entirely surrounded by the Land of Israel."*

C.   *And said Rabbah bar bar Hannah, "I myself have seen that place, and the distance is the same as that between Be Kube and Pumbedita."*

I.7   A.   *Does it then follow that the initial Tannaite authority before us takes the view that when bringing a writ of divorce from the places named here, one need not make the stated declaration? Then is not this what is under dispute between the two authorities: The one authority takes the view that the operative consideration is, because* [Israelites overseas] *are inexpert* in the requirement that the writ be prepared for the particular person for whom it is intended, *and the residents of these areas have learned what to do; and the other authority holds that the operative consideration is,* because valid witnesses are not readily found to confirm the signatures [and the declaration of the agent serves to authenticate the signatures of the witnesses], *and in these places, too, witnesses are not readily found.*

B. *Not at all. Rabbah can work matters out in accord with his theory, and Raba can work matters out in accord with his theory.*

C. *Rabbah can work matters out in accord with his theory: All parties concur that the reason for the required declaration is that* [Israelites overseas] are inexpert in the requirement that the writ be prepared for the particular person for whom it is intended, *and here, what is at issue is, the initial authority holds that since these are located near the Land of Israel, they learn what is required; then Rabban Gamaliel comes along to say that those located in areas surrounded by the Land of Israel have learned the rules, while those nearby have not, then R. Eliezer comes along to indicate that those located in areas surrounded by the Land of Israel also are not exempt,* so as not to make a distinction among territories all assigned to the category of "overseas."

D. *Raba can work matters out in accord with his theory: All parties concur that the reason for the required declaration is that* valid witnesses are not readily found to confirm the signatures. *The initial Tannaite authority takes the view that these locales, since they are located near the border, will produce witnesses; Rabban Gamaliel comes along to say that in the areas surrounded by the Land of Israel, witnesses are going to be readily turned up, while in the areas near the Land, that is not the case; then R. Eliezer comes along to say that also in the areas surrounded by the Land of Israel, that is not the case,* so as not to make a distinction among territories all assigned to the category of "overseas."

I.8 A. *We have learned in the Mishnah:* **And sages say, "He must state, 'In my presence it was written, and in my presence it was signed,' only in the case of him who delivers a writ of divorce from overseas, and him who takes [one abroad]":**

B. *Does it then follow that the initial Tannaite authority before us takes the view that one who takes a writ of divorce overseas is not required to make the stated declaration? Then is not this what is at issue? The one authority maintains that the operative consideration is,* because [Israelites overseas] are inexpert in the requirement that the writ be prepared for the particular person for whom it is intended, **[4B]** *and the residents of these areas have learned what to do; and the other authority holds that the operative consideration is,* because valid witnesses are not readily found to confirm the signatures [and the declaration of the agent serves to authenticate the signatures of the witnesses], *and in these places, too, witnesses are not readily found.*

C. *Rabbah can work matters out in accord with his theory, and Raba can work matters out in accord with his theory.*

D. *Rabbah can work matters out in accord with his theory: All parties concur that the reason for the required declaration is that* [Israelites overseas] are inexpert in the requirement that the writ be prepared for the particular person for whom it is intended, *and here, what is at issue is, whether we make a decree extending the obligation that applies to one who brings a writ from overseas to the Land of Israel to the person who takes a writ from the Land of Israel overseas, and the rabbis cited below maintain that we do make a decree covering one who takes such a writ overseas on account of the decree covering bringing such a decree to the Land of Israel.*

E. *Raba can work matters out in accord with his theory: All parties concur that the reason for the required declaration is that* valid witnesses are not readily found to confirm the signatures.

I.9 A. *We have learned in the Mishnah:* **And he who delivers [a writ of divorce] from one overseas province to another must state, "In my presence it was written, and in my presence it was signed."**

B. Lo, if he takes it from one place to another in the same overseas province, he does not have to make the required declaration. *Now that poses no problem to Raba [who can explain why], but it does present a conflict with the position of Rabbah!*

C. *Do not draw the conclusion that* if he takes it from one place to another in the same overseas province, he does not have to make the required declaration. *Rather, draw the conclusion that* if he brings it from one province to another in the Land of Israel, he does not have to make that declaration.

D. *But that position is spelled out explicitly in the Mishnah paragraph itself:* **He who delivers a writ of divorce in the Land of Israel does not have to state, "In my presence it was written, and in my presence it was signed"!**

E. *If I had only that statement to go by, I should have concluded that that is the case only after the fact, but to begin with, that is not the rule. So we are informed to the contrary.*

F. *There are those who set up the objection in the following language:* **[And he who delivers [a writ of divorce] from one overseas province to another must state, "In my presence it was written, and in my presence it was signed":]** Lo, if he takes it from one place to another in the same overseas province, he does not have to make the required declaration. *Now that poses no problem to Rabbah [who can explain why], but it does present a conflict with the position of Raba!*

G. *Do not draw the conclusion that* if he takes it from one province to another in the Land of Israel he does not have to make the declaration, *but say:* Lo, if it is within the same province overseas, he does not have to make that declaration, but if it is from one province to another in the Land of Israel, *what is the law?* He has to make the declaration.

H. *Then the Tannaite formulation ought to be:* **And he who delivers [a writ of divorce]** without further articulation.

I. In point of fact, even if one brings a writ of divorce from one province to another in the Land of Israel, *he also does not have to make the declaration, for, since there are pilgrims, witnesses will always be available.*

J. *That poses no problem for the period at which the house of the sanctuary is standing, but for the period in which the house of the sanctuary is not standing, what is to be said?*

K. *Since courts are well established, there still will be plenty of witnesses.*

I should gladly present the remainder of this monumental composition (not a mere composite but a cogent and continuous statement), which runs on for twenty units, but enough has been given to establish the character of the whole, and readers do not have to share my intense admiration for the Bavli as a piece of writing to follow the argument I present here. So let us turn to the sample at hand. At their reading of M. Gittin 1:1, where the Talmuds intersect but diverge in the reading of the Mishnah paragraph, we are able to identify what is at issue. Here is an occasion on which we can see the differences between the Yerushalmi's and the Bavli's representation of a conflict of principles contained within a Mishnah ruling.

Now to look at the two Talmuds' reading of the same Mishnah rule: The Yerushalmi maintains that at issue is the inexpertness of overseas courts vs. a lenient ruling to avoid the situation of the abandoned wife; the Bavli, inexpertness of overseas courts vs. paucity of witnesses. How these diverse accounts differ in intellectual character and also program is hardly revealed by that brief precis. That explains why I give a great part of its massive and brilliant discussion. Only then will my insistence on the real difference, the Talmuds' fundamental difference in the intellectual morphology and structure that form the substrate of each writing, emerge in all its clarity. When we see how the two Talmuds respond to the same question, we realize that the Bavli is different from the Yerushalmi not in detail but in very character. Despite commonalities of form, which validate comparison, the two Talmuds in fact are utterly unlike pieces of writing. The second of the two Talmuds makes its own statement not merely because it very often says different things from the Yerushalmi, or because it says different things in different ways (though both are the case).

The Talmud of Babylonia stands on its own not only because its framers think differently; nor merely because their modes of thought and analysis in no way correspond to those of the Yerushalmi. The governing reason is that, for the framers of the Bavli, what is at stake *in thought* is different from *the upshot of thought* as conceived by the authors of the Yerushalmi's compositions and compilers of its composites. Specifically, for the sages who produced the Bavli, the ultimate compilers and redactors of the document, what at issue is not laws but law: how things hold together at the level of high abstraction. After we have compared the Talmuds at this crucial point, I shall point to the evidence that sustains that theory of the document.

To accomplish the work, I set side by side the whole of the Yerushalmi's discussion and part of the Bavli's. The comparison makes the case, and a quick reference back to the passage we have just examined will justify the generalizations I offer at the end.

[I.A] Now here is a problem. In the case of one who brings a deed of gift from overseas, does he have to state, "Before me it was written and before me it was signed"? [Why is the rule stricter for writs of divorce?]

[B] R. Joshua b. Levi said, "The case [of writs of divorce] is different, for [overseas] they are not expert in the details of preparing writs of divorce [properly]."

[C] Said R. Yohanan, "It is a lenient ruling which [sages] have provided for her, that she should not sit an abandoned wife [unable to remarry]."

[D] And is this a lenient ruling? It is only a stringent one, for if the messenger did not testify, "In my presence it was written, and in my presence it was signed," you are not indeed going to permit the woman to remarry [at all], [so what sort of a lenient ruling do we have here]?

[E] Said R. Yosé, "The strict requirement which you have imposed on the matter at the outset, requiring the messenger to testify, 'Before me it was written and before me it was signed,' turns out to be a lenient ruling which you have

I.1 A. What is the operative consideration here?

B. Said Rabbah, [2B] "Because [Israelites overseas] are inexpert in the requirement that the writ be prepared for the particular person for whom it is intended."

C. Raba said, "Because valid witnesses are not readily found to confirm the signatures [and the declaration of the agent serves to authenticate the signatures of the witnesses]."

D. *So what is at issue between these two explanations?*

E. *At issue between them is a case in which two persons brought the writ of divorce [in which case Raba's consideration is null], or a case in which a writ of divorce was brought from one province to another in the Land of Israel [in which case the consideration of Rabbah is null], or from one place to another in the same overseas province.*

I.2 A. *And from the perspective of Rabbah, who has said, "Because [Israelites overseas] are inexpert in the requirement that the writ be prepared for the particular person for whom it is intended," there should still be a requirement that the writ of divorce is brought by two persons, such as is* set for the case at the end. For if the husband later on should come and call into question the validity of the document, his cavil will be null."

[F] [As to the denial of credibility to the husband's challenge to the validity of the writ of divorce,] R. Mana contemplated ruling, "That applies to a complaint dealing with matters external to the body of the document itself."

[G] But as to a complaint as to the body of the document itself [do we believe him]? [Surely we take seriously his claim that the document is a forgery.]

[H] And as to a complaint [against the writ] which has no substance [one may not take the husband's cavil seriously].

[I] And even in the case of a cavil which has substance [should he not be believed]? [Surely he should be believed.]

[J] Said R. Yosé b. R. Bun, "[No, the original statement stands in all these cases]. [That is to say,] since you have said that the reason you have applied in the case a more stringent requirement at the outset, that the messenger must declare, 'Before me it was [written, and be

the requirement in respect to all acts of testimony that are spelled out in the Torah [in line with Deut. 19:15]!

B. An individual witness is believed where the question has to do with a prohibition [for example, as to personal status, but not monetary matters].

C. *Well, I might well concede that we do hold,* an individual witness is believed where the question has to do with a prohibition, *for example, in the case of a piece of fat, which may be forbidden fat or may be permitted fat, in which instance the status of a prohibition has not yet been assumed. But here, with regard to the case at hand, where the presence of a prohibition is assumed, namely, that the woman is married, it amounts to a matter involving prohibited sexual relations, and a* matter involving sexual relations is settled by no fewer than two witnesses.

fore me it was] signed,' is that you have imposed a lenient ruling at the end, for if the husband later on should come and call into question the validity of the document, his cavil will be null, and we must conclude that there is no difference at all whether the complaint against the validity of the document pertains to matters external to the body of the document or to matters internal to the body of the document, nor is there any difference whether the complaint deals with matters of no substance or matters of substance. [Once the necessary formula is recited by the messenger, the document has been validated against all future doubts.]"

[K] And yet should one not take account that invalid witnesses may have signed the document?

[L] Said R. Abun, "The husband is not suspect of disrupting [the wife's future marriage] in a matter which is in the hands of Heaven, [but is suspect of doing so only in a matter which lies before a court]. [Hence we do not take account of the husband's issuing such a

D. Most overseas Israelites are expert in the rule that the document has to be written for the expressed purpose of divorcing this particular woman.

E. *And even R. Meir, who takes account of not only the condition of the majority but even that of the minority [in this case, people not expert in that rule], concedes the ordinary scribe of a court knows the law full well, and it was rabbis who imposed the requirement. But here* [3A] *so as to prevent the woman from entering the status of a deserted wife [unable to remarry], they made the rule lenient.*

F. *Is this really a lenient ruling? It is in fact a strict ruling, since, if you require that the writ of divorce be brought by two messengers, there is no possibility of the husband's coming and challenging its validity and having it invalidated, but if only one person brings the document, he can still do so!*

G. Since the master has said, "As to how many persons must be present when the messenger hands over the writ of divorce to the wife, there is a dispute between R. Yohanan and R. Hanina. One party maintains it must be at least two, the other three." *Now, since that*

complaint as is en-
tered at G.]

[M] "In a court proceeding
he is suspect of dis-
rupting the wife's
[future marriage]. For
since he knows full
well that if he should
come and register a
complaint against the
validity of the docu-
ment, his complaint
will be deemed null,
even he sees to it
[when he prepares the
writ] that it is signed
by valid witnesses."

*is the fact, the messenger
will clarify the
husband's intentions to
begin with, and the
husband under such
circumstances is not
going to come and try to
invalidate the writ and
so get himself into
trouble later on.*

Readers will stipulate that the Bavli proceeds in the same fair and balanced manner to expose the dispute of Yohanan and Joshua b. Levi: if this, then what about that; if that, then what about this; how does this deal with that, how does that deal with this – and so on through a movement, a minuet really, of perfect classical order, proportion, balance. But enough has been given to provide a full grasp of the Bavli's intellectual morphology. Here the Yerushalmi, as much as the Bavli, presents a sustained argument, not just a snippet of self-evidently informative information, as at its reading of M. B.M. 1:1. So we now examine a fully exposed argument in the Yerushalmi as against its counterpart in the Bavli.

The Yerushalmi presents two theses, A-C, then challenges the second of the two, D-E. This produces a secondary inspection of the facts of the matter, F-I, and a resolution of the issues raised, J; then another secondary issue, K-M. Is there an *Auseinandersetzung* between the two conflicting parties, Joshua b. Levi and Yohanan? Not at all. There is, in fact, no exchange. Instead of a dialogue, formed into an ongoing set of challenges, we have the voice of the Talmud intervening, "And is this a lenient ruling at all?" There is no pretense that Joshua asks a question to Yohanan, or Yohanan to Joshua. The controlling voice is that of the Talmud itself, which sets up pieces of information and manipulates them. B. I.5, by contrast, presents us with one of the Bavli's many superb representations of issues, and we see that the goal of contention is not argument for its own sake, nor is the medium the message, as some have imagined.

Here is an instance of what I maintain characterizes the Bavli and not the Yerushalmi: the search for the unitary foundations of the diverse laws, through an inquiry into the premises of discrete rules, the comparison and contrast of those premises, the statement of the emergent principles, and the comparison and contrast of those principles with the ones that derive from other cases and their premises – a process, an inquiry, without end into the law behind the laws. What the Yerushalmi ignores but the Bavli urgently seeks, beyond its presentation of the positions at hand, is to draw attention to the premises of those positions, the reasoning behind them, the evidence that supports them, the argument that transforms evidence into demonstration, and even the authority, among those who settle questions by expressing opinions, who can hold the combination of principles or premises that underpin a given position.

B. at I.1 states the contrary explanations and identifies the issues between them. Then one position is examined, challenged, defended – fully exposed. The second position is given equal attention, also challenged, also defended, in all, fully exposed. The two positions having been fairly stated and amply argued, we proceed to the nub of the matter: If X is so right, then why has Y not adopted his position? And if Y, then why not X? This second level of exchange allows each position to be redefended, reexplained, reexposed – all on fresh grounds. Now at this point, we have identified two or more principles that have been combined to yield a position before us, so the question arises, what authority, among those who stand behind the law, holds these positions, which, while not contradictory, also are not commonly combined in a single theory of the law? I.5 then exposes the several possibilities – three major authorities, each with his several positions to be spelled out and tested against the allegations at hand.

When we observe that one Talmud is longer than the other, or one Talmud gives a fuller account than the other, we realize that such an observation is trivial. The real difference between the Talmuds emerges from this – and I state with emphasis: *the Bavli's completely different theory of what it wishes to investigate.* And that difference derives from why the framers of the Bavli's compositions and composites did the work to begin with. The outlines of the intellectual character of the work flow from the purpose of the project, not the reverse; and thence, the modes of thought, the specifics of analytical initiative – all these are secondary to intellectual morphology. So first comes the motivation for thought, then the morphology of thought, then the media of thought, in that order.

That explains what I mean by saying, the difference between the Yerushalmi and the Bavli is the difference between jurisprudence and philosophy: the one is a work of exegesis in search of clarity of rules and, at its best, in quest of the jurisprudential system, the other, an exercise of sustained, critical, and dialectical argument and analysis in quest of philosophical truth. To state matters simply, the Yerushalmi presents and explains the laws, the rule for this, the rule for that – pure and simple; "law" bears is conventional meaning of jurisprudence. The Bavli presents the law, now in the philosophical sense of, the abstract issues of theory, the principles at play far beneath the surface of detailed discussion, the law behind the laws. And that, we see, is not really "law," in any ordinary sense of jurisprudence; it is law in a deeply philosophical sense: the rules that govern the way things are, that define what is proportionate and orderly and properly composed.

The reason that the Bavli does commonly what the Yerushalmi does seldom and then rather clumsily – the balancing of arguments, the careful formation of a counterpoint of reasons, the excessively fair representation of contradictory positions (why doesn't X take the position of Y? why doesn't Y take the position of X? Indeed!) – is not that the Bavli's framers are uninterested in conclusions and outcome. It is that for their Talmud, the deep structure of reason is the goal, and the only way to penetrate into how things are at their foundations is to investigate how conflicting positions rest on principles to be exposed and juxtaposed, balanced, and, if possible, negotiated, if necessary, left in the balance.

The analogy to music past and immediate makes the point. The Yerushalmi is an eighteenth-century fugue, the Bavli, a later twentieth-century symphonic metamorphosis: not merely more complicated, but rather, a different conception altogether of what music is – and can do. And while, in the end, neither kind of music is the only valid kind, taste and judgment do come into play; while we value and enjoy the simplicities of the baroque, the profundities, the inventiveness, the abstraction of our own day's music speak to us and reshape our hearing. So, too, while anyone can appreciate the direct and open clarity of the Yerushalmi (in those vast spaces of the text that are clear and accessible), no one can avoid the compelling, insistent, scrupulously fair but unrelenting command of the Bavli: see to the center of things, the core of mind, the workings of intellect in its own right.

What I find interesting therefore is that even when the facts are the same, the issues identical, and the arguments matched, the Bavli's author manages to lay matters out in a very distinctive way. And that way yields as a sustained, somewhat intricate argument (requiring us to keep in the balance both names and positions of authorities and also the objective issues and facts) what the Yerushalmi's method of representation gives us as a rather simple sequence of arguments. If we say that the Bavli is "dialectical," presenting a moving argument, from point to point, and the Yerushalmi is static, through such a reductive understatement we should vastly misrepresent the difference. The Yerushalmi's argument unfolds; the Bavli's argument assumes a formally static position at I.2. Rather, the Bavli's presentation is one – as we have seen before – of thrust and parry, challenge and response, assertion and counter assertion; theoretical possibility and its exposure to practical facts ("if I had to rely...I might have supposed..."); and, of course, the authorities of the Bavli (not only the framers) in the person of Abbayye are even prepared to rewrite the received Tannaite formulation. That initiative can come, I should think, only from someone totally in command of the abstractions and able to say, the details have to be this way; so the rule of mind requires; and so it shall be.

The Yerushalmi's message is that the Mishnah yields clear and present rules; its medium is the patient exegesis of Mishnah passages, the provision and analysis of facts required in the understanding of the Mishnah. That medium conveys its message about not the Mishnah alone, but – through its silences, which I think are intellectual failures of millenial dimensions – about the laws. The Bavli, for its part, conveys its message in a coherent and persistent manner through its ever-recurring medium of analysis and thought. We miss the point of the message if we misconstrue the medium: it is not the dialectical argument, and a mere reportage of questions and answers, thrust and parry, proposal and counterproposal – that does not accurately convey the medium of the Bavli, not at all. Where we ask for authority behind an unstated rule and find out whether the same authority is consistent as to principle in other cases altogether, where we show that authorities are consistent with positions taken elsewhere – here above all we stand in the very heart of the Bavli's message, but only if we know what is at stake in the medium of inquiry. Happily, our sages of blessed memory leave no doubts about what is at stake.

The Bavli's voice is unique – and so is its message. But the message emerges in the medium. The Bavli attained intellectual hegemony over the mind of Israel, the holy people, because its framers so set forth their medium that the implicit message gained immediacy in the heat of argument – so that, as a matter of fact, argument about the law served as a mode of serving God through study of the Torah. But its true power derived from the message: that the truth is one. Now to set forth, in the correct context, precisely what that sentence means. And the sole valid context is, of course, the one defined for itself by the Bavli: the Mishnah, to which the Bavli's framers turned for the structure and substance of their statement. What has all this to do with the mind of God? We still stand some distance from the answer to that question. First, let me identify what is unique in the Bavli's voice, that is, its hermeneutics. Only then will the theological premises of the hermeneutics demand exposure.

9

The Bavli's Unique Hermeneutics

Were there no Mishnah, there would be no Talmuds. The purpose of both Talmuds was simply to clarify and amplify selected passages of the Mishnah. Since the Mishnah is about life, and the Talmuds, about the Mishnah, the one way in which the Talmuds can make a statement that is not contingent and subordinate is through hermeneutics; there, and only there, their task of commentary yields the opportunity for autonomous discourse. While the Mishnah records rules governing the conduct of the holy life of Israel, the holy people, the Talmuds concern themselves with the details of the Mishnah. The one is descriptive and free-standing, the others analytical and contingent. But while the Talmud of the Land of Israel sticks close to its primary document and amplifies it, the Talmud of Babylonia takes its own path. The Bavli vastly transcends the Mishnah and forms an eloquent statement of its own, one that, to be sure, is spoken in silence, between the lines, in what is done rather than what is said.

The medium for the expression of the Bavli's statement of its own therefore was dictated by the form and assignment of the document. Since the Talmud was a commentary in form, hermeneutics served as the mode of expression for whatever, within or beyond the commentary, the framers wished to say. When we understand how the Bavli's own statement is made, which is, its principles for the reading of the received writing, then we can identify the hermeneutics, and perceive the theological statement conveyed by the hermeneutics. What makes the second Talmud unique is contained in the ways in which its hermeneutics differed from that of the first, and, it follows, the full message of the Bavli will become clear to us only when we have compared that document to its predecdessor and noticed the points of difference.

The Talmud of Babylonia speaks in one, unique voice and takes shape out of a unique singular and economical hermeneutics; there is no other like it.[1] Quite how a vast prolix (sometimes tedious) and dense writing turns out to say some few things, and to say them with such power as to impose its judgment upon an entire prior writing and also on the intellect of an entire religious world to come – that is what requires attention.[2] For it is the fact that, in the Judaism of the Dual Torah, the faithful meet God in the Torah, and the Talmud of Babylonia forms the centerpiece of the Torah.   Together with its associated Midrash compilations, the Bavli's compilers and the writers of its compositions found the way to form the mind and define the intellect of the faithful.

This they did not do through original statements of doctrine or law, since, as we have seen in Chapter Four, they went over the ground of received ideas in their established formulation. It was rather through the public display of right reasoning, the exposition of argument. Exposing the traits of rationality again and again in concrete exercises, the framers of the document said one thing about many things, much as, we have seen, the framers of Sifra did. But what they said gained heights of abstraction, aimed at transcendent truths formed in a lofty perspective;

---

[1]Claims of uniqueness of course can never be satisfactorily shown to be valid because we should have first examined all possible candidates of comparability. Having completed the comparison of the Bavli to the Yerushalmi (not to mention Scripture, the Mishnah, the Tosefta, and the prior Midrash compilations, which required no sustained inquiry), I did compare the Talmud with counterpart writings of Zoroastrianism in *Judaism and Zoroastrianism at the Dusk of Late Antiquity. How Two Ancient Faiths Wrote Down Their Great Traditions*, submitted to Athlone Press, London. For the Bavli in canonical context, see the seven-volume monograph, *The Bavli's Unique Voice. A Systematic Comparison of the Talmud of Babylonia and the Talmud of the Land of Israel* (Atlanta, 1993: Scholars Press for South Florida Studies in the History of Judaism), I-VII. I. *Bavli and Yerushalmi Qiddushin Chapter One Compared and Contrasted;* II. *Yerushalmi's, Bavli's, and Other Canonical Documents' Treatment of the Program of Mishnah-Tractate Sukkah Chapters One, Two, and Four Compared and Contrasted. A Reprise and Revision of* The Bavli and Its Sources; III. *Bavli and Yerushalmi to Selected Mishnah Chapters in the Division of Moed. Erubin Chapter One, and Moed Qatan Chapter Three;* IV. *Bavli and Yerushalmi to Selected Mishnah Chapters in the Division of Nashim. Gittin Chapter Five, Nedarim Chapter One, and Niddah Chapter One;* V. *Bavli and Yerushalmi to Selected Mishnah Chapters in the Division of Neziqin. Baba Mesia Chapter One and Makkot Chapters One and Two;* VI. *Bavli and Yerushalmi to a Miscellany of Mishnah Chapters. Gittin Chapter One, Qiddushin Chapter Two, and Hagigah Chapter Three;* and VII. *What Is Unique about the Bavli in Context? An Answer Based on Inductive Description, Analysis, and Comparison.*

[2]But we have already noted how Sifra's authors say the same thing about many different things, and the same is so of the Mishnah itself. So what distinguishes the Bavli is not its capacity to impose a single program upon diverse data, but the character of that program. That accounts for the inquiry of Chapter Seven.

Sifra's hermeneutics conveyed a judgment about the proper ordering of the world, the right source of taxonomy. The Bavli's hermeneutics conveyed judgments of a considerably weightier character.

From their example we may conclude that by showing people how to think, then, in the context of a revealed Torah, the Bavli's framers maintained that one can also guide them to what to think: by reason of right reasoning formed into right attitudes, right thoughts lead to right deeds. In the "how" of thought, the "what" found form and substance. But I maintain – to recapitulate the thesis of this book – the modes of thought came to expression in hermeneutics, the guides to reading the Torah. That is what contained the rationality that translated inchoate religion – rite, belief, attitude, symbol, myth, proposition, and emotion alike, even in its initial theological formation – into a cogent and compelling statement about the nature of mind itself. Now to make that statement stick, I have first to describe the Bavli's unique voice, then – in Chapters Nine and Ten – interpret some of its specific recurrent hermeneutical exercises.

The demonstration is feasible because of one characteristic of the document. The Bavli is uniform, beginning to end. Different from, much more than, a haphazard compilation of episodic traditions, upon examination this Talmud shows itself to be a cogent and purposive writing. Through a single, determinate set of rhetoric devices, which themselves signal the definition of the writing and the rules of reading that writing, a single program of inquiry is brought to bear on many and diverse passages of two inherited documents, the Mishnah and Scripture. The voice is one and single because it is a voice that everywhere expresses the same limited set of sounds. It is singular because these notes are arranged in one and the same way throughout. The words ever-changing, the music forms a singular chant. Even the very study of the Bavli for ages to come conveyed that remarkable fact: it is a sung writing, never read, always recited in its own chant and song.

Their writing therefore required not reading but response. That explains, also, the reason that the form of "reading" their document was singing: knowing the music, one could supply the right words; obviously, I identify the hermeneutics with that music. Right knowledge of how to decipher the script – musical notes, really – afforded access to the melody and its meaning, the music and the words. So the words written down form keys, signals to the modes of analysis.

The Talmud's statement of the Torah – Oral and Written, method and message alike – took a form unique in its context. All other Judaic writings (with the sole exception of the prior Talmud) made their statements whole and complete; what we see is what there is. No Midrash compilation of antiquity requires knowledge extrinsic to that text or some other text (Scripture, for instance) to yield its sense. By its distinctive formalization of speech, the Mishnah forms its own best commentary. When we know how it sends out its signals, we also can receive its messages. Other writings – The Fathers and The Fathers According to Rabbi Nathan, the Tosefta read in relationship to the Mishnah – all contain a complete and wholly accessible (the facts being known) statement. The framers of the Bavli took a different route, one that required readers to participate in the writing of the statement that was to be made. It was a path, therefore, that would lead from the lonely reader reading a fully exposed writing to a conversation between master and disciple, a community of meaning formed out of the chorus, singing the text. The master sang the melody, the disciples the contrapuntal statement; the music then bore the message of the text.

For in that document the framers of the Bavli wrote down not fully exposed statements but only notes toward the formulation of a complete thought. They set down the annotated but abbreviated script – by which future masters and disciples might reconstruct for themselves the drama of inquiry and argument. I am inclined to think part of the Bavli's remarkable success lay in the space it left open for the reader to join in the writing – the recreation – of the book. What is conveyed through the instrument of singsong – more really, the readers' sing-along – is the rhetoric, and, the rhetoric being everywhere uniform, what is opened by a protocol of rhetoric is not the case but the principle on which the case is to be decided; from principle we descend to underlying premise.

The character of the writing, not only its contents, therefore, set forth the systemic statement. The Bavli's one voice, sounding through all tractates, is the voice of exegetes of the Mishnah. The document is organized around the Mishnah, and that order is not merely formal, but substantive. At *every* point, if the framers have chosen a passage of Mishnah exegesis, that passage will stand at the head of all further discussion. *Every* turning point in every sustained composition and even in a large composite of compositions brings the editors back to the Mishnah, *always* read in its own order and *invariably* arranged in its own sequence. So the Bavli's authors and future readers sing together in a single way about some few things.

It follows that well-crafted and orderly rules governed the character of the sustained discourse that the writing in the Bavli sets forth. All framers of composites and editors of sequences of composites found guidance in the same limited repertoire of rules of analytical rhetoric: some few questions or procedures, directed always toward one and the same prior writing. Not only so, but a fixed order of discourse dictated that a composition of one sort, A, always come prior to a composite of another type, B. A simple logic instructed framers of composites, who sometimes also were authors of compositions, and who other times drew upon available compositions in the making of their cogent composites. So we have now to see the Bavli as entirely of a piece, cogent and coherent, made up of well-composed large-scale constructions.

The Bavli's one voice speaks in only a few, well-modulated tones: a scale of not many notes at all, comparable to our eight-tone scale. But the tonal scale of the Bavli cannot sustain comparison with our musical scale, because while with our eight tones, we can produce an infinity of melodies, the Bavli's signals yielded only a few, rather monotonous ones; and that is the very success of the document in holding together a vast range of subjects within a determinate and limited hermeneutics. True, these few, monotonous melodies sometimes continue for so long a line as to produce the effect of tedium; but they do echo in the mind. In a probe I made,[3] I found that nearly 90 percent of the whole comprises Mishnah commentary of various kinds. Not only so, but the variety of the types of Mishnah commentary is limited. Cogent composites – a sequence of well-linked comments – are further devoted to Scripture or to topics of a moral or theological character not closely tied to the exegesis of verses of Scripture; these form in the aggregate approximately 10 percent of the whole number of composites. So the Bavli has one voice, and it is the voice of a person or persons who propose to speak about one document and to do so in some few ways. Let me spell out what this means.

First, we are able to classify *all* composites (among the more than three thousand that I examined for the purpose of this description of the document) in three principal categories: [1] exegesis and amplification of the law of the Mishnah; [2] exegesis and exposition of verses of, or topics in, Scripture; [3] free-standing composites devoted to topics other than those defined by the Mishnah or Scripture. These classifications were not forced or subtle; the grounds for making them were consistent; appeal throughout was to gross and merely formal characteristics, not to subjective judgments of what unstipulated consideration might underly, or define, the intention of the framer of a passage.

Second, with that classification in place, it is a matter of simple fact that much more than four-fifths of all composites of the Bavli address the Mishnah and systematically expound that document. These composites are subject to subclassification in two ways: Mishnah exegesis and speculation and abstract theorizing about the implications of the Mishnah's statements. The former type of composite, further, is to be

---

[3]*The Rules of Composition of the Talmud of Babylonia. The Cogency of the Bavli's Composite* (Atlanta, 1991: Scholars Press for South Florida Studies in the History of Judaism).

classified in a few and simple taxa, for example, composites organized around [1] clarification of the statements of the Mishnah, [2] identification of the authority behind an anonymous statement in the Mishnah, [3] scriptural foundation for the Mishnah's rules; [4] citation and not seldom systematic exposition of the Tosefta's amplification of the Mishnah. That means that most of the Bavli is a systematic exposition of the Mishnah. The abstract that you read will conform to this description in the proportion and order of its comments on the Mishnah.

Third, the other fifth (or still less) of a given tractate will comprise composites that take shape around [1] Scripture or [2] themes or topics of a generally theological or moral character. Distinguishing the latter from the former, of course, is merely formal; very often a scriptural topic will be set forth in a theological or moral framework, and very seldom does a composite on a topic omit all reference to the amplification of a verse or topic of Scripture. The proportion of a given tractate devoted to other-than-Mishnah exegesis and amplification is generally not more than 10 percent.

The upshot is simple and demands heavy emphasis: *The Bavli speaks about the Mishnah in essentially a single voice, about fundamentally few things.* Its mode of speech as much as of thought is uniform throughout. Diverse topics produce slight differentiation in modes of analysis. The same sorts of questions phrased in the same rhetoric – a moving, or dialectical, argument, composed of questions and answers – turn out to pertain equally well to every subject and problem. The Talmud's discourse forms a closed system, in which people say the same thing about everything. The fact that the Talmud speaks in a single voice supplies striking evidence for three propositions:

(1)   that the Talmud does speak in particular for the age in which its units of discourse took shape;

(2)   that that work was done toward the end of that long period of Mishnah reception that began at the end of the second century and came to an end at the conclusion of the sixth century;

(3)   that the medium for the Talmud's message was, and could only have been, the hermeneutics that defined the writing and how it was to be read.

Since I maintain that the Bavli sets forth the theology of the received Judaism, and since, by definition, theology forms a cogent and rigorous statement out of the congeries of received ideas and attitudes, I have to ask whether the Judaism that the Bavli sets forth is a tradition, as people commonly suppose, or whether it is a free-standing statement of a system, a philosophy that has reached expression in proper proportion and full, harmonious, reasoned form. At issue is whether the writing forms a passive medium for the preservation of truth received, or an active partner in the shaping of truth. My view – to recapitulate the entire argument of the book – is that Judaism in the statement of the Bavli is not traditional but philosophical, that, given the origin and character of the truth the Bavli claimed to present, it is a theological writing, joining philosophical method to a religious message, and that the Bavli gives us a statement for the future, not a mere reprise of a received heritage of the past. What makes me take that view?

The ubiquitous character of the Talmud's single and continuous voice argues for one of two points of origin. First, powerful and prevailing conventions may have been formed in the earliest stages of the reception and study of the Mishnah, then carried on thereafter without variation or revision. Or, second, the framing of sayings into uniform and large-scale constructions of discourse – composites – may have been accomplished only toward the end of the period marked by the formation of the Talmud's units of discourse and their conglomeration into the Talmud as we know it. In the former case, we posit that the mode of reasoned analysis of the Mishnah and the repertoire of issues to be addressed to any passage of the Mishnah were defined early on, then persisted for four or five hundred years – the span of time that separates us from Columbus. The consequent, conventional mode of speech yielded that nearly total uniformity of discourse characteristic of numerous units of discourse of the Talmud at which the interpretation of a law of the Mishnah is subject to discussion. In the latter case we surmise that a vast corpus of sayings, some by themselves, some parts of larger conglomerates, was inherited at some point toward the end of the two hundred years under discussion. This corpus of miscellanies was then subjected to intense consideration as a whole, shaped and reworded into the single, cogent, and rhetorically consistent Talmudic discourse before us.

As between these two possibilities, the Bavli's rules of discourse make the latter by far the more likely. The reason is that I cannot find among the units of discourse in the Talmud evidence of differentiation among the generations of names or schools. The Bavli is not a layered document, the result of a long sedimentary process. There is no interest, for instance, in the chronological sequence in which sayings took shape and in which discussions may be supposed to have been carried on. That is to say, the Talmudic unit of discourse approaches the explanation of a passage of the Mishnah without systematic attention to the layers in which ideas were set forth, the schools among which discussion must have been divided, the sequence in which statements about a Mishnah law were made.

That fact points to formation at the end, not agglutination in successive layers of intellectual sediment. In a given unit of discourse, the focus, the organizing principle, the generative interest – these are defined solely by the issue at hand. The argument moves from point to point, directed by the inner logic of argument itself. A single plane of discourse is established. All things are leveled out, so that the line of logic runs straight and true. Accordingly, a single conception of the framing and formation of the unit of discourse stands prior to the spelling out of issues. More fundamental still, what people in general wanted was not to create topical anthologies – to put together instances of what this one said about that issue – but to exhibit the logic of that issue, viewed under the aspect of eternity. Under sustained inquiry we always find a theoretical issue, freed of all temporal considerations and the contingencies of politics and circumstance.

Once these elemental literary facts make their full impression, everything else falls into place as well. Arguments did not unfold over a long period of time, as one generation made its points, to be followed by the additions and revisions of another generation, in a process of gradual increment and agglutination running on for two hundred years. That theory of the formation of literature cannot account for the unity, stunning force, and dynamism of the Talmud's dialectical arguments. To the contrary, someone (or small group) at the end determined to reconstruct, so as to expose, the naked logic of a problem. For this purpose, oftentimes, it was found useful to cite sayings or positions in hand from earlier times. But these inherited materials underwent a process of reshaping, and, more aptly, refocusing. Whatever the original words – and we need not doubt that at times we have them – the point of everything in hand was defined and determined by the people who made it all up at the end. The whole shows a plan and program. Theirs are the minds behind the whole. In the nature of things, they did their work at the end, not at the outset. There are two possibilities. The first is that our document emerges out of a gradual increment of a sedimentary process. Or it emerges as the creation of single-minded geniuses of applied logic and sustained analytical inquiry. But there is no intermediate possibility.

Look at any of the Talmud's sustained discussions and ask, how have they been put together? The answer invariably is, in a logical and orderly way, following the rules of rational exposition of a proposition, and that means, utterly without regard to who said what, where, when, or why; everything is recast so that the flow of ideas, from point to point, dictates the order of sayings. Nothing could be moved from its present position without changing the sense of everything (and producing gibberish). It follows – so it seems to me – that the whole is the work of the one who decided to make up the discussion on the atemporal logic of the point at issue. Otherwise the discussion would be not continuous but disjointed, full of seams and margins, marks of the existence of prior conglomerations of materials that have now been sewn together. What we have are not patchwork quilts, but woven fabric.

Along these same lines, we may find discussions in which opinions of Palestinians, such as Yohanan and Simon b. Laqish, will be joined together side by side with opinions of Babylonians, such as Rab and Samuel. The whole, once again, will unfold in a smooth way, so that the issues at hand define the sole focus of discourse. The logic of those issues will be fully exposed. Even in our brief encounter with the opening pages of tractate Gittin, we saw ample evidence of that fact. Considerations of the origin of a saying in one country or the other will play no role whatsoever in the rhetoric or literary forms of argument. There will be no possibility of differentiation among opinions on the basis of where, when, by whom, or how they are formulated, only on the basis of what, in fact, is said. The upshot is that we may fairly ask about the message of the method of those who followed this one and single, prevailing method: a fixed set of rules on choice of language, a fixed repertoire of problems, a fixed received text governing the whole – the Bavli as we have it.

On the page of the Bavli, the role of individuals is both ubiquitous – numerous statements are joined to specific names – and also unimportant. The paramount voice is that of "the Talmud." It is that voice that invokes named sayings and formulates challenges to them. The rhetoric of the Talmud may be described very simply: a preference for questions and answers, a willingness then to test the answers and to expand through secondary and tertiary amplification, achieved through further questions and answers. The whole gives the appearance of the script for a conversation to be reconstructed, or an argument of logical possibilities to be reenacted, in one's own mind. In this setting we of course shall be struck by the uniformity of the rhetoric, even though we need not make much of the close patterning of language.

The voice of "the Talmud," moreover, authoritatively defines the mode of analysis. The inquiry is consistent and predictable; one argument differs from another not in supposition but only in detail. When individuals' positions occur, it is because what they have to say serves the purposes of "the Talmud" and its uniform inquiry. The inquiry is into the logic and the rational potentialities of a passage. To these dimensions of thought, the details of place, time, and even of an individual's philosophy, are secondary. All details are turned toward a common core of discourse. This, I maintain, is possible only because the document as whole takes shape in accord with an overriding program of inquiry and comes to expression in conformity with a single plan of rhetorical expression. To state the proposition simply: It did not just *grow*, but rather, someone *made* it up.

The Talmudic argument is not indifferent to the chronology of authorities. But the sequence in which things may be supposed to have been said – an early third-century figure's saying before a later fourth-century figure's saying – in no way explains the construction of protracted dialectical arguments. The argument as a whole, its direction and purpose, always govern the selection, formation, and ordering of the parts of the argument and their relationships to one another. The dialectic is determinative. Chronology, if never violated, is always subordinated. Once that fact is clear, it will become further apparent that "arguments" – analytical units of discourse – took shape at the end, with the whole in mind, as part of a plan and a program. That is to say, the components of the argument, even when associated with the names of specific authorities who lived at different times, were not added piece by piece, in order of historical appearance. They were put together whole and complete, all at one time, when the dialectical discourse was made up. By examining a few units of discourse, we see the unimportance of the sequence in which people lived, hence of the order in which sayings (presumably) became available.

But what is the message of the method, which is to insist upon the Mishnah's near monopoly over serious discourse? To begin with, the very character of the Talmud tells us the sages' view of the Mishnah. The Mishnah presented itself to them as constitutive, the text of ultimate concern. So while, for one example, the Mishnah speaks of a quarrel over a coat, the Talmud talks of the Mishnah's provision of an oath as a means of settling the quarrel in a fair way: substance transformed into process. What the framers of the Bavli wished to say about the Mishnah will guide us toward the definition of the message of their method, but it will not tell us what that message was, or why it was important.

Now that we know that the Bavli is a document of remarkable integrity, repeatedly insisting upon the harmony of the parts within a whole and unitary structure of belief and behavior, we ask what the Bavli says: the one thing that is repeated in regard to many things. To identify the message of the Bavli, we have to locate its method, for it is through the method of the Bavli that we hear its one voice – for that uniformity of expression and thought is what the method brings to expression – and, when we grasp that voice and what it is saying, we shall know the statement that the Bavli's framers wish to make. And the only way forward is to see what is special about the Bavli, which is to say, what distinguishes it from its precedessor, the Yerushalmi. When we know the difference, we shall account also for the destiny of this document: why the Bavli became the summa of Judaism and its authoritative source.

If I had to state in a single phrase the governing hermeneutics of the Talmud, it is this: *The task of interpretation is to uncover the integrity of the truth that God has manifested in the one and unique revelation, the Torah (Oral and Written).* By integrity I mean not merely the result of facile harmonization but the rigorous demonstration that the Torah, at its foundations, makes a single statement, whole, complete, cogent, and coherent; harmonious; unified and beyond all division. The message of the first document of the Oral Torah, the Mishnah, was the hierarchical unity of all being in the One on high. Then the right medium for that message is the Bavli on account of the character of its hermeneutics, best summarized as its quest for abstraction. Matching the Mishnah's ontology of hierarchical unity of all being is the Bavli's principle that many principles express a single one, many laws embody one governing law, which is the law behind the laws. In more secular language, the intellectual medium of the Bavli accomplishes the transformation of jurisprudence into philosophy. How do the two documents work together to establish through many facts a single statement of the governing fact of being? The Mishnah establishes a world in stasis: lists of like things, subject to like rules. The Bavli portrays a world in motion: lists of like things form series; but series, too, conform to rules. The Mishnah sets forth lists, the Bavli, series.

Demonstrating in conclusion and in message that the truth is one, whole, comprehensive, cogent, coherent, harmonious, showing that fact of intellect – these sustained points of insistence on the character of mind and the result of thought form the goal of the Bavli's framers. It is by comparison to the Yerushalmi that we recognize the salient intellectual traits of the Bavli. Where we identify initiatives characteristic of the Bavli and unusual in the Yerushalmi, there we describe the Bavli in particular. On that basis, we point as indicative to the paramount trait, emerging from a variety of episodic distinctions, of the Bavli, its quest through abstraction for the unity of the law, the integrity of truth. Specifically, in the comparison with the Yerushalmi we appreciate that the Bavli's quest for unity leads to the inquiry into the named authorities behind an unassigned rule, showing that a variety of figures can concur, meaning, names that stand for a variety of distinct principles can form a single proposition of integrity. That same quest insists on the fair and balanced representation of conflicting principles behind discrete laws, not to serve the cause of academic harmony (surely a lost cause in any age!), but to set forth how, at their foundations, the complicated and diverse laws may be explained by appeal to simple and few principles; the conflict of principles then is less consequential than the demonstration that diverse cases may be reduced to only a few principles.

Take, for example, the single stylistically indicative trait of the Bavli, its dialectical, or moving, argument. The dialectical argument opens the possibility of reaching out from one thing to something else, not because people have lost sight of their starting point or their goal in the end, but because they want to encompass, in the analytical argument as it gets under way, as broad and comprehensive a range of cases and rules as they possibly can. The movement from point to point in reference to a single point that accurately describes the dialectical argument reaches a goal of abstraction, leaving behind the specificities of not only cases but laws, carrying us upward to the law that governs many cases, the premises that undergird many rules, and still higher to the principles that infuse diverse premises; then the principles that generate other, unrelated premises, which, in turn, come to expression in other, still-less intersecting cases. The meandering course of argument comes to an end when we have shown how things cohere. That is what we have learned about the Bavli in this comparison of the two Talmuds.

But the Yerushalmi is not the only, or even the principal, point of comparison for the Bavli. The Mishnah, to which the Bavli formally is devoted as a commentary, and which most of the Bavli really does serve as just that, surely claims a high place in the hierarchy of valid comparisons. For, after all, a writing that is attached to another document surely demands comparison and contrast with that other document. Only one point of comparison makes any difference at all: the contrast of the Bavli's and the Mishnah's fundamental intellectual agenda. These, I shall now show, are fully complementary. Both bring to expression in a huge mass of instantiations a few simple propositions, all of which come down to one statement: truth is one. The integrity of the truth forms the singular statement of the Judaism of the Dual Torah, and each in its way, the Mishnah and the Bavli make that statement – and, at their foundations, that statement alone.

The Mishnah's version of the integrity of truth focuses upon the unity of all being in hierarchical ontology. A single metaproposition encompasses the multitude of the Mishnah's proposition, which is, all classes of things stand in a hierarchical relationship to one another, and, in that encompassing hierarchy, there is place for everything. The theological proposition that is implicit but never spelled out, of course, is that one God occupies the pinnacle of the hierarchy of all being; to that one God, all things turn upward, from complexity to simplicity; from that one God, all things flow downward, from singularity to multiplicity. To understand that simple statement, we begin with a definition of a metaproposition.

A proposition presents the result of an analysis of a given problem. When analyses of a variety of problems yield diverse propositions that as a matter of fact turn out to say the same one thing about many diverse things, that one thing said in many ways about many things forms not a proposition but a metaproposition. It is a proposition that derives from all subsets of propositions and states in an abstract and general way – whether explicitly or merely by indirection – the one proposition contained within many demonstrations of propositions. We know that we have identified the metapropositional program of a writing if, when we say what we think is at stake, in the most general terms, in a variety of specific syllogisms, we turn out to be saying the same thing again and again. We may test our hypothetical metaproposition by asking whether, in those many things, we may identify any other proposition to define the stakes of a demonstration; or whether some other encompassing proposition may serve as well as the one we propose over as broad a range of data as we examine. Where may we expect to find not only propositions but a statement that coheres throughout: a statement in behalf of all propositions? A coherent legal system, for one example, not only sets forth rules for diverse circumstances but, through the rules, also may lay out a philosophy of the social order, an account of what is always fair and just; then all of the cases, each with its generalization, turn out to repeat in different ways a single encompassing statement.

So, too, while the author of a document makes statements about a great many subjects, a well-crafted document by a strong-minded writer will find the author saying much the same thing about all things. Then the key to good writing will be the power to make the same point again and again without boring the reader or belaboring the obvious. Indeed, an important and truly well-conceived piece of writing addressed to a long future will precipitate productive debates about not only details but what that some one thing said in many ways is meant to propose. Great writing leaves space for readers. That is the mark of a strong argument, a well-crafted formulation of a considered viewpoint, the expression of a deeply reflected-upon attitude, or, in intellectual matters, a rigorously presented proposition. To find out what we might imagine some one thing a writer may say about many things, we ask simply, "What is at stake if this point is validated?" or simply, "If so, so what?" If time and again we find that treatment of a given subject yields as its final and most general and abstract point a proposition that turns out also to emerge from an unrelated treatment of some other subject, altogether, then we have what I call a metaproposition, meaning, a proposition that transcends a variety of propositions and that occurs in all of them.

Obviously, defining the metapropositional statement that an author repeatedly sets forth involves an element of eisegesis, even subjectivity.

That is invariably a starting point. On the one side, others may see some other metaproposition that circulates throughout a piece of writing, different from one that I might propose. On the other side, still others may perceive no metaproposition at all. How to test a thesis on the metaproposition of a diverse piece of writing? One irrefutable demonstration is that a single rhetoric prevails, for that legitimates asking whether saying everything in some one way, writers also say one thing about many things. To define that some one thing, and to find out whether or not a proposed metaproposition in fact circulates throughout such a writing, first of all, a massive survey must show where, how, and why one proposes that one and same proposition that – according to a proposed metaproposition – an author persists in setting forth in the context of a great many diverse discussions.

If it can be shown that most, or even all, of a large and various corpus of writing turns out to be saying in a single, uniform way that one thing through its treatment of a great many things, then we are justified in claiming to have set forth that proposition beyond the propositions, that metaproposition, that animates a document. It is the one that the authors have composed the document to set forth and in a vast number of ways to demonstrate. But let me forthwith turn to the two problems just now noted. What about the possibility that another metaproposition may be shown to inhere, different from the one that as a matter of hypothesis is set forth at the outset? Or what if a proposed metaproposition is shown not to be present at all? Then the experiment has failed. And how are we going to test the validity of two or more proposed metapropositions, and so to know whether or not the metaproposition that is suggested is the right one? The answer lies in a detailed demonstration that the proposed metaproposition is the best possible one, in the context of a variety of possibilities, to encompass the data at hand. And God lives in the details. Have we an example of a metapropositional statement set forth in a single, public, anonymous, and authoritative writing, and can we define the contents of one such statement? Indeed we do and we can. A remarkably cogent and simple metaproposition, a recurrent statement that defines what is at stake in detailed syllogistic argument, inheres in the Mishnah and proves paramount throughout. The pervasive telos of thought in the Mishnah is such that many things are made to say one thing, which concerns the nature of being.

Specifically, the Mishnah's authority repeatedly demonstrates that all things are not only orderly, but are ordered in such wise that many things fall into one classification. So one thing may hold together many things of diverse classifications. These two matched and complementary propositions – [1] many things are one, [2] one thing encompasses many

– complement each other. In forming matched opposites, the two provide a single, complete, and final judgment of the whole of being, social, natural, supernatural alike. Nearly the whole of the document's tractates in one way or another repeat that simple point. The metaproposition is never expressed but it is everywhere demonstrated by showing, in whatever subject is treated, the possibility always of effecting the hierarchical classification of all things: each thing in its taxon, all taxa in correct sequence, from least to greatest.

Showing that all things can be ordered, and that all orders can be set into relationship with one another, we of course transform method into message. The message of hierarchical classification is that many things really form a single thing, the many species a single genus, the many genera an encompassing and well-crafted, cogent whole. Every time we speciate, we affirm that position. Each successful labor of forming relationships among species, for example, making them into a genus, or identifying the hierarchy of the species, proves it again. Not only so, but when we can show that many things are really one, or that one thing yields many (the reverse and confirmation of the former), we say in a fresh way a single immutable truth, the one of this philosophy concerning the unity of all being in an orderly composition of all things within a single taxon. Exegesis always is repetitive – and a sound exegesis of the systemic exegesis must then be equally so, everywhere explaining the same thing in the same way.

To state with emphasis what I conceive to be that one large argument – the metaproposition – that the Mishnah's authorship sets forth in countless small ways: *The very artifacts that appear multiple in fact form classes of things, and, moreover, these classes themselves are subject to a reasoned ordering, by appeal to this-worldly characteristics signified by properties and indicative traits.*

Monotheism hence is to be demonstrated by appeal to those very same data that for paganism prove the opposite. The way to one God, ground of being and ontological unity of the world, lies through "rational reflection on ourselves and on the world," this world, which yields a living unity encompassing the whole. That claim, presented in an argument covering overwhelming detail in the Mishnah, directly faces the issue as framed by paganism. Immanent in its medium, it is transcendent in its message.

To show how the metaproposition is stated through the treatment of a wide range of subjects, concrete recapitulations of this abstract statement are now required. So I turn to a very brief reprise of my demonstration, concerning the Mishnah, of the sustained effort to demonstrate how many classes of things – actions, relationships, circumstances, persons, places – are shown really to form one class. Just as God, in creation, ordered all things, each in its class under its name, so in the Mishnah classification works its way through the potentialities of chaos to explicit order. The issue concerns nature, not supernature, and sorts out and sifts the everyday data of the here and the now. It will prove its points, therefore, by appeal to the palpable facts of creation, which everyone knows and can test. So recognition that one thing may fall into several categories and many things into a single one comes to expression, for the authorship of the Mishnah, in secular ways. One of the interesting ones is the analysis of the several taxa into which a single action may fall, with an account of the multiple consequences, for example, as to sanctions that are called into play, for a single action. The right taxonomy of persons, actions, and things will show the unity of all being by finding many things in one thing, and that forms the first of the two components of what I take to be the philosophy's teleology.

Mishnah-tractate Keritot 3:9

A. There is one who ploughs a single furrow and is liable on eight counts of violating a negative commandment:
B. [Specifically, it is] he who (1) ploughs with an ox and an ass [Deut. 22:10], which are (2,3) both Holy Things, in the case of (4) [ploughing] mixed seeds in a vineyard [Deut. 22:9], (5) in the Seventh Year [Lev. 25:4], (6) on a festival [Lev. 23:7] and who was both a (7) priest [Lev. 21:1] and (8) a Nazirite [Num. 6:6] [ploughing] in a grave yard.
C. Hanania b. Hakhinai says, "Also: He is [ploughing while] wearing a garment of diverse kinds" [Lev. 19:19, Deut. 22:11].
D. They said to him, "This is not within the same class."
E. He said to them, "Also the Nazir [B8] is not within the same class [as the other transgressions]."

Here is a case in which more than a single set of flogging is called for. B's felon is liable to three hundred twelve stripes, on the listed counts. The ox is sanctified to the altar, the ass to the Temple upkeep (B2,3). Hanania's contribution is rejected since it has nothing to do with ploughing, and sages' position is equally flawed. The main point, for our inquiry, is simple. The one action draws in its wake multiple consequences. Classifying a single thing as a mixture of many things then forms a part of the larger intellectual address to the nature of mixtures. But it yields a result that, in the analysis of an action, far transcends the metaphysical problem of mixtures, because it moves us toward the ontological solution of the unity of being.

So much for actions. How about substances? Can we say that diverse things, each in its own classification, form a single thing? Indeed so. Here is one example, among a great many candidates, taken from Mishnah-tractate Hallah. The tractate takes as its theme the dough-offering to which the framers assume Num. 15:17-21 refers: "Of the first of your coarse meal you shall present a cake as an offering." The tractate deals with the definition of dough liable to the dough-offering, defining the bread, the process of separating dough-offering, and the liability of mixtures.

Mishnah-tractate Hallah 1:1, 3

1:1   A.   [Loaves of bread made from] five types [of grain] are subject to dough-offering:

        B.   (1) wheat, (2) barley, (3) spelt, (4) oats, and (5) rye;

        C.   lo, [loaves of bread made from] these [species] are subject to dough-offering,

        D.   and combine with each other [for the purpose of reckoning whether or not a batch of dough comprises the minimum volume subject to dough-offering (M. Hal. 1:4, 2:6, M. Ed. 1:2)].

        E.   And products of these species are forbidden for common use until Passover under the category of new produce [produce harvested before the waving of the first sheaf (Lev. 23:14)].

        F.   And grasses of these species may not be reaped until the reaping of the first sheaf.

        G.   And if they took root prior to the waving of the first sheaf, the waving of the first sheaf releases them for common use;

        H.   but if they did not take root prior to the waving of the omer, they are forbidden for common use until the next omer.

1:3   A.   Grain in the following categories is liable to dough-offering when made into dough but exempt from tithes:

        B.   gleanings, forgotten sheaves, produce in the corner of a field, that which has been abandoned, first tithe from which heave-offering of the tithe has been removed, second tithe, and that which is dedicated to the Temple which has been redeemed, the left-over portion of grain which was harvested for the offering of the first sheaf, and grain which has not reached a third of its anticipated growth.

        C.   R. Eliezer says, "Grain which has not reached one-third of its growth is exempt from dough-offering when made into dough."

M. Hal. 1:1 addresses the issuing of whether or not five species of grain join together to produce dough of sufficient volume to incur liability to the dough-offering. Since they share in common the trait that they are capable of being leavened (*himus*), they do. So the genus encompasses all of the species, with the result that the classification process is neatly illustrated. "Joining together" or connection then forms a statement that these many things are one thing. M. 1:2 makes the same point about the five species. The interstitial cases at M. Hal. 1:3 are subject to ownership other than that of the farmer. But that fact does not change their status as to dough-offering. We take no account of the status with regard to ownership, past or present use as another type of offering, or the stage of growth of the grain whence the dough derives. This then forms the other side of the taxonomic labor: indicators that do not distinguish. The upshot is as I said: many things are one thing; one rule applies to a variety of classes of grains.

In the impalpable and invisible realm of classification and status, we can conjure, but cannot touch or feel or see, the lines of structure and division. Order is imputed and imagined. What about the visible world of space? Here we can frame a question that permits a highly tangible representation of the complexity of unity and diversity, the demonstration that one thing encompasses many things, so many things form one thing. The question is asked in this way: When is a field a field, and when is it two or ten fields? That taxonomic problem of how many are one, or how one is deemed many, is addressed at Mishnah-tractate Peah, which concerns itself with giving to the poor produce abandoned at the corner of a field. Then we have to know what constitutes a field, hence the question of when one thing is many things, or when many things are one thing, framed in terms of spatial relations:

Mishnah-tractate Peah 2:1, 5; 3:5

2:1	A.	And these [landmarks] establish [the boundaries of a field] for [purposes of designating] peah:
	B.	(1) a river, (2) pond, (3) private road, (4) public road, (5) public path, (6) private path that is in use in the hot season and in the rainy season, (7) uncultivated land, (8) newly broken land, (9) and [an area sown with] a different [type of] seed.
	C.	"And [as regards] one who harvests young grain [for use as fodder – the area he harvests] establishes [the boundaries of a field]," the words of R. Meir.
	D.	But sages say, "[The area he harvests] does not establish [the boundaries of a field], unless he has also ploughed [the stubble] under."
2:5	A.	One who sows his field with [only] one type [of seed], even if he harvests [the produce] in two lots,
	B.	designates one [portion of produce as] peah [from the entire crop].
	C.	If he sowed [his field] with two types [of seeds], even if he harvests [the produce] in only one lot,
	D.	he designates two [separate portions of produce as] peah, [one from each type of produce].
	E.	He who sows his field with two types of wheat –
	F.	[if] he harvests [the wheat] in one lot, [he] designates one [portion of produce as] peah.
	G.	[But if he harvests the wheat in] two lots, [he] designates two [portions of produce as] peah.
3:5	A.	[Two] brothers who divided [ownership of a field which previously they had jointly owned]
	B.	give two [separate portions of produce] as peah [each designates peah on behalf of the produce of his half of the field].
	C.	[If] they return to joint ownership [of the field],

D.   [together] they designate one [portion of produce] as peah [on behalf of the entire field].
E.   Two [men] who [jointly] purchased a tree [together] designate one [portion of produce] as peah [on behalf of the entire tree] –
F.   But if one purchased the northern [half of the tree], and the other purchased the southern [half of the tree],
G.   the former designates peah by himself, and the latter designates peah by himself.

The principle of division rests upon the farmer's attitude and actions toward a field. If the farmer harvests an area as a single entity, that action indicates his attitude or intentionality in regard to that area and serves to mark it as a field. For each patch of grain the householder reaps separately a peah share must be designated; the action indicates the intentionality to treat the area as a single field. But natural barriers intervene; rivers or hills also may mark off a field's boundaries, whatever the farmer's action and therefore a priori intentionality or attitude. So in classifying an area of ground as a field, there is an interplay between the givens of the physical traits and the attitude, confirmed by action, of the farmer.

I have repeatedly claimed that the recognition that one thing becomes many does not challenge the philosophy of the unity of all being, but confirms the main point. Why do I insist on that proposition? The reason is simple. If we can show that differentiation flows from within what is differentiated – that is, from the intrinsic or inherent traits of things – then we confirm that at the heart of things is a fundamental ontological being, single, cogent, simple, that is capable of diversification, yielding complexity and diversity. The upshot is to be stated with emphasis. *That diversity in species or diversification in actions follows orderly lines confirms the claim that there is that single point from which many lines come forth.* Carried out in proper order – [1] the many form one thing, and [2] one thing yields many – the demonstration then leaves no doubt as to the truth of the matter. Ideally, therefore, we shall argue from the simple to the complex, showing that the one yields the many, one thing, many things, two, four.[4]

Mishnah-tractate Shabbat 1:1

1:1 A.   [Acts of] transporting objects from one domain to another, [which violate] the Sabbath, (1) are two, which [indeed] are four [for one who is] inside, (2) and two which are four [for one who is] outside.
B.   How so?
C.   [If on the Sabbath] the beggar stands outside and the householder inside,

---

[4]That is also what is at stake in the issue of when a list is a series, addressed by B. Zebahim to Mishnah-tractate Zebahim Chapter Five, above, Chapter Five.

D.   [and] the beggar stuck his hand inside and put [a beggar's bowl] into the hand of the householder,

E.   or if he took [something] from inside it and brought it out,

F.   the beggar is liable, the householder is exempt.

G.   [If] the householder stuck his hand outside and put [something] into the hand of the beggar,

H.   or if he took [something] from it and brought it inside,

I.   the householder is liable, and the beggar is exempt.

J.   [If] the beggar stuck his hand inside, and the householder took [something] from it,

K.   or if [the householder] put something in it and he [the beggar] removed,

L.   both of them are exempt.

M.   [If] the householder put his hand outside and the beggar took [something] from it,

N.   or if [the beggar] put something into it and [the householder] brought it back inside,

O.   both of them are exempt.

M. Shab. 1:1 classifies diverse circumstances of transporting objects from private to public domain. The purpose is to assess the rules that classify as culpable or exempt from culpability diverse arrangements. The operative point is that a prohibited action is culpable only if one and the same person commits the whole of the violation of the law. If two or more people share in the single action, neither of them is subject to punishment. At stake therefore is the conception that one thing may be many things, and if that is the case, then culpability is not incurred by any one actor. The consequence of showing that one thing is many things is set forth with great clarity in the consideration not of the actor but of the action. One class of actions is formed by those that violate the sanctity of the Sabbath. Do these form many subdivisions, and, if so, what difference does it make? Here is a famous passage that shows how a single class of actions yields multiple and complex speciation, while remaining one:

Mishnah-tractate Shabbat 7:1-2

7:1   A.   A general rule did they state concerning the Sabbath:

B.   Whoever forgets the basic principle of the Sabbath and performed many acts of labor on many different Sabbath days is liable only for a single sin-offering.

C.   He who knows the principle of the Sabbath and performed many acts of labor on many different Sabbaths is liable for the violation of each and every Sabbath.

D.   He who knows that it is the Sabbath and performed many acts of labor on many different Sabbaths is liable for the violation of each and every generative category of labor.

E.   He who performs many acts of labor of a single type is liable only for a single sin-offering.

7:2   A.   The generative categories of acts of labor [prohibited on the Sabbath] are forty less one:

      B.   (1) he who sews, (2) ploughs, (3) reaps, (4) binds sheaves, (5) threshes, (6) winnows, (7) selects [fit from unfit produce or crops], (8) grinds, (9) sifts, (10) kneads, (11) bakes;

      C.   (12) he who shears wool, (13) washes it, (14) beats it, (15) dyes it;

      D.   (16) spins, (17) weaves,

      E.   (18) makes two loops, (19) weaves two threads, (20) separates two threads;

      F   (21) ties, (22) unties,

      G.   (23) sews two stitches, (24) tears in order to sew two stitches;

      H.   (25) he who traps a deer, (26) slaughters it, (27) flays it, (28) salts it, (29) cures its hide, (30) scrapes it, and (31) cuts it up;

      I.   (32) he who writes two letters, (33) erases two letters in order to write two letters;

      J.   (34) he who builds, (35) tears down;

      K.   (36) he who puts out a fire, (37) kindles a fire;

      L.   (38) he who hits with a hammer; (39) he who transports an object from one domain to another –

      M.   lo, these are the forty generative acts of labor less one.

Now we see how the fact that one thing yields many things confirms the philosophy of the unity of all being. For the many things all really are one thing, here, the intrusion into sacred time of actions that do not belong there. M. Shab. 7:1-2 presents a parallel to the discussion, in Mishnah-tractate Sanhedrin, of how many things can be shown to be one thing and to fall under a single rule, and how one thing may be shown to be many things and to invoke multiple consequences. It is that interest at M. 7:1 which accounts for the inclusion of M. 7:2, and the exposition of M. 7:2 occupies much of the tractate that follows.

Accordingly, just as at Mishnah-tractate Sanhedrin the specification of the many and diverse sins or felonies that are penalized in a given way shows us how many things are one thing and then draws in its wake the specification of those many things, so here we find a similar exercise. It is one of classification, working in two ways, then: the power of a unifying taxon, the force of a differentiating and divisive one. The list of the acts of labor then gives us the categories of work, and performing any one of these constitutes a single action in violation of the Sabbath. How, exactly, do these things work themselves out? If one does not know that the Sabbath is incumbent upon him, then whatever he does falls into a single taxon. If he knows that the Sabbath exists and violates several Sabbath days in succession, what he does falls into another taxon. If one knows that the Sabbath exists in principle and violates it in diverse ways, for example, through different types of prohibited acts of labor, then many things become still more differentiated. The consideration throughout, then, is how to assess whether something is a single or multiple action as to the reckoning of the consequence.

I asked at the outset how we might know whether our proposed metaproposition if right or wrong. The evidence in behalf of my reading of the Mishnah covers nearly the entirety of the document. It is not episodic but structural, in that entire tractates can be demonstrated to take shape around issues of hierarchical classification and the principles that guide correct classification. It does not seem to me plausible that it is merely by accident that these sustained efforts, covering the vast surface of the writing – sixty-one usable tractates (omitting reference to tractates Eduyyot and Abot) and more than five hundred and fifty chapters – go through the same process time and again. Hierarchization defines the problematic throughout.[5]

It is therefore the incontrovertible fact that the framers of the Mishnah set forth not only cases, examples, propositions as to fact, but also, through the particulars, a set of generalizations about classification and the relationships of the classes of things that yield   a metaproposition. The whole composition of thought is set forth, in the correct intellectual manner, through the patient classification of things by appeal to the traits that they share, with comparison and contrast among points of difference then yielding the governing rule for a given classification. And the goal was through proper classification of things to demonstrate the hierarchical order of being, culminating in the proposition that all things derive from, and join within, (in secular language) one thing or (in the language of philosophy of religion) the One, or (in the language of Judaism) God.

The Bavli's version of the integrity of truth aims to show in countless cases the cogency of (jurisprudential) laws in (philosophical) law. And it is through the right hermeneutics that that is demonstrated, the message conveyed in a rational manner. Having shown that diverse topics of the Mishnah are so represented as to make a single set of cogent points about hierarchical classification, I turn directly to the problem of the Bavli: Can the same claim be made of the Mishnah's greatest single commentary, that it, too, says one thing about many things? The answer to the "can" lies in rhetoric: Do the people talk in the same way about many subjects? The answer – by this point obvious, after seven parts of a monograph on the uniqueness of discourse in the Bavli – is that they do. Then what is it that our sages say time and again?

We forthwith turn to a case in point. It is the two Talmuds' reading of Mishnah-tractate Qiddushin 2:2. The suitor declares an act of

---

[5]As I have shown in *Judaism as Philosophy. The Method and Message of the Mishnah* (Columbia, 1991: University of South Carolina Press).

betrothal, but only on a condition. If the condition is not met, the betrothal is null. But if the condition is disadvantageous to the woman and she accepts it, and the condition is not met, then the woman is better off than before: Do we still regard failure to meet the condition as a cause of nullifying the betrothal? That is the issue of the Mishnah rule. The two positions are A-G vs. H. Then we see how the Talmuds find it fitting to discuss that dispute. As always in my presentation of the classics of Judaism, I find that (as in the casae of architecture) God lives in the details.

Yerushalmi to Mishnah-tractate Qiddushin
2:2

[A] "Be betrothed to me for this cup of wine," and it turns out to be honey –

[B] "of honey," and it turns out to be wine,

[C] "with this silver denar," and it turns out to be gold,

[D] "with this gold one," and it turns out to be silver,

[E] "on condition that I am rich," and he turns out to be poor,

[F] "on condition that I am poor," and he turns out to be rich –

[G] she is not betrothed.

[H] R. Simeon says, "If he deceived her to [her] advantage, she is betrothed."

[I] "On condition that I am a priest," and he turns out to be a Levite,

[J] "on condition that I am a Levite," and he turns out to be a priest,

[K] "a netin," and he turns out to be a mamzer,

[L] "a mamzer," and he turns out to be a netin,

[M] "a town-dweller," and he turns out to be a villager,

[N] "a villager," and he turns out to be a town-dweller,

[O] "on condition that my house is near the bath," and it turns out to be far away,

[P] "far," and it turns out to be near;

[Q] "on condition that I have a daughter or a slave girl who is a hairdresser," and he has none,

[R] "on condition that I have none," and he has one;

[S] "on condition that I have no children," and he has;

[T] "on condition that he has," and he has none –

[U] in the case of all of them, even though she says, "In my heart I wanted to become betrothed to him despite that fact," she is not betrothed.

[V] And so is the rule if she deceived him.

The Yerushalmi treats the issue before us in the following passage:

[II.A] R. Simeon says, "If he deceived her to her advantage, she is betrothed" [M. 2:2H].

[B] R. Yohanan said, "R. Simeon concurs that if he deceived her about an advantage as to genealogy, she is not betrothed."

[C] Said R. Yosé, "The Mishnah itself has made the same point: **'On condition that I am a priest,'** and he turns out to be a Levite [etc.] **[M. 2:21].**

[D] Now there is no *problem* in the case in which he claimed to be a **priest and turns out to be a Levite [that she is not betrothed].**

[E] [But if he claimed to be] a Levite and he turned out to be a priest, [there, too, she is not betrothed, for] she has the right to say, "I do not want his superior airs to lord it over me."

That sum and substance of the matter completes the Yerushalmi's treatment. Here is the Bavli's counterpart; I do not repeat the Mishnah paragraph.

II.1 A. **R. Simeon says, "If he deceived her to [her] advantage, she is betrothed":**

B. *But doesn't R. Simeon accept the following:* **wine, and it turned out to be vinegar, vinegar, and it turned out to be wine – both parties have the power to retract [M. B.B. 5:6K-L]?** *Therefore, there are people who are perfectly happy with wine, others with vinegar; so here, too, some are happy with silver and not with gold at all.*

We immediately find a different case, but one in which the same premise operates as the premise of the rule here: people accept a deception that leaves them better off; why should Simeon exact the full measure of truth?

C. *Said R. Shimi bar Ashi, "I bumped into Abbayye, who was in session and explaining this matter to his son: Here with what case do we deal? It is one in which* a man said to his agent, 'Go, lend me a silver denar, and with it betroth Miss So-and-so in my behalf,' and the agent went and lent him a gold denar. *One authority maintains that the man was meticulous about the instructions, and the other, that* all he was doing was giving him good advice on how to proceed ['showing him the place'].*"

The solution is to redfine the case at hand, showing how the issue is different from what it seemed to be when we asked out question. But then we submit the redefinition to the test of the actual language before us: does the claim conform to the facts?

D. *If it is true that the Mishnah speaks of an agent, then the language should be not,* **Be betrothed to me,** *but rather,* **Be betrothed to him!** *And so too, not* **If he deceived her to [her] advantage,** *but rather,* **If he deceived** *him to [his]* **advantage!**

E. *But to begin with it was of gold* [Freedman: the agent knew full well that he was giving a gold denar].

Now there is a second effort to clarify the matter in such a way as to leave both parties with good arguments. Here we see the real goal: it is to make sure that both contending masters' opinions are equally defensible. And that means, they must form their dispute around two valid, but conflicting principles, as F now accomplishes:

> F.   *Rather, said Raba, "I let the lion of the group explain it – and who might that be? It is R. Hiyya bar Abin: Here with what case do we deal? One in which* she said to her agent, 'Go and receive for me my token of betrothal from Mr. So-and-so, who said to me, "Be betrothed to me with a denar of silver,"' and he went and the other gave him a denar of gold. *One authority maintains that the woman was meticulous about the instructions, and the other, that* all she was doing was giving him good advice on how to proceed ['showing him the place']."
>
> G.   *And what is the meaning of the language,* **and it turns out to be***?*
>
> H.   *It was wrapped up in a cloth [and only when the woman got it did she know what it was].*

We have accomplished our first goal: showing that both sides in the Mishnah operate in the same range of rationality; each has a valid view; principles are at stake, and harmonies consist of equally valid principles, which apply to specific cases in diverse, sometimes conflicting, ways. But we move outward from our case and its principles to a broadening of the issue to its deeper premise: the character of a stipulation given to an agent. If I hire someone to do something for me, and I tell him or her, go do it in such and such a place, is that specification of the place part of the instruction, or is it just good advice as to a suitable location for the mission? How, in other words, do we explain the meaning and use of language?

> 2.   A.   *Said Abbayye, "R. Simeon, Rabban Simeon b. Gamaliel, and R. Eleazar, all take the view that, in a case such as this, in giving these instructions, all he was doing was giving him good advice on how to proceed ['showing him the place'].*"
>
>   B.   *R. Simeon: as we have just now said.*

We now survey a variety of unrelated cases, which rest on distinct principles of law but turn out to share common premises as to language and its meaning. The upshot is, it is in language that we find the deepest unities of being; the words we use form the bridge from mind to mind; and from our minds to God's mind, which we know because the Torah tells us how God speaks and what God says. It is a long perspective indeed that I ask you to take, but I think, the right one: the Torah is the one reliable account that we have of who God is and what God does, how God thinks and the rules that govern God's, and our, rationality. That is what is at stake, when we investigate the meaning of language in the concrete details of laws and cases. So we move on to this inquiry into how a variety of cases turns out to concern the profound premise: what do people mean by what they say?

C. *R. Simeon, Rabban Simeon b. Gamaliel: as we have learned in the Mishnah:* [49A] **An unfolded document [has] the signatures within [at the bottom of a single page of writing]. And one which is folded has the signatures behind [each fold]. An unfolded document, on which its witnesses signed at the back, or a folded document, on which its witnesses signed on the inside – both of them are invalid. R. Hananiah b. Gamaliel says, "One which is folded, on the inside of which its witnesses signed their names, is valid, because one can unfold it." Rabban Simeon b. Gamaliel says, "Everything is in accord with local custom"** [M. B.B. 10:1]. *Now in reflecting on this matter [we said], well, doesn't the first authority concur,* **Everything is in accord with local custom?** *And said R. Ashi, "This refers to a place in which a plain one was customary, and a folded one was made, or a place in which a folded one was customary, and a plain one was made. All parties concur that the one who gave instructions was meticulous about the matter. Where is the point of dispute? Where both forms are acceptable, and the husband said to the scribe, 'Make a plain one,' but the scribe went and made a folded one. One authority maintains that the husband was meticulous about the instructions, and the other, that all he was doing was giving him good advice on how to proceed ['showing him the place'].*"

D. *R. Eleazar: as we have learned in the Mishnah:*

E. **The woman who said, "Receive my writ of divorce for me in such-and-such a place," and he [the messenger] received it for her in some other place –**

F. **it is invalid.**

G. **R. Eliezer declares it valid** [M. Git. 6:3K-M].

H. *Therefore* all he was doing was giving him good advice on how to proceed ["showing him the place"].

3. A. Said Ulla, "The Mishnah's controversy concerns only a monetary advantage, but as to a genealogical advantage, all parties concur that she is not betrothed. *How come? 'I really don't want a shoe that is bigger than my foot.'*"

B. *So, too, it has been taught on Tannaite authority:* **R. Simeon concedes that if he deceived her to her advantage in a matter of genealogy, she is not betrothed** [T. Qid. 2:5I].

C. *Said R. Ashi, "A close reading of our Mishnah paragraph yields the same conclusion, for the Tannaite formulation is as follows:*

D. **"'....on condition that I am a priest,' and he turns out to be a Levite,**

E. **"'....on condition that I am a Levite,' and he turns out to be a priest,**

F. **"'...a netin,' and he turns out to be a mamzer,**

G. **"'...a mamzer,' and he turns out to be a netin** [M. 2:3A-D].

H. *"And in these matters, R. Simeon does not take issue."*

I. *Objected Mar bar R. Ashi, "Well, note the further Tannaite formulation:*

J. **"'...on condition that I have a daughter or a slave girl who is an adult [alt.: a hairdresser],' and he has none,**

K. **"'...on condition that I have none,' and he has one –**

L. *"and these represent monetary advantages, and yet here, too, R. Simeon does not take issue! Rather, he differs in the first clause, and likewise in*

> *the second, and here, too, he differs in the first clause and so, too, in the second!'*

M.   *But how are the matters comparable? In that case, both items represent a monetary advantage, so he differs in the first clause, and the same in the second. But here, where it is a matter of a genealogical advantages, if he did differ, it should have been made explicit in the Tannaite formulation.*

N.   *And if you prefer, I shall say, here, too, genealogical advantage is what is at issue. Do you imagine that* **an adult** *is meant literally? It means, of superior standing, for the betrothed woman can say, "It is not acceptable to me that she should take my words from me and go and tell them around the neighborhood."*

In the following case, I find a fine articulation of the answer to the question, what is it that the Bavli's sages keep saying through the medium of hermeneutics, which is, as I have already iterated, cases rest on premises, which point toward principles; principles carry us to other premises, that yield other cases; and diverse cases, with their premises and their principles, then can be shown to coalesce in, if not harmonious statements, then statements of fixed and few differences at the level of high abstraction. We then reduce the range of diversity to a few differences; demonstrate the harmony of discrete rules; show the operation of some few laws, so moving jurisprudence upward to the level of philosophy. In the context defined by the Mishnah, the proposition of the Mishnah about the ontological unity of being is matched by the persistent results of the process of thought instantiated throughout the Bavli, demonstrating the intellectual unity of thought. I forthwith turn to a case in point, at M. Erub. 2:2H:

[II.A] **R. Simeon says, "If he deceived her to her advantage, she is betrothed" [M. 2: 2H].**	II.1 A.	**R. Simeon says, "If he deceived her to [her] advantage, she is betrothed":**
	B.	*But doesn't R. Simeon accept the following:* **wine, and it turned out to be vinegar, vinegar, and it turned out to be wine – both parties have the power to retract [M. B.B. 5:6K-L]**? *There-fore, there are people who are perfectly happy with wine, others with vinegar; so here, too, some are happy with sil-ver and not with gold at all.*

C.   *Said R. Shimi bar Ashi,*
      "I bumped into Abbayye,
      who was in session and
      explaining this matter to
      his son: Here with what
      case do we deal? It is
      one in which a man
      said to his agent, 'Go,
      lend me a silver denar,
      and with it betroth
      Miss So-and-so in my
      behalf,' and the agent
      went and lent him a
      gold denar. *One au-*
      thority maintains that
      the man was meticulous
      about the instructions,
      and the other, that all he
      was doing was giving
      him good advice on
      how to proceed
      ['showing him the
      place'].*"

D.   *If it is true that the*
      Mishnah speaks of an
      agent, then the language
      should be not, **B e**
      betrothed to me, *but*
      rather, **Be betrothed to**
      him! *And so, too, not* **If**
      he deceived her to
      [her] advantage, *but*
      rather, **If he deceived**
      h i m   t o   [h i s]
      advantage!

E.   *But to begin with it was*
      of gold [Freedman: the
      agent knew full well
      that he was giving a
      gold denar].

F.   *Rather, said Raba, "I am*
      the lion of the group
      explain it — and who
      might that be? It is R.
      Hiyya bar Abin: here
      with what case do we
      deal? One in which she
      said to her agent, 'go
      and receive for my my
      token of betrothal
      from Mr. So-and-so,

who said to me, "be betrothed to me with a denar of silver,"' and he went and the other gave him a denar of gold. *One authority maintains that the woman was meticulous about the instructions, and the other, that* all she was doing was giving him good advice on how to proceed ['showing him the place']."

G. *And what is the meaning of the language,* **and it turns out to be?**

H. *It was wrapped up in a cloth [and only when the women got it did she know what it was].*

II.2 A. *Said Abbayye, "R. Simeon, Rabban Simeon b. Gamaliel, and R. Eleazar, all take the view that, in a case such as this, in giving these instructions, all he was doing was giving him good advice on how to proceed ['showing him the place']."*

B. *R. Simeon: as we have just now said.*

C. *R. Simeon, Rabban Simeon b. Gamaliel: as we have learned in the Mishnah:* **[49A] An unfolded document [has] the signatures within [at the bottom of a single page of writing]. And one which is folded has the signatures behind [each fold]. An unfolded document, on which its witnesses signed at the back, or a folded document,**

on which its wit-
nesses signed on the
inside – both of them
are invalid. R. Hana-
niah b. Gamaliel says,
"One which is folded,
on the inside of
which its witnesses
signed their names, is
valid, because one
can unfold it." Rab-
ban   Simeon   b.
Gamaliel   says,
"Everything is in ac-
cord with local cus-
tom" [M. B.B. 10:1].
*Now in reflecting on this
matter [we said], well,
doesn't the first author-
ity concur,* **Everything
is in accord with local
custom**? *And said R.
Ashi, "This refers to a
place in which a plain
one was customary, and
a folded one was made,
or a place in which a
folded one was custom-
ary, and a plain one was
made. All parties concur
that the one who gave
instructions was meticu-
lous about the matter.
Where is the point of
dispute? Where both
forms are acceptable, and
the husband said to the
scribe, 'Make a plain
one,' but the scribe went
and made a folded one.
One authority maintains
that the husband was
meticulous about the in-
structions, and the other,
that all he was doing
was giving him good
advice on how to pro-
ceed ['showing him
the place']."*

D.   *R. Eleazar: as we have
learned in the Mishnah:*

[B] R. Yohanan said, "R. Simeon concurs that if he deceived her about an advantage as to genealogy, she is not betrothed."

[C] Said R. Yosé, "The Mishnah itself has made the same point: **'On condition that I am a priest,' and he turns out to be a Levite [etc.] [M. 2:21].**

[D] Now there is no *problem* in the case in which he claimed to be **a priest and turns out to be a Levite, [that she is not betrothed].**

[E] [But if he claimed to be] a Levite and he turned out to be a priest, [there, too, she is not betrothed, for] she has the right to say, "I do not want his superior airs to lord it over me."

E. **The woman who said, "Receive my writ of divorce for me in such-and-such a place," and he [the messenger] received it for her in some other place –**

F. **it is invalid.**

G. **R. Eliezer declares it valid [M. Git. 6:3K-M].**

H. *Therefore* all he was doing was giving him good advice on how to proceed ['showing him the place']."

3. A. Said Ulla, "The Mishnah's controversy concerns only a monetary advantage, but as to a genealogical advantage, all parties concur that she is not betrothed. *How come? 'I really don't want a shoe that is bigger than my foot.'"*

B. *So, too, it has been taught on Tannaite authority:* **R. Simeon concedes that if he deceived her to her advantage in a matter of genealogy, she is not betrothed [T. Qid. 2:5I].**

C. *Said R. Ashi, "A close reading of our Mishnah paragraph yields the same conclusion, for the Tannaite formulation is as follows:*

D. **"'...on condition that I am a priest,' and he turns out to be a Levite,**

E. **"'...on condition that I am a Levite,' and he turns out to be a priest,**

F.   "'...a netin,' and he turns out to be a mamzer,

G.   "'...a mamzer,' and he turns out to be a netin [M. 2:3A-D].

H.   *"And in these matters, R. Simeon does not take issue."*

I.   *Objected Mar bar R. Ashi, "Well, note the further Tannaite formulation:*

J.   "'...on condition that I have a daughter or a slave girl who is an adult [alt.: a hairdresser],' and he has none,

K.   "'...on condition that I have none,' and he has one –

L.   *"and these represent monetary advantages, and yet here, too, R. Simeon does not take issue! Rather, he differs in the first clause, and likewise in the second, and here too, he differs in the first clause, and here too!'*

M.   *But how are the matters comparable? In that case, both items represent a monetary advantage, so he differs in the first clause, and the same in the second. But here, where it is a matter of a genealogical advantages, if he did differ, it should have been made explicit in the Tannaite formulation.*

N.   *And if you prefer, I shall say, here, too, genealogical advantage is what is at issue. Do you imagine that* **an adult** *is meant literally? It*

> *means, of superior standing, for the" betrothed woman can say, "It is not acceptable to me that she should take my words from me and go and tell them around the neighborhood.*

The Yerushalmi's composition wants to make the point that Simeon will go along with an advantageous claim as to genealogy, a point that the Mishnah rule itself is shown to register. And that concludes the Yerushalmi's message.

The Bavli covers the same ground, but much more, and in a more complex manner. First, we address the generalization, not a particular detail. And we frame the issue in another context altogether, that of a transaction in wine. So the Bavli accomplishes its principal purpose of moving always toward the general, transcending the details of a case in favor of its principle, moving beneath the surface of a particular toward its abstract premise. And that is accomplished not in so many words but implicitly, in the simple statement before us. Not only so, but, if this did not accomplish the purpose, II.2 states matters in general terms all over again – but the terms now shift to another matter altogether. How do we interpret instructions that a person gives an agent? Now, it is clear, that issue inheres in a variety of cases, which we review; it can be shown to inhere in ours as well. But Abbayye's statement, II.2.B does not go back into our case in detail; it suffices to allude to II.1.F. Then we go into another matter altogether, Simeon b. Gamaliel's ruling on the rules covering the preparation of documents; then yet another item, the receipt of a writ of divorce.

Now all these cases have in common is the premise that we have articulated, and it is the glory of the Bavli to demonstrate that fact, time and again. Does that mean the Bavli's Mishnah exegesis falls below the standard of clarity attained in the Yerushalmi? Not at all, for at II.3 we state explicitly the exegetical proposition that the Yerushalmi has established. But here, too, we present that proposition in a remarkably fresh way. Ashi sustains the proposed proposition (on which Y. concurs), but then his son, Mar, takes issue with that reading; once more, a proposition is transformed into a point of contention, a thesis is offered that requires us to read the Mishnah paragraph in a contrary way, and that thesis is grounded on a close and careful reading of the formulation of the language of the Mishnah itself. And in these ways, and in others that will become clear when we consider the Talmuds' reading of Mishnah-tractate Hagigah Chapter Three, the Bavli's voice is unique.

What follows carries us once more to the same broad level of generalization about the Talmuds' differences, and the Bavli's distinctive traits and unique voice. In the contrast of the two Talmuds' reading of M. Hag. 3:1 we see how the Bavli's composites' authors aim at showing the integrity of truth, by which I mean, the cogency, indeed, the harmony, of laws in a comprehensive and unifying law. For the two Talmuds' treatment of M. Hag. 3:1B, I give only the principal part of Bavli's reading; its secondary expansion, through I.8, should be noted as well, but the abstract here suffices to make the point.

[II.A] [As to M. 3:1B, not immersing one utensil inside another,] R. La [= B.'s Ila] in the name of R. Yohanan: "If the unclean object was as heavy as a liter, they do not immerse it [inside of another one, since it will weigh down on the container and so interpose between the container and the immersion pool's water]."	I.1 A. [They immerse utensils inside of other utensils for purification for use with food in the status of heave-offering, but not for purification for use with food in the status of Holy Things:] Why not for use with [food in the status of] Holy Things?
[B] Abba Saul says, "Also in the case of utensils used for the preparation of food in the status of heave-offering, they immerse [one such vessel inside of another] only in the case of a wicker basket [in which other utensils may be placed]. [But other utensils may not serve as containers for immersion.]"	B. Said R. Ila, "Because the weight of the inner utensil interposes [between the outer utensil and the water itself]." [Abraham: It prevents the water from reaching every part of the utensils, thus invalidating the immersion of both the outer and the inner utensils.]
	C. But since the concluding clause of the Mishnah invokes the consideration of interposition, it would follow that the opening clause is not based on the consideration of interposition, for the Tannaite formulation states: **The rule for Holy**

Things is not like the rule for heave-offering. For in the case of [immersion for use of] Holy Things one unties a knot and dries it off, immerses and afterward ties it up again. And in the case of heave-offering one ties it and then one immerses.

D. *Both the opening and the closing rules invoke the consideration of interposition, but it was necessary to underline that that consideration operates throughout. For had we been informed of that consideration only for the opening clause, I might have supposed that the operative consideration that it is not permitted to immerse utensils within utensils for food in the status of Holy Things is the weight of the utensils, which causes interposition, but in the latter case, where there is no such consideration of the weight of a utensil, I might have thought it would not be a matter of interposition even for Holy Things. Moreover, if the Mishnah had informed us of the latter clause alone, I might have imagined that the reason that one may not immerse utensils within utensils for food in the status of Holy Things is because of the consideration that [21B] a knot tightens in the water, while in the first of the*

two clauses, where the
water makes the utensil
float, that would be no
matter of interposition;
accordingly, it was nec-
essary to make the point
in both instances.

[C] Said R. Yohanan,
     "Abba Saul and R.
     Simeon have both said
     the same thing.

[D] "For we have learned
     there: **He who kept
     hold on a man or on
     utensils and im-
     mersed them – they
     are unclean** [since the
     water has not touched
     the place by which he
     holds on to them]. **If
     he rinsed his hand in
     the water, they are
     clean. R. Simeon says,
     'He should loose his
     hold on them so that
     the water may come
     into them'**"[M. Miq.
     8:5D-F].

[E] Said R. Yohanan, "It is
     reasonable to suppose
     that R. Simeon will
     concur with the view
     of Abba Saul. But
     Abba Saul will not
     concur with R.
     Simeon. [Simeon will
     be concerned with the
     weight of the utensil.
     Abba Saul will not
     concur with Simeon
     that rinsing off prior
     to immersion will not
     suffice. Abba Saul will
     accept rinsing off prior
     to immersion.]"

[F] Rabbis of Caesarea in
     the name of R.
     Yohanan: "The de-
     cided law follows the
     view of Abba Saul."

[G] And so it has been taught: "The law accords with his view."

[H] Said R. Jonah, "The Mishnah [which regards M. 3:1B, immersion of one utensil inside another as valid for heave-offering but not Holy Things as a gradation that treats Holy Things as superior to heave-offering] follows the view of R. Meir.

[I] "But in the view of sages they may do so [in the case of a large wicker basket] even for food in the status of Holy Things."

I.2 A. *R. Ila is consistent with opinions stated elsewhere [when he invokes the consideration of interposition], for* said R. Ila said R. Hanina bar Pappa, "There are ten points at which Holy Things exceed in strictness food in the status of heave-offering that are set forth in our Mishnah; the first five apply to both Holy Things and unconsecrated food prepared according to the rules governing the cleanness of Holy Things, the latter five apply to Holy Things but not to unconsecrated food prepared according to the rules governing the cleanness of Holy Things.

B. *"How come? In connection with the first five, there is the possibility of uncleanness such as is decreed by the Torah, so, in these cases, rabbis made a precautionary decree covering both Holy Things and unconsecrated food prepared in accord with the rules governing the cleanness of Holy Things. In connection with the latter five, in which there is no risk of uncleanness such as is decreed by the Torah, rabbis made precautionary decrees with respect to Holy Things but not with respect to the governance of unconsecrated food prepared in accord with the*

rules of uncleanness
governing Holy
Things."

C.   Raba said, "Since the
second five are governed
by the consideration of
interposition, the former
five cannot be governed
by the consideration of
interposition; and as to
the clause discussed at
the outset, the operative
consideration is this: It
is a precautionary de-
cree, against immers-
ing needles and hooks
in a utensil the mouth
of which is not the size
of the spout of a skin
bottle [such as would
permit free entry of
water], *as we have
learned in the Mishnah:*
**The intermingling of
immersion pools is
through a hole the
size of the spout of a
water-skin, in the
thickness and capac-
ity – [22A] two fingers
turned around in full.
[If there is doubt
whether it is the size
of the spout of a wa-
ter-skin or not the
size of the spout of a
water-skin, it is unfit,
because it derives
from the Torah] [M.
Miq. 6:5A-D]."**

D.   *[Raba] accords with that
which* R. Nahman said
Rabbah bar Abbuha
said, "There are eleven
points at which Holy
Things exceed in
strictness food in the
status of heave-offer-
ing that are set forth in
our Mishnah; the first
six apply to both Holy

Things and unconse-
crated food prepared
according to the rules
governing the clean-
ness of Holy Things,
the latter five apply to
Holy Things but not to
unconsecrated food
prepared according to
the rules governing
the cleanness of Holy
Things."

E.   *So what's at issue*
       between Raba's and R.
       Ila's statements?

F.   *At issue between them is*
       the case of a basket or
       net that was filled
       with utensils and im-
       mersed. *In the opinion*
       of him who has said that
       the operative considera-
       tion is interposition, that
       consideration applies
       here, too; according to
       him who maintains that
       it is a precautionary
       decree, against im-
       mersing needles and
       hooks in a utensil the
       mouth of which is not
       the size of the spout of
       a skin bottle [such as
       would permit free en-
       try of water], *well, that*
       consideration would not
       come into play here.

I.3   A.   *Raba is consistent with*
           views expressed else-
           where, for said Raba,
           "A basket or net that
           was filled with uten-
           sils and immersed –
           the utensils are clean.
           But an immersion pool
           that one divided by
           using a basket or a net
           – he who immerses
           therein has gained
           nothing from the im-
           mersion. *For lo, while*

*the earth is wholly perfo-
rated* [in that water
flows through hollows
of the earth, and water
appearing anywhere is
bound to be connected
to a large aquifer
elsewhere, the con-
nection is not valid
(Abraham)], *nonethe-
less, we require that the
forty seahs of valid water
be collected in a single
place. And that is the
rule in reference to a
utensil that is clean, but
in respect to a utensil
that is unclean, since the
immersion serves quite
well for the entire uten-
sil, it serves also for the
utensils that are in it.
For we have learned in
the Mishnah:* **A bucket
which is full of uten-
sils, which one
dunked – lo, they [the
utensils] are clean.
And if it did not im-
merse, the water is
not mingled [with
that of the immersion
pool], until it [the wa-
ter in the bucket] is
mingled [with the
water of the pool] by
[a stream) the size of
the spout of a water-
skin [M. Miq. 6:2].** "

Now we note that precisely the same consideration operates in both
answers to the question, the consideration of interposition. Not only so,
but the same authority, Ila, stands behind the matter. What Y. does with
that statement is simple. The fact is extended by Abba Saul to another
circumstance, then two authorities are shown to have concurred, with
some secondary analysis of that allegation. So the main point is allowed
to stand without significant challenge. So much for the Yerushalmi.

What the Yerushalmi treats as a settled fact, the Bavli handles as a
challenge to discerning intellect. Ila's statement is tested against the

evidence of the wording of the rule itself, something the Yerushalmi's compositions' framers rarely do. This challenge from the wording is resolved at D, in a familiar initiative: had matters not been spelled out time and again, I might have read the language of the Mishnah to yield a point that is in fact not true. A second step follows, which is to test the consistency of the authorities at hand: they invoke here the same principle that they invoke elsewhere. The payoff of such an inquiry is to link discrete cases into a common law – again, the quest for the law behind the laws in the guise of a testing of the consistency of authorities' positions, and I.2, 3 accomplish that goal. But this leads to a secondary issue, since Raba is cited in connection with the evidence concerning Ila, and the issues between their positions are spelled out. Then, I.3, Raba is himself shown to be consistent. What follows at I.4 is a mere footnote, but I.5 takes up the quest for the law behind the laws, now proposing that the difference of opinion between Raba and Ila links to a difference of opinion among Tannaite authorities as well, and that difference turns out to pertain to the same problem as the one at our Mishnah, so is not farfetched at all. When we reach the law behind the laws, we stand at the goal of the Bavli's labors: to add to the Mishnah yet another singular truth about the truth, which is to say, the Torah.

Both the Mishnah and the Bavli undertake to uncover and expose, in the laws of the Torah, the philosophy that the Torah reveals. That is the upshot of the two documents' powerful and reasoned, fully instantiated polemic: many things yield one thing, and this is that one thing. Stated in the language of revelation, the Torah through many things says one thing, through many commandments, sets forth one commandment, through diversity in detail makes a single, main point. And we know what that point is. By "the integrity of truth," in secular language, we say the same thing that we express when, in mythic language, we speak, as does Sherira Gaon at the end of a long apologetic tradition, of "the one whole Torah of Moses, our rabbi." But now, by "one" and by "whole," very specific statements are made: jurisprudence reaches upward toward philosophy, on the one side, and the teachings and rules of the Torah are wholly harmonious and cogent, on the other. In the language that I have used here, the upshot is very simple: mind is one, whole, coherent; thought properly conducted yields simple truth about complex things.

Comparing the Mishnah and the Bavli, as much as contrasting the Yerushalmi and the Bavli, have brought us to this conclusion. The outcome of the contrast, then, is not merely the difference that the Yerushalmi is brief and laconic while the Bavli speaks in fully spelled-out ways. Nor is it the difference that, in general, the Yerushalmi's presentations are not dialectical, and the Bavli's are, for even though that difference may in general prove fixed, on occasion the Yerushalmi will expand an argument through question and answer, parry and counterthrust, and the analogy of a duel will apply to the Yerushalmi, if not consistently.

The difference is intellectual and, appropriately, comes to the surface in hermeneutics: the Bavli's composites' framers consistently treat as a question to be investigated the exegetical hypotheses that the Yerushalmi's compositions' authors happily accept as conclusive. All of the secondary devices of testing an allegation – a close reading of the formulation of the Mishnah, an appeal to the false conclusion such a close reading, absent a given formulation, might have yielded, to take the examples before us – serve that primary goal. The second recurrent difference – as we have seen time and again in Parts One through Six – is that the Bavli's framers find themselves constantly drawn toward questions of generalization and abstraction (once more: the law behind the laws), moving from case to principle to new case to new principle, then asking whether the substrate of principles forms a single, tight fabric. The Yerushalmi's authors rarely, if ever, pursue that chimera.

But what gives the Bavli its compelling, ineluctable power to persuade, the source of the Bavli's intellectual force is that thrust for abstraction, through generalization (and in that order, generalization, toward abstraction). To spell out in very simple terms what I conceive to be at issue: The way that the law behind the laws emerges is, first, generalization of a case into a principle, then, the recasting of the principle into an abstraction encompassing a variety of otherwise free-standing principles. This observation calls to mind, as I have briefly shown just now, how the Mishnah's cases time and again point toward a single abstraction, the hierarchical order of all being. Here, in the Bavli, I find the counterpart and completion of the Mishnah's deepest layer of thought, which is, the intellectual medium to match the philosophical message. The union of philosophy and religion is effected through the Talmud's theology under the canopy of hermeneutics. Now to the details, where God dwells.

10

The Hermeneutical Difference and Its Meaning
Order, Harmony, Proposition

> The methodological understanding of permanently fixed life expressions we call explication. As the life of the mind only finds its complete, exhaustive, and therefore, objectively comprehensible expression in language, explication culminates in the interpretation of the written records of human existence. This art is the basis of philology. The science of this art is hermeneutics.
>
> Wilhelm Dilthey[1]

The language that contains the evidence of "the life of the mind" for our sages of blessed memory is – and can only be – the language of the Torah, which is to say, the language of God: all the words of God we have. If for "the written records of human existence" we substitute the words "the Torah," we have, whole and complete, the hermeneutical task: finding the rules that form of words sentences, of sentences coherent thoughts, and of coherent thoughts the sum of God's mind so far as in the Torah we know and gain access to it. In the intelligent reading of the Torah we meet God; in the rules of reading, we uncover the theology of Judaism. The logic of God – the theology of Judaism – that affords knowledge that God has manifested then consists in identifying the Torah's hermeneutics and articulating its principles in accessible, theological language.

The agendum of hermeneutics encompasses the issue of the author's original meaning. In the case of the Torah, of course, the stakes are very high. But, as we have already seen, "our sages of blessed memory" do not concede that the Author's original meaning and intent cannot be

---

[1]Cited by K.M. Newton, *Interpreting the Text*, p. 42.

recapitulated, for, they maintain to the contrary, the very language that is used, on the one side, and the character of the document on the other (we cannot say "writing" since part of the document is oral and only later on written down), together afford ready access to the original meaning and intent. Sages begin with the firm conviction that they know that meaning because they know how to find it out. When we follow them from their reading upward to the rules that manifestly govern that reading, and when we then recapitulate those rules in the setting of not reading but believing – the implications for knowledge of the mind of God, the modes of thought of God, the rationality of God – then through God's self-manifestation in the Torah, we know God, or, more to the point, whatever it is about God that God wishes us to know. From the fact that God gave the Torah, all things flow. To the fact that God gave the Torah, all things return.

To see how this is expressed in a detailed examination of some passages of the Talmud of Babylonia, we systematically take up a simple program, first, the sustained hermeneutics that asks us to find flaws and remove them by explaining them away, second, the hermeneutical medium of argument, and, third, the hermeneutical task of showing the rationality of disputes.

To begin with, of course, we have to distinguish between literary criticism of technicalities of phrasing the writing and a hermeneutics aimed at discovering in the Torah the mind of God. They relate, but they are not the same thing. Specifically, sages' interest is not in the literary traits of sayings but in their logic. The sense of "logic" here is: sensible wording and clear articulation of sense, coherence with other sayings on the same subject or problem, cogency at the level of principle with other congruent sayings, and identity at the level of premise with the premises of other, free-standing principles and their cases. The rules of thought that govern the inquiry into the logic of these Tannaite sayings they take to be self-evident, and, for them, self-evidence is the trait of the Torah (whether Oral, whether Written), by reason of the divine Authorship. That is not to say they did not conduct a massive program of literary criticism; they did; but the program formed only a small part of their larger labor.

The unnamed authors of the Bavli's compositions of course read the language of the Mishnah with great care, watching for prolixity and verbosity, and here is a very simple example of how they did their work:

I.1.   A.   *What need do I have to repeat in the Mishnah,*
        B.   **this one says, "I found it!" –**
        C.   **and that one says, "I found it!" –**
        D.   **this one says, "It's all mine!" –**
        E.   **and that one says, "It's all mine!"?**

F.   *Let the Tanna repeat only a single* [plea]. [Surely one plea would have been sufficient.]

G.   *It is only a single [formulation] that the Tanna has repeated* [Daiches: it is only one plea], namely,

H.   "this one says, 'I found it and it's all mine...,' and that one says, 'I found it and it's all mine....'"

B. B.M. 1:1/I.1[2]

But nothing in this simple exercise of literary criticism suggests the ambition and originality of the Bavli's composites' authors' reading of the Mishnah. They not only recapitulated the program of the prior Talmud's reading of the Mishnah, they vastly extended and deepened it.

Let me begin my portrait of how in the Talmud sages demonstrate the Torah's perfection with an array of specific propositions, all of them joined together in what is a perfectly representative example. Here we see how many distinct propositions may flow together to make a single point. Just as sages do not say obvious or redundant things, so of course the Mishnah has to be shown to speak always with plausible purpose and a fresh point. To see how that obvious fact stands behind a persistent pattern in Mishnah exegesis, once more indicative of a hermeneutics that leads to one kind of reading of the Mishnah, rather than some other, I give a single example of how the repertoire of considerations – no banality, no repetition, no eccentricity in the Mishnah – governs a sustained exposition of a Mishnah paragraph:

Bavli Bava Mesia 9:1

A.   **[103A] He who leases a field from his fellow [as tenant farmer or sharecropper],**

B.   **in a place in which they are accustomed to cut [the crops], he must cut them.**

C.   **[If the custom is] to uproot [the crops], he must uproot them.**

---

[2]I choose most of my examples from the Babas – Baba Qamma, Baba Mesia, and Baba Batra – because these are the tractates of civil law and commonly define the earliest steps in the curricula of Talmud academies. Not only are they representative of the document as a whole, but they also have slight counterpart in the earlier Talmud, where the three Babas are meager and undeveloped, scarcely a Talmud at all. Since I wish to underline the autonomy of the second Talmud, therefore the distinctive character of its statement, I therefore choose cases where there is only rare intersection with the first one. But I underline once more: I claim only that what we examine here is routine and ordinary in the second Talmud, rare and extraordinary in the first – not that the Yerushalmi never exhibits classifications of discourse that the Bavli always puts forth. "Never" and "always" are not terms that serve very well in analysis of these writings. Not only so, but the quality of the text tradition that delivers from antiquity to our own hands the actual wording of these writings is thin and unreliable; hence we can make no claim at all that appeals to "always" or "never."

D.   [If the custom is] to plough after [reaping and so to turn the soil], he must plough.

E.   All is in accord with the prevailing custom of the province.

F.   Just as they split up the grain, so they split up the straw and stubble.

G.   Just as they split up the wine, so they split up [103B] the [dead] branches and reed props.

H.   And both [parties to the agreement] must provide reed props.

We commence with a complementary Tannaite formulation, to be brought into juxtaposition with the Mishnah rule:

I.1   A.   *A Tannaite authority repeated:* In a locality in which people are accustomed to cut off the crops, one has not got the right to uproot them; to uproot them, one has not got the right to cut them off, and either party may prevent the other [from diverging from the usual practice].

B.   "To cut off the crops, one has not got the right to uproot them": For lo, he may say, "I want the field to be manured with stubble," and the other may claim, "It is too much work to uproot the plants."

C.   "To uproot them, one has not got the right to cut them off": [The landlord] can say, "I want my field to be cleared of stubble," and the tenant can say, "I need the stubble [for my cattle, and I don't want it to stay in the ground]."

The point of redundancy is now identified and removed:

D.   "And either party may prevent the other": Why bother to make this point?

E.   The sense is, "what is the reason," namely, "what is the reason that in a locality in which people are accustomed to cut off the crops, one has not got the right to uproot them? and vice versa? It is because either party may prevent the other."

We now consider the clause by close reading of the given Mishnah sentences:

II.1   A.   [If the custom is] to plough after [reaping and so to turn the soil], he must plough:

B.   *That's obvious!*

C.   *No, it was necessary to make the point because in a place where people do not weed while the grain is standing, and the lessee went and weeded it, I might have thought that he can plead, "I weeded it so as not to have to plough later on." Therefore we are taught that that condition has to be stipulated at the outset.*

The Mishnah contains emphatic words, for example, "all...," and these are assumed to exhibit intent and bear particular meaning; then here again we have to be told why the emphasis, if it is not to be dismissed as mere style:

III.1   A.   **All is in accord with the prevailing custom of the province:**

        B.   *What is it that "all" is meant to encompass?*

        C.   *It is meant to encompass that teaching that rabbis have stated on Tannaite authority:*

        D.   **[He who leases a field from his fellow and there were trees in the field,] in a place in which people are accustomed to rent out trees along with the field, lo, they are deemed to belong to the lessee. And in a place in which people are accustomed to rent out trees by themselves, lo, they belong to the lessor [T. B.M. 9:4A-F].**

        E.   **In a place in which people are accustomed to rent out trees along with the field, lo, they are deemed to belong to the lessee** – *that is perfectly self-evident!*

        F.   *The rule is required to cover a case in which everyone ordinarily leases fields for a third share, while he went and leased it for a quarter share. I might have thought that the lessor can plead, "I charged you a lower rental in the assumption that you would have no share in the produce of the trees." Therefore we are informed that such a stipulation should have been made at the outset.*

        G.   **And in a place in which people are accustomed to rent out trees by themselves, lo, they belong to the lessor** – *that is perfectly self-evident!*

        H.   *The rule is required to cover a case in which everyone ordinarily leases fields for a quarter share, while he went and leased it for a third share. I might have thought that the lessor can plead, "I paid you a higher rental in the assumption that I would have a share in the produce of the trees." Therefore we are informed that such a stipulation should have been made at the outset.*

Here is marshaled much of the Talmud's hermeneutical repertoire, examples of the types of literary phenomena that attract attention and illustrative formulations of the solutions to specific problems that recur throughout the document. Having seen the way the matter works in its natural environment, let us turn to some of the specific hermeneutical rules and how they are instantiated.

True, as we saw, the framers of the Bavli's compositions and composites did not invent the proposition that the Mishnah is a thing of perfection. The first Talmud had fully exposed that proposition. But (whether or not they learned anything at all from the first Talmud), the writers of the second Talmud's compositions and, occasionally, the compilers of its composites, vastly expanded the range of proof. This they did by setting forth a more ambitious criterion for perfection and then systematically identifying possible flaws and repeatedly, in some few ways, demonstrating that the candidates for condemnation in fact deserved admiration. Routine inquiries of a critical character time and again yield the general proposition that the oral part of the Torah exhibits no imperfections. Authors of compositions took special interest in text criticism, showing, identifying, and correcting imperfections. Since, here, we are dealing with not what is attributed to God but what is assigned to named sages or to their consensus, no restrictions of tact or respect placed limitations on sages' close and unforgiving reading. They watched above all for inconsistency, banality, eccentricity, repetition, and verbosity, quickly pointing out candidates for ridicule. The hermeneutics that instructed on the reading of the Mishnah required constant attention to the possibility that the Mishnah repeated itself, contradicted itself, represented eccentric opinion, or simply expressed its ideas in a slovenly way – not only the Mishnah, but its named authorities.

Indeed, the principle of interpretation of the Mishnah focused not on the Mishnah in particular (except when it came to the wording of a Mishnah paragraph) but on the intellectual work of the sages of the document. At stake time and again in the reading of the Mishnah is, how could Judah contradict himself? Or why should Meir make such a pointless, because obvious and redundant, statement? Or why should Simeon take an eccentric position? Or does the Mishnah rule stand for only one authority, not for the consensus of the collegium? The upshot of the work is to identify the Torah's perfection with not the Mishnah but the authorities cited by the Mishnah, on the one side, and those persons who, or sayings that, have the status of Mishnah authorities, on the other. The hermeneutics governed the reading of words, memorized or written; the reading that was to take place was not a book but authoritative statements, in whatever medium they were preserved. The identification of the Torah vastly transcended the written part and the oral part in relationship to the written; now the demonstration of the flawless Torah extended to the positions, convictions, and persons of the sages who formed the media for the formulation of the Torah, sentence by sentence.

The rather ample set of abstracts of which the present and the coming chapter are composed stand for types of readings, each of them repeated many times through the Bavli. My effort is to show in a precise, textual manner the product of the hermeneutics, which allows us to form a theory of its character, moving a step onward still to an account of the theological outcome of the successful reading of a given passage. Here we begin with an example of how the Bavli composition will address the flaws of inconsistency, banality, and eccentricity:

Bavli Baba Mesia 8:8

A.   He who rents out a house to his fellow for a year –
B.   [if] the year was intercalated [and received an extra month of Adar],
C.   it is intercalated to the advantage of the tenant.
D.   [If] he rented it to him by the month,
E.   [if] the year was intercalated,
F.   it is intercalated to the advantage of the landlord.

G.   M^cSH B: In Sepphoris a person hired a bathhouse from his fellow for twelve golden [denars] per year, at the rate of one golden denar per month [and the year was intercalated].

H.   [102B] The case came before Rabban Simeon b. Gamaliel and before R. Yosé.

I.   They ruled, "Let them divide the month added by the intercalation of the year."

I.1   A.   *Is the precedent [G-I] then cited to contradict the rule [A-C]?*

Since the rule is that the month is not divided between the landlord and tenant, the precedent that is cited obviously contradicts the rule. That of course is not conceivable in a perfect writing, and a quick solution is found: rewrite the precedent.

B.   *The passage contains a lacuna and this is its intended sense:* And if he had said to him, "For twelve golden coins per year, a golden denar per month," let them divide it. **M^cSH B: In Sepphoris a person hired a bathhouse from his fellow for twelve golden [denars] per year, at the rate of one golden denar per month [and the year was intercalated]. The case came before Rabban Simeon b. Gamaliel and before R. Yosé. They ruled, "Let them divide the month added by the intercalation of the year."**

So much for the facile removal of contradictions. Many other modes of harmonization are available, as the case requires: distinctions, for example, between the rule that derives from, or pertains to, a law deriving from the Torah and one deriving from authority of sages; between one case and another case, which can be shown to be different and therefore subject to its own rule; and the like.

The same passage allows us to see how the Talmud addresses the problem of human banality: saying obvious things in obvious ways, not to mention repetitiousness and redundancy and the like. The same passage bears a gloss in the name of Rab, which is immediately classified as stupid by reason of banality:

C.   *Said Rab, "If I had been there, I would have assigned the whole of the added month to the landlord."*

D.   *What does he thereby intend to tell us? Is it that one takes as authoritative only the final statement in a transaction that leads to an agreement? Rab has already made that point. For R. Huna said, "They say in the household of Rab, 'If the agreed price is an istera, a hundred maahs, then a hundred maahs are due; if a hundred maahs, an istira, then an istera is what is due.'"*

E.   *Were that the only formulation of Rab's view, I should have reached the conclusion that in that case, the second formulation is meant to spell out the first; therefore we are informed that that is not the case.* [But in the more generic formulation of the rule, in the present context, we realize his view encompasses a broader variety of cases, so that,

when the two terms are contradictory, we simply follow the second
that is used.]

The next step in this absolutely paradigmatic composition leads to a
separate kind of initiative. Samuel now presents a different theory of the
case at hand. The premise of his proposed rule is contrary to the premise
that we interpret the context of an agreement in which a number of
statements have been made so that only the final statement that is made
is operative. But elsewhere, Samuel has taken precisely the position the
opposite of which is now imputed to him on the basis of what he has
said:

F.   *And Samuel said, "[With reference to the decision of Simeon b. Gamaliel*
        and Yosé,] we deal in that decision with a case in which the landlord comes
        to lay claim at the middle of the month, but if he should come and lay claim
        at the beginning of the month, the whole of the fee for the month is
        assigned to the landlord. Should he come at the end of the month, the
        whole of it is to the tenant." [Possession establishes title. If the
        landlord demands rent in the middle of the extra month, the tenant
        has the first half rent free; he pays for the second; the house belongs
        to the landlord, and ownership for the next half month is subject to
        dispute.]

G.   *But then does Samuel reject the view that one takes as authoritative only*
        the final statement in a transaction that leads to an agreement?

H.   *But lo, both Rab and Samuel maintain,* "[In a case in which one says to
        the other,] 'I am selling you a kor for thirty selas,' he can retract
        even at the last seah. But if he says, 'I am selling you a kor for
        thirty, at a sela per seah,' then as the buyer takes each, he makes
        acquisition of it."

The solution to the problem is another medium of harmonization; now
we invoke the rule that operates in that other case, and it turns out to
have nothing to do with the proposed theory behind Samuel's position;
then the intersecting case does not contain the occasion for Samuel to
contradict himself after all:

I.   There, the reason is that he has taken possession, and here, too, he
        has taken possession.

To conclude, we continue the tangent begun at I with the introduction of
the facts and issues of the intersecting case. Now the position contrary to
Rab's and Samuel's, which is that of Nahman, is set forth:

J.   And R. Nahman said, "Land remains in the presumptive possession
        of its owner."

This, too, forms a candidate for the trash bin of banalities: sages do not
repeat what prior sages already have said, that is an unthinkable flaw:

K. *What does he thereby intend to tell us? Is it that one takes as authoritative only the final statement in a transaction that leads to an agreement? Rab has already made that point.*

There is a solution to that problem, as we see at the conclusion.

L. *He indicates that that is the rule even if the terms were reversed* [because we rely not on the order only, but on the prevailing presumption].

What are now eliminated in these exchanges are banality, eccentricity, and redundancy. As is clear, at stake in the operating rules of interpretation is not a text at all but a set of conceptions and formulations, whether these derive from the Mishnah, or from Scripture, or from sages; whether the sages are named in the Mishnah or clearly identified as later and of a lower standing than those of the Mishnah.

The single most common solution to the problem of redundancy spelled out why, though two or more positions looked repetitious of one another, they in fact were required, since each made a point omitted by the other. This commonplace formulation, a *serikhuta* ("demonstration of the necessity of two apparently redundant statements"), forms one of the basic tools of Mishnah criticism and occurs on every second or third page of the Talmud when Mishnah criticism is under way; it equally serves to show why when a given sage says the same thing about two things, he must do so, lest we misunderstand that thing. What seems to overlap does not actually exhibit the flaw of repetition, because the two apparently parallel or even repetitive statements deal with different situations, make different points, or invoke different principles altogether.

We come now to the dialectical argument, to which we have already been exposed. For enough of the Talmud has been cited thus far to show how the document works out its program of Mishnah commentary. But in so doing, we have yet to examine the single most interesting trait of the writing, which is the dialectical argument. That protracted, sometimes meandering, always moving argument raises a question and answers it, then raises a question about the answer, then does the same; it moves hither and yon; it is always one, but it is never the same, and it flows across the surface of the Talmud. The dialectical argument is one principal means by which the second Talmud accomplishes its goal; it is rare in the first Talmud, common and definitive in the second. The passage that we consider occurs at Bavli to M. B.M. 1:1-2/IV.1-6 = B. B.M. 5B-6A. Our interest is in the twists and turns of the argument and what is at stake in the formation of a continuous and unfolding composition:

IV.1 A.   **[5B] This one takes an oath that he possesses no less a share of it than half, [and that one takes an oath that he possesses no less a share of it than half, and they divide it up]:**

Our first question is one of text criticism: analysis of the Mishnah paragraph's word choice. We say that the oath concerns the portion that the claimant alleges he possesses. But the oath really affects the portion that he does not have in hand at all:

> **B.**   *Is it concerning the portion that he claims he possesses that he takes the oath, or concerning the portion that he does not claim to possess?* [Daiches: The implication is that the terms of the oath are ambiguous. By swearing that his share in it is not "less than half," the claimant might mean that it is not even a third or a fourth (which is "less than half"), and the negative way of putting it would justify such an interpretation. He could therefore take this oath even if he knew that he had no share in the garment at all, while he would be swearing falsely if he really had a share in the garment that is less than half, however small that share might be.]
>
> **C.**   *Said R. Huna, "It is that he says, 'By an oath! I possess in it a portion, and I possess in it a portion that is no less than half a share of it.'"* [The claimant swears that his share is at least half (Daiches)].

Having asked and answered the question, we now find ourselves in an extension of the argument; the principal trait of the dialectical argument is now before us: [1] but maybe [2] the contrary is the case, so what about [3] – that is, the setting aside of a proposition in favor of its opposite:

> **D.**   *Then let him say, "By an oath! The whole of it is mine!"*
>
> **E.**   *But are we going to give him the whole of it?* [Obviously not, there is another claimant, also taking an oath.]
>
> **F.**   *Then let him say, "By an oath! Half of it is mine!"*
>
> **G.**   *That would damage his own claim* [which was that he owned the whole of the cloak, not only half of it].
>
> **H.**   *But here, too, is it not the fact that, in the oath that he is taking, he impairs his own claim?* [After all, he here makes explicit the fact that he owns at least half of it. What happened to the other half?]
>
> **I.**   *[Not at all.] For he has said, "The whole of it is mine!"* [And, he further proceeds,] *"And as to your contrary view, by an oath, I do have a share in it, and that share is no less than half!"*

Now what we have here is not a set piece of two positions, with an analysis of each; it is, rather, an analytical argument, explaining why this, not that, then why not that but rather this; and onward. It is not an endless argument, an argument for the sake of arguing, or evidence that important to the Bavli is process but not position. To the contrary, the passage is resolved with a decisive conclusion, not permitted to run on. But the dialectical composition proceeds – continuous and coherent from point to point, even as it zigs and zags:

2.   A.   Now, since this one is possessed of the cloak and standing right there, and that one is possessed of the cloak and is standing right there, why in the world do I require this oath?

Until now we have assumed as fact the premise of the Mishnah's rule, which is that an oath is there to be taken. But why assume so? Surely each party now has what he is going to get. So what defines the point and effect of the oath?

B.   Said R. Yohanan, "This oath [to which our Mishnah passage refers] happens to be an ordinance imposed only by rabbis,

C.   "so that people should not go around grabbing the cloaks of other people and saying, 'It's mine!'" [But, as a matter of fact, the oath that is imposed in our Mishnah passage is not legitimate by the law of the Torah. It is an act taken by sages to maintain the social order.]

We do not administer oaths to liars; we do not impose an oath in a case in which we may end up turning an honest man into a liar either. So we ask how we can agree to an oath in this case at all?

D.   *But why then not advance the following argument: Since such a one is suspect as to fraud in a property claim, he also should be suspect as to fraud in oath taking?*

E.   *In point of fact, we do not advance the following argument: Since such a one is suspect as to fraud in a property claim, he also should be suspect as to fraud in oath taking, for if you do not concede that fact, then how is it possible that the All-Merciful has ruled,* "One who has conceded part of a claim against himself must take an oath as to the remainder of what is subject to claim"?

F.   *Why not simply maintain, since such a one is suspect as to fraud in a property claim, he also should be suspect as to fraud in oath taking?*

G.   *In that other case, [the reason for the denial of part of the claim and the admission of part is not the intent to commit fraud, but rather,] the defendant is just trying to put off the claim for a spell.*

We could stop at this point without losing a single important point of interest; everything is before us. But having fully exposed the topic, its problem, and its principles, we take a tangent indicated by the character of the principle before us: when a person will or will not lie or take a false oath. We have a theory on the matter; what we now do is expound the theory, with special reference to the formulation of that theory in explicit terms by a named authority:

H.   This concurs with the position of Rabbah. [For Rabbah has said, "On what account has the Torah imposed the requirement of an oath on one who confesses to only part of a claim against him? It is by reason of the presumption that a person will not insolently deny the truth about the whole of a loan in the very presence of the creditor and so entirely deny the debt. He will admit to part of the debt and deny part of it. Hence we invoke an oath in a case in which one does so, to coax out the truth of the matter."]

I.   For you may know, [in support of the foregoing,] that R. Idi bar Abin said R. Hisda [said]: "He who [falsely] denies owing money on a loan nonetheless is suitable to give testimony, but he who denies that he holds a bailment for another party cannot give testimony."

Predictably, we cannot allow matters to stand without challenge, and the challenge comes at a fundamental level, with the predictable give-and-take to follow:

J.   But what about that which R. Ammi bar Hama repeated on Tannaite authority: "[If they are to be subjected to an oath,] four sorts of bailees have to have denied part of the bailment and conceded part of the bailment, namely, the unpaid bailee, the borrower, the paid bailee, and the one who rents."

K.   *Why not simply maintain, since such a one is suspect as to fraud in a property claim, he also should be suspect as to fraud in oath taking?*

L.   *In that case as well, [the reason for the denial of part of the claim and the admission of part is not the intent to commit fraud, but rather,] the defendant is just trying to put off the claim for a spell.*

M.   *He reasons as follows: "I'm going to find the thief and arrest him." Or: "I'll find [the beast] in the field and return it to the owner."*

Once more, "if that is the case" provokes yet another analysis; we introduce a different reading of the basic case before us, another reason that we should not impose an oath:

N.   *If that is the case, then why should one who denies holding a bailment ever be unsuitable to give testimony? How come we don't just maintain that the defendant is just trying to put off the claim for a spell. He reasons as follows: "I'm going to look for the thing and find it."*

O.   *When in point of fact we do rule,* He who denies holding a bailment is unfit to give testimony, *it is in a case in which witnesses come and give testimony against him that at that very moment, the bailment is located in the bailee's domain, and he fully is informed of that fact, or, alternatively, he has the object in his possession at that very moment.*

The solution to the problem at hand also provides the starting point for yet another step in the unfolding exposition. Huna has given us a different resolution of matters. That accounts for No. 3, and No. 4 is also predictable:

3.   A.   *But as to that which R. Huna has said* [when we have a bailee who offers to pay compensation for a lost bailment rather than swear it has been lost, since he wishes to appropriate the article by paying for it, (Daiches)], "They impose upon him the oath that the bailment is not in his possession at all,"

B. *why not in that case invoke the principle, since such a one is suspect as to fraud in a property claim, he also should be suspect as to fraud in oath taking?*

C. *In that case also, he may rule in his own behalf, "I'll give him the money."*

4. A. *Said R. Aha of Difti to Rabina, "But then the man clearly transgresses the negative commandment:* 'You shall not covet.'"

B. *"You shall not covet" is generally understood by people to pertain to something for which one is not ready to pay.*

Yet another authority's position now is invoked, and it draws us back to our starting point: the issue of why we think an oath is suitable in a case in which we ought to assume lying is going on; so we are returned to our starting point, but via a circuitous route:

5. A. **[6A]** *But as to that which R. Nahman said, "They impose upon him [who denies the whole of a claim] an oath of inducement," why not in that case invoke the principle, since such a one is suspect as to fraud in a property claim, he also should be suspect as to fraud in oath taking?*

B. *And furthermore, there is that which R. Hiyya taught on Tannaite authority:* "Both parties [employee, supposed to have been paid out of an account set up by the employer at a local store, and storekeeper] take an oath and collect what each claims from the employer," *why not in that case invoke the principle, since such a one is suspect as to fraud in a property claim, he also should be suspect as to fraud in oath taking?*

C. *And furthermore, there is that which R. Sheshet said,* "We impose upon an unpaid bailee [who claims that the animal has been lost] three distinct oaths: first, an oath that I have not deliberately caused the loss, that I did not put a hand on it, and that it is not in my domain at all," *why not in that case invoke the principle, since such a one is suspect as to fraud in a property claim, he also should be suspect as to fraud in oath taking?*

We now settle the matter:

D. *It must follow that we do not invoke the principle at all, since such a one is suspect as to fraud in a property claim, he also should be suspect as to fraud in oath taking.*

What is interesting is why walk so far to end up where we started: Do we invoke said principle? No, we do not. What we have accomplished on our wanderings is a survey of opinion on a theme, to be sure, but opinion that intersects at our particular problem as well. The moving argument serves to carry us hither and yon; its power is to demonstrate that all considerations are raised, all challenges met, all possibilities explored. This is not a set-piece argument, where we have proposition, evidence, analysis, conclusion; it is a different sort of thinking altogether, purposive and coherent, but also comprehensive and compelling for its admission of possibilities and attention to alternatives.

If I had to choose only one consequence of the formation of the Talmud through dialectical arguments more than through any other mode of thought and writing, it would be the power of that mode of the representation of thought to show us – as no other mode of writing can show us – not only the result but the workings of the logical mind. When we follow a proposal and its refutation, the consequence thereof, and the result of that, we ourselves form partners to the logical tensions and their resolutions; we are given an opening into the discourse that lies before us. As soon as matters turn not upon tradition, to which we may or may not have access, but reason, specifically, challenge and response, proposal and counterproposal, "maybe matters are just the opposite?" we find an open door before us. For these are not matters of fact but of reasoned judgment, and the answer, "well, that's my opinion," in its "traditional form," namely, that is what Rabbi X has said so that must be so, finds no hearing. Moving from facts to reasoning, propositions to the process of counter argument, the challenge resting on the mind's own movement, its power of manipulating facts one way rather than some other and of identifying the governing logic of a fact – that process invites the reader's or the listener's participation. In general, the Yerushalmi presents facts and explains them; the Bavli presents a problem with its internal tensions in logic and offers a solution to the problem and a resolution of the logical conflicts. Then the hermeneutics of the Bavli comes to the surface in this case, as in all of its parallel cases.

The dialectical argument forms a means to an end. The goal of all argument remains one and immovable: to show the unity of the law. The hermeneutics of this Talmud aims at showing us how to read the laws in such a way as to discern how many things really say one thing. This is of course invariably expressed in practical, rarely in theoretical form; the hermeneutics, as I said in the last chapter, takes the form of a detailed exposition of this and that; our task is through regression from stage to stage to identify within the case the principles of exposition that lead to the rules of reading. In the present instance, the only one we require to see a perfectly routine and obvious procedure, we mean to prove the point that if people are permitted to obstruct the public way, if damage was done by them, they are liable to pay compensation. First, we are going to prove that general point on the basis of a single case. Then we shall proceed to how a variety of authorities, dealing with diverse cases, sustain the same principle:

Bavli Baba Mesia 10:5/O-X

O.   He who brings out his manure to the public domain –
P.   while one party pitches it out, the other party must be bringing it in to manure his field.

Q.   They do not soak clay in the public domain,
R.   and they do not make bricks.
S.   And they knead clay in the public way,
T.   but not bricks.
U.   He who builds in the public way –
V.   while one party brings stones, the builder must make use of them in building –
W.   and if one has inflicted injury, he must pay for the damages he has caused.
X.   Rabban Simeon b. Gamaliel says, "Also: He may prepare for doing his work [on site in the public way] for thirty days [before the actual work of building]."

We begin with the comparison of the rule before us with another Tannaite position on the same issue, asking whether an unattributed, therefore authoritative, rule stands for or opposes the position of a given authority; we should hope to prove that the named authority concurs:

I.1   A.   *May we say that our Mishnah paragraph does not accord with the view of R. Judah? For it has been taught on Tannaite authority:*
B.   R. Judah says, "At the time of fertilizing the fields, a man may take out his manure and pile it up at the door of his house in the public way so that it will be pulverized by the feet of man and beast, for a period of thirty days. For it was on that very stipulation that Joshua caused the Israelites to inherit the land" [T. B.M. 11:8E-H].
C.   You may even maintain that he concurs with the Mishnah's rule [that while one party pitches it out, the other party must be bringing it in to manure his field]. R. Judah concedes that if one has caused damage, he is liable to pay compensation.

If we take the position just now proposed, then Judah will turn out to rule every which way on the same matter:

D.   *But has it not been taught in the Mishnah:* If the storekeeper had left his lamp outside, the storekeeper is liable [if the flame caused a fire]. R. Judah said, "In the case of a lamp for Hanukkah, he is exempt" [M. B.Q. 6:6E-F], because he has acted under authority. *Now surely that must mean,* under the authority of the court [and that shows that one is not responsible for damage caused by his property in the public domain if it was there under the authority of the court]!
E.   *No, what it means is, on the authority of carrying out one's religious obligations.*
F.   *But has it not been taught on Tannaite authority:*
G.   In the case of all those concerning whom they have said, "They are permitted to obstruct the public way," if there was damage done, one is liable to pay compensation. But R. Judah declares one exempt from having to pay compensation.
H.   *So it is better to take the view that our Mishnah paragraph does not concur with the position of R. Judah.*

The point of interest has been introduced: whether those permitted to obstruct the public way must pay compensation for damages they may cause in so doing. Here is where we find a variety of cases that yield a single principle:

2.   A.   *Said Abbayye, "R. Judah, Rabban Simeon b. Gamaliel, and R. Simeon all take the position that in the case of all those concerning whom they have said, 'They are permitted to obstruct the public way,' if there was damage done, one is liable to pay compensation.*

       B.   *"As to R. Judah, the matter is just as we have now stated it.*

Simeon b. Gamaliel and Simeon now draws us to unrelated cases:

       C.   *"As to Rabban Simeon b. Gamaliel, we have learned in the Mishnah:* **Rabban Simeon b. Gamaliel says, 'Also: He may prepare for doing his work [on site in the public way] for thirty days [before the actual work of building].'**

       D.   *"As to R. Simeon, we have learned in the Mishnah:* **A person should not set up an oven in a room unless there is a space of four cubits above it. If he was setting it up in the upper story, there has to be a layer of plaster under it three handbreadths thick, and in the case of a stove, a handbreadth thick. And if it did damage, the owner of the oven has to pay for the damage. R. Simeon says, 'All of these measures have been stated only so that if the object did damage, the owner is exempt from paying compensation if the stated measures have been observed' [M. B.B. 2:2A-F]."**

We see then that the demonstration of the unity of the law and the issue of who stands, or does not stand, behind a given rule, go together. When we ask about who does or does not stand behind a rule, we ask about the principle of a case, which leads us downward to a premise, and we forthwith point to how that same premise underlies a different principle yielding a case – so how can X hold the view he does, if that is his premise, since at a different case he makes a point with a principle that rests on a contradictory premise.

Having seen how the several hermeneutical principles appear on their own terms, let us now examine a case in which all of them come into play in the formation of a large and continuous composition. We see successively these concerns: [1] the rationality of disputes; [2] the consistency of authorities; [3] the persistence through the layers of the law of the same organizing issues. We begin with the first of these points and then see how the others follow in sequence.

The Mishnah and the Talmud are comparable to the moraine left by the last age: studded with boulders; for the Talmud, these are those many disputes that litter the pages and impede progress. That explains why much of the Talmud is taken up with not only sorting out disputes, but also showing their rationality, meaning, reasonable people have perfectly valid reasons for disagreeing about a given point, since both parties share the same premises but apply them differently; or they really do not differ at all, since one party deals with one set of circumstances, the other with a different set of circumstances. In the following, we set side by side the principles that a sale made in error is null, on the one side, and the possibility of fraud, on the other; on the one basis or on the other, we confirm or nullify a sale:

Bavli Baba Batra 92A

I.1   A.   *It has been stated:*
       B.   He who sells an ox to his fellow and it turned out to be a habitual gorer –
       C.   Rab said, "Lo, this is a sale made in error [and null, the seller returning the purchase money]."
       D.   And Samuel said, "The seller can say to him, 'I sold it to you for slaughter.'" [There has been no misrepresentation of the merchandise; the sale is valid.]

How do we resolve the dispute? On the one side, Rab allows the sale to be canceled, on grounds that there has been a sale made in error; on the other, Samuel maintains it is not a sale made in error, because the seller assumed the buyer bought the beast for meat, not for labor. If so, cannot the facts of the case resolve the dispute?

       E.   *But examine the case: If it is someone who ordinarily buys a beast for slaughtering, then his presumed intent was to buy this beast for slaughtering, and if it was someone who would ordinarily have bought the beast for use in ploughing, then it was for the purpose of ploughing! [So what's the point of the dispute?]*
       F.   *What we are dealing with here is someone who purchases for both purposes.*
       G.   *Well, why not examine how much money was paid [which will also indicate the purchaser's intent]?*
       H.   *The dispute concerns a case in which the price of a beast sold for meat went up and stands at the same level as the price for an animal for ploughing.*
       I.   *Yeah, then what difference does it make anyhow?*
       J.   What difference it makes is in regard to the trouble [of butchering the beast].
       K.   *So what sort of case [would be involved in making the seller give the money back] anyhow?* **[92B]** *If there is no money for paying the buyer back, let the ox be retained for the money, as people say, "From someone who owes you money, accept as payment even bran."*
       L.   *The dispute concerns itself with a case in which there really is money to pay the buyer back. In that case, Rab said, "Lo, this is a sale made in error [and null, the seller returning the purchase money]," the operative criterion being majority practice, and the majority buys oxen for ploughing.*

M.   And Samuel said, "The seller can say to him, 'I sold it to you for slaughter,'" *the operative criterion being majority practice, only in matters of religious prohibitions, but not in matters involving money.*

What we now have is a resolution to the dispute that shows the full rationality of the dispute. Rab's view is reasonable; most people buy animals for work, not for food; that is then assumed the case here. Samuel concurs with the case and the principle, but he has another principle in mind altogether: majority practice would govern where it pertains; here it is impertinent. So there really is no dispute at all.

That statement of facts now leads to a separate initiative, one which challenges the facts just now introduced. We move to a new case altogether, and the movement underlines the profound unity of the law; cases may join in one way or in some other; none stands all by itself, a naked detail out of all sensible context:

I.2   A.   [To the proposition that we follow majority practice, only in matters of religious prohibitions, but not in matters involving money,] *an objection was raised as follows:* **The woman who was widowed or divorced – she says, "You married me as a virgin" – and he says, "Not so, but I married you as a widow" – if there are witnesses that [when she got married,] she went forth to music, with her hair flowing loose, her marriage contract is two hundred [M. Ket. 2:1A-D].** *The operative consideration, then, is that there are witnesses. Lo, if there were no witnesses, then the claim could not be established. Now why should that be the case? Let us rather invoke the principle that the operative criterion is the condition of the majority of women, and the majority of women are virgins when they get married!*

      B.   *Said Rabina, "It is because one may well say that, while the majority of women are virgins when they are married and a minority are widows, still, on the other hand, when a woman is married as a virgin, that fact is publicized, and since in this case the fact is not confirmed, the principle of following the status, so far as she is confirmed, is damaged.*

      C.   *So what in the world do we need witnesses for? Since the fact that she was married as a virgin is not established, they are false witnesses!*

      D.   *Rather, the majority of those who marry as virgins are known to have been in that condition when they were married, but since the condition of this one is not known, the majority principle in her case is damaged.*

      E.   *Come and take note: If someone sold to someone else a slave who turned out to have been a thief or gambler, the sale is valid. If it turned out he was a thug or outlaw, the buyer may say to him, "This is yours, take him back." Now in the opening clause, [93A] what is the operative consideration? Is it not that most slaves are like that? Doesn't this prove that, even in financial matters, we are guided by the rule characteristic of the majority?*

      F.   *No, not all of them are like that.*

      G.   *Come and take note:* **An ox [deemed harmless] which gored a cow [which died] and her newly born calf was found [dead] beside her – and it is not known whether, before it gored her, she gave birth,**

or after it gored her, she gave birth – [the owner of the ox] pays
half-damages for the cow, and quarter-damages for the offspring
[M. B.Q. 5:1]. *Now why should this be the case? Why not say,* follow
the status of the majority of most cows, and most cows that are
pregnant give birth [so this one has, too]? *Therefore in this case the
miscarriage assuredly was caused by the goring.*

H. *There the reason that the majority rule does not apply is that we are not
certain whether the ox approached from the front, in which case the
miscarriage came about because of shock, or whether it came from behind,
and the miscarriage was due to goring;* the indemnity falls into the
category of money, the ownership of which is subject to doubt, and
where we deal with a case of money the ownership of which is
subject to doubt, it must be divided among the claimants.

It would be difficult to point to a better example of the hermeneutics of
the Talmud, a sustained effort to draw together discrete cases into a
single cogent pattern, on the one side, and to show the rationality of
disputes, the negotiability of moot points, on the other. A third
important element is to show that later authorities, when they differ,
differ along established lines; the law contains reasonable disputes, but,
on the disputed points, earlier and later generations concur in dividing
down predictable lines. And here, again, we move to new cases along
well-explored lines:

I.3 A. *May we say that [Rab's and Samuel's dispute] follows the lines of the
conflict among the following Tannaite authorities:*
B. An ox which was grazing, and a dead ox was found beside it, it
must not be said, even though the one is gored and the other is
known to gore, the one bitten and the other is known to bite,
"Obviously one gored or bit the other."
C. R. Aha says, "A camel that was covering females among the
camels, and one of the camels was found dead – it is obvious that
the one killed the other" [T. B.Q. 3:6L-R].
D. *Taking as our premise that the principles of following the majority and
confirming the legal status are pretty much the same thing* [most animals
don't gore, so every animal is assumed not to gore until proved to
the contrary, and the ox that is known to gore is confirmed as a
goring ox (Slotki)], *may we say that Rab concurs with R. Aha and
Samuel with the initial Tannaite authority?*

The proposal in its own terms may not be permitted to stand; distinctions
are there to be drawn:

E. *Rab will say to you, "Well, as a matter of fact, I take the position that I do
even within the premises of the position of the initial Tannaite authority.
For the initial Tannaite authority takes the position that he does only
because we are not going to be guided by the confirmed legal status, but we
are guided by the condition of the majority."* [Slotki: And thus in this
case it is to be assumed that the other oxen, who form the majority,
have done the killing.]

F.   *And Samuel can say to you, "Well, as a matter of fact, my position accords even with R. Aha's. For R. Aha takes the position that he does there only because we are guided by the principle of confirming the legal status of a given beast, and since it is confirmed in that status, we are guided by it; but one is not guided by the principle of the condition of the majority."*

G.   *Come and take note:* **He who sells produce [consisting of grain] to his fellow [not specifying whether it is for food or for seed], and they did not sprout, and even if it was flax seed, he is not liable to make it up.** *What is the meaning of* **and even if it was flax seed?** *Is it not, even as to flax seed, most of which is purchased for sowing, even here we are not governed by the principle that we follow what the majority do in a given case?*

H.   *It is a matter subject to conflict among Tannaite statements, for it has been taught on Tannaite authority:* **He who sells produce to his fellow and the latter sowed it but the seeds did not sprout, if it was garden seeds, which are not eaten, the seller is responsible to make it up. If it was flax seed, he is not liable to make it up. R. Yosé says, [93B] "He has to pay back the value of the seed." They said to him, "Well, plenty of people buy it for other purposes"** *[T. B.B. 6:1]. Now who are the Tannaite authorities [who dispute the issue of whether we are governed by the rule that covers the majority]? Shall we say they are only R. Yosé and "they said to him"? But both of them are governed by the consideration of the rule that describes the majority, the one, the majority of purchasers, the other, the majority of seed* [most people buy flax seed for purposes other than sowing; most flax seed is sold for sowing, though to a minority of buyers (Slotki)]. [Slotki: So neither of these concurs with Samuel.]

I.   *The dispute is either between the initial Tannaite authority and R. Yosé or between the initial Tannaite authority and "they said to him."*

A sufficiency of cases allows me to conclude by permitting this final example to speak for itself. The upshot is an account of the entire range of possible challenges and their counters (the dialectical argument) that leads to the demonstration of the rationality of disputes, their limitation and reasonable character: disputes concern established principles, shared by all parties, but interpreted differently by each participant to the argument. So everybody agrees about everything that matters and disagrees about anything that does not.

It is time now to specify the hermeneutics that I think comes to full exposure in these cases and the many like them. The framers of the Talmuds take as their task the reading of one component of the Torah alone, the oral part. This they identify not only with a particular, formed document, the Mishnah, but also with received sayings that bear the sign TN' that stands for Tannaite status. These sayings they did not assume to have been collected in some one document, awaiting a reading start to finish. Rather, all sayings of Tannaite status, whether in the Mishnah, whether not, required the same attention. We already have observed how the two Talmuds equally engage in a process of dismantling the

Mishnah into selected paragraphs or even lone sentences, these to be read in their own, fresh context. Now we realize that the Mishnah's deconstruction forms only one phase of the larger, systematic definition of that of which the Torah's oral part consists. And that consists of sentences, at most paragraphs, but not whole chapters, and certainly not whole "books." It follows that the first rule of reading was, we read sentences on their own, but also in relationship to other sentences; documentary lines are null; large-scale, coherent propositions, such as the Mishnah read by itself composes and fully exposes, are null.

Five congeries of hermeneutical rules yielding theological facts govern throughout, all of them serving to express the hermeneutics that convey the theological principles of Judaism. The first three made their appearance in Chapter Nine, the final two here.

[1] DEFINING THE TORAH AND THE CONTEXT FOR MEANING: The Torah consists of free-standing statements, sentences, sometimes formed into paragraphs, more often not; and we are to read these sentences both on their own – for what they say – and also in the context created by the entirety of the Torah, Oral and Written. Therefore the task is to set side by side and show the compatibility of discrete sentences; documents mean nothing, the Torah being one. The entirety of the Torah defines the context of meaning. All sentences of the Torah, equally, jointly, and severally, form the facts out of which meaning is to be constructed.

[2] SPECIFYING THE RULES OF MAKING SENSE OF THE TORAH: Several premises govern in our reading of the sentences of the Torah, and these dictate the rules of reading. The first is that the Torah is perfect and flawless. The second is that the wording of the Torah yields meaning. The third is that the Torah contains, and can contain, nothing contradictory, incoherent, or otherwise contrary to common sense. The fourth is that the Torah can contain no statement that is redundant, banal, silly, or stupid. The fifth is that our sages of blessed memory when they state teachings of the Torah stand for these same traits of language and intellect: sound purpose, sound reasoning, sound result, in neat sentences. The task of the reader (in secular language) or the master of the Torah (in theological language, in context the two are one and the same) then is to identify the problems of the Torah, whether Written or Oral, and to solve those problems. Knowing what will raise a difficulty, we also know how to resolve it.

[3]   IDENTIFYING THE CORRECT MEDIUM OF DISCOURSE: Since
       our principal affirmation is that the Torah is perfect, and the
       primary challenge to that affirmation derives from the
       named classifications of imperfection, the proper mode of
       analytical speech is argument. That is because if we seek
       flaws, we come in a combative spirit: proof and conflict, not
       truth and consequence. Only by challenging the Torah
       sentence by sentence, at every plausible point of
       imperfection, are we going to show in the infinity of detailed
       cases the governing fact of perfection. We discover right
       thinking by finding the flaws in wrong thinking, the logical
       out of the failings of illogic. Only by sustained confrontation
       of opposed views and interpretations will truth result.

So much for the perfection of the Torah. How, in context, does it
"restore the heart"? Here is the hermeneutics that shows the answer.

[4]   THE HARMONY OF WHAT IS SUBJECT TO DISPUTE, THE
       UNITY AND INTEGRITY OF TRUTH: Finding what is rational
       and coherent: The final principle of hermeneutics is to
       uncover the rationality of dispute. Once our commitment is
       to sustained conflict of intellect, it must follow that our goal
       can only be the demonstration of three propositions,
       everywhere meant to govern: [1] disputes give evidence of
       rationality, meaning, each party has a valid, established
       principle in mind; [2] disputes are subject to resolution; [3]
       truth wins out. The first proposition is most important. If
       we can demonstrate that reasonable sages can differ about
       equally valid propositions, for instance, which principle
       governs in a particular case, then schism affords evidence of
       not imperfection but profound coherence. The principles are
       affirmed, their application subjected to conflict. So, too, if
       disputes worked out in extended, moving arguments,
       covering much ground, can be brought to resolution, as is
       frequently the case in either a declared decision or an
       agreement to disagree, then the perfection of the Torah once
       more comes to detailed articulation.
[5]   KNOWING GOD THROUGH THE THEOLOGY EXPRESSED IN
       HERMENEUTICS: And, finally, in a protracted quest for the
       unity of the truth, detailed demonstration that beneath the
       laws is law, with a few wholly coherent principles inherent
       in the many, diverse rules and their cases – in that sustained
       quest, which defines the premise and the goal of all

Talmudic discourse we meet God: in mind, in intellect, where that meeting takes place.

Index

Aaron, 84-85, 137, 154

Abba, 63, 198

Abba bar Nathan, 184

Abba Saul, 143, 244, 248

Abbahu, 98

Abbayye, 78, 101-102, 198, 208, 232-233, 236-237, 241, 266

Abodah Zarah, 24, 37

Abot, 15, 84, 123-124, 129-130, 133, 160, 230

Abraham, 137, 154, 242, 248

Abun, 194, 204

act of labor, 228-229

adultery, 102, 157-158

agglutination, 216

Aha, 269-270

Aha of Difti, 263

All-Merciful, 261

altar, 61, 63, 146-149, 154-157, 224

American Translation, 39

Ammi bar Hama, 262

Amora, 34, 43

analogy, 105, 158, 184, 190, 207, 250

angel of death, 78, 128

anoint, 130, 157

anonymity, 34, 60, 63, 189, 197, 214, 222

apocalyptic, 133, 137

appendix, 153

Aqiba, 66, 85, 100-102, 147

Arab, 78

Aramaic, 60, 77, 99, 106, 114, 194

argument a fortiori, 85, 162

Aristotle, 17-19, 24, 37, 52, 54

Ashi, 102, 198, 234, 238-239, 241

atonement, 61

authorship, 23, 45, 51, 79, 145-146, 149-151, 156-166, 172-173, 223-224, 252

autonomy, 109, 135, 174, 177, 253

B. Qiddushin, 73

Ba, 187

Baba Batra, 253, 267

Baba Mesia, 3, 78, 80, 84, 210, 253, 256, 264

Baba Qamma, 253

Babylonia, 3, 8, 12-13, 15-16, 28-30, 32-33, 36, 39, 41, 47, 51,

South Florida Studies in the History of Judaism

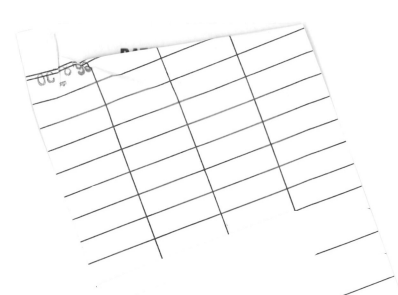

DEMCO 38-297